Brand Lands,
Hot Spots &
Cool Spaces

Brand Lands, Hot Spots & Cool Spaces

Welcome to the Third Place and the Total Marketing Experience

Christian Mikunda
Translated by Andrea Blomen

KOGAN
PAGE

London & Sterling, VA

Publisher's note

Every possible effort has been made to ensure that the information contained in this book is accurate at the time of going to press, and the publishers and authors cannot accept responsibility for any errors or omissions, however caused. No responsibility for loss or damage occasioned to any person acting, or refraining from action, as a result of the material in this publication can be accepted by the editor, the publisher or any of the authors.

First published in Germany in 2002 as *Marketing spüren: Willkommen am Dritten Ort* by Redline Wirtschaft bei Ueberreuter
First published in Great Britain and the United States in 2004 by Kogan Page Limited

120 Pentonville Road
London N1 9JN
United Kingdom

22883 Quicksilver Drive
Sterling VA 20166–2012
USA

www.kogan-page.co.uk

©2002, 2004 Wirtschaftsverlag Carl Ueberreuter, Frankfurt/Wien

The right of Dr Christian Mikunda to be identified as the author of this work has been asserted by him in accordance with the Copyright, Designs and Patents Act 1988.

ISBN 0 7494 4256 5

British Library Cataloguing-in-Publication Data

A CIP record for this book is available from the British Library.

Library of Congress Cataloging-in-Publication Data

Mikunda, Christian.
  [Marketing spuren. English]
  Brand lands, hot spots, and cool places : welcome to the third place and the total marketing experience / Christian Mikunda.
      p. cm.
  "First published in Germany in 2002 as Marketing spuren : Willkommen am dritten Ort"--Verso t.p.
Includes bibliographical references and index.
  ISBN 0-7494-4256-5
  1. Special events--Marketing. 2. Special events--Planning. I Title.
GT3405.M5513 2004
659--dc22
                          2004005768

Typeset by Saxon Graphics Ltd, Derby
Printed and bound in Great Britain by Scotprint, Haddington

For Denise and Julian

Contents

List of figures

List of plates

About the author

Dr Christian Mikunda, internationally acclaimed dramatist, guru, psychologist and trend scout, specializes in advising companies throughout Europe, the United States and Asia on mood management in public spaces. Having developed his theories for film and TV production, today he works in teams involving some of the world's most influential architects such as Daniel Libeskind and Massimiliano Fuchsas. Through his consultancy, CommEnt, he advises TV stations, shopping malls, hotel chains, museums, branded product manufacturers and city centres. One of Europe's best-known and highly paid speakers and a frequent guest on TV shows, he describes himself as a 'performing scientist'. His on-the-road marketing seminars have taken place in New York, London, Paris, Las Vegas, Los Angeles, Tokyo, Orlando, Minneapolis, Vienna, Coburg, Manchester and Zurich. He lectures at the University of Vienna and has been a visiting professor at Tubingen University, Germany and a guest speaker at Harvard University.

In 1986 Christian Mikunda published his first book *Kino spüren: Strategien der emotionalen Filmgestaltung* (reprinted in 2002 by WUV Vienna). He then went on to produce television features and image films, and coach people in television at ZDF, ORF and ARD in dramaturgy and picture composition. His second book, *Der verbotene Ort, oder Die inszenierte Verführung*, is considered essential reading for anyone in business dramaturgy today. It has now even been published in Chinese and Korean and was recently reprinted by Ueberreuter Wirtschaft.

www.mikunda.com

Acknowledgements

'Is the book finished yet?' asks my son for the fifth time today. Denise cannot even remember what our lives were like before writing the book. Which is why my greatest thanks go to my lovely wife Denise Mikunda-Schulz, MA and my son, Julian Darwin Mikunda. Denise, herself an author, took care of the translation and revision of *Brand Lands*. Anyone who has tried to get clearance for picture copyrights from all around the world will know what this really means. *Brand Lands, Hot Spots and Cool Spaces* is my third book, but it is the first to feature a dedication at the beginning: to Denise and Julian. My wife's grandmother, Margaretha Niglas, and my mother, Inge Mikunda, contributed their fair share to running our daily lives during these difficult times. I am eternally grateful for their selfless support.

My secretary, Inge Pintarich, not only has everything at CommEnt under perfect control, she also even cuts a peeled apple up into small pieces for me on a daily basis. Full of ideas, my most important personal assistant, Alexander Vesely, psychotherapist and film-maker, has taken on the responsibility for the visual concept of *Brand Lands*. Both these colleagues' commitment goes far beyond the usual scope normally expected at a company. The renowned television set designer and scenographer Jürgen Hassler and his company Make it Real became my most important partners for CommEnt outside the company. Cooperation with him is always inspiring, relaxed and professional. He is the creative partner for developing Third Places with whom I have wanted to work for 10 years now.

I must thank those who commissioned me for the many experiences I used in this book. These people were discussion partners, initiators of analyses, travel sponsors. Leo Fellinger and Kurt Loidl, MA, of Porsche Austria, in cooperation with Engelbert Egger of GEO, enabled us to do some research work in Japan and Europe, where we were supported by entire teams of interpreters, drivers and agents on site. Dr David Bosshart, director of the renowned Swiss Gottlieb Duttweiler Institute, and Reinhard Peneder and his team at Umdash Shop Concepts are committed commissioners of learning expeditions around the globe. Without them I would never have seen a large proportion of the Third Places described here. Finally, Friedrich Blaha, the office furniture tycoon and owner of biz-Büro Innovations Zentrum, has furnished a room to develop his brand land with walls displaying the entire know-how laid out in this book. Readers can surely imagine how much his consultant loves him for that.

These days, the recently deceased doyen of shop concepts, Professor Wilhelm Kreft, a fatherly friend and author of a 900-page standard work, is uppermost in my mind. Everyone in the publishing trade knows my German publisher, Jürgen Diessl, and his trademark leather cap. Highly committed and always in high spirits, he signs his e-mails 'With exquisite regards'. Ms Andrea Blomen, my translator, received the manuscript from him and converted it into english with lots of *esprit*. The initiator of the English version is Maria Pinto-Peuckmann, to whom I will be forever grateful. I especially thank the many people who contributed to the acquisition of pictures, especially photographer Robert Herbst, gastronomes Leo Doppler, Rolf Hiltl and Pierre Nierhaus, Gabriela Benz of Le Meridien, Dr Michael Braun of Swarovski and Allison Straw of Selfridges.

When first meeting face to face with my publisher at Kogan Page in London, I had lost my voice on a long lecture-tour. Probably sounding somewhat like Mickey Mouse, I tried to explain my theories to Pauline Goodwin. How wonderful that she trusted me anyway. Thank you Pauline, and the whole team at Kogan Page.

Introduction

The visitor single-mindedly enters the museum grounds of the Peggy Guggenheim Foundation in Venice. He 'discharges' his not inconsiderable admission fee and sweeps through the security check into the familiar garden that – as always – immediately 'beams' him into a state of relaxed exhilaration. In the exhibition building he spends several minutes in front of a colourful picture by Miró, briefly stops in front of a Kandinsky to subsequently pause in front of his favourite Magritte painting – which shows day and night at the same time. Then, however, he immediately heads for the terrace overlooking the Canale Grande. Many other visitors are already leaning against the stone balustrade against the backdrop of chugging vaporetti and gondolas in that Venetian light. A company just launching a new drink with a strange, green colour proffer samples to taste, and 20 minutes pass in a twinkling.

On first-time visits one might still explore the valuable collection of 20th century paintings and sculptures in detail. But since then the emotional mood of these museum premises has become more important than the exhibition proper. After brief stop-overs at favourite paintings visitors prefer to sit in the ivy-clad stone arcade right next to the graves of Peggy Guggenheim and her innumerable dogs, spend ages rummaging through the museum store, drink a café latte at the museum's cafeteria and touch the huge glass stone in the elaborately designed gate of the Foundation by way of a farewell every time they leave. Although not an ardent admirer of modern painting, someone might nevertheless became a regular patron of the museum, paying the admission fee, making a few purchases and eating or drinking something.

Home away from home

The Peggy Guggenheim Foundation is one of those places where the legitimate marketing targets – increasing sales and prolonged visiting time – meet with humanity's longing for semi-public, themed – or better, staged – habitats. These are places where one temporarily feels at home, that are emotionally so powerful they allow their visitors to recharge themselves with emotion. The Peggy Guggenheim is a Third Place.

Following thoroughly designed flats and aesthetically appealing workplaces, these so-called Third Places fall into the category of new leisure. The First Place, the fully styled home, was an invention made as early as in the 19th century. 'Show me how you live and I will tell you who you are,' a writer once said. The aesthetics of the home turned into an expression of one's own self – this was when lifestyle was born. People lived modestly in Biedermeier style or bombastically exotic as advocated by the 'painting prince' Makart in Vienna. In each case the added value of aesthetics was still entirely under the control of the individual – the staged habitat was the home.

This was due to change when North America discovered the motivating force of an aesthetic working environment in the 1960s. This is how the Second Place emerged, taking the form of generously spaced open-plan offices with plenty of light, air and greenery, or experiments with colourfully painted factory halls. Staff fell ill more rarely, identified more strongly with the company, were more motivated and, hence, more productive – much to their boss's delight. Consequently, the workplace had now also turned into a 'staged habitat' to a certain degree.

In the 1980s the then new trend towards experience-oriented marketing increasingly spilled over to public spaces. People started 'staging' stores and restaurants, revamping museums and erecting the first experience hotels. The sensuality and homeliness of these places induced people to perceive these semi-public spaces as personal habitats as well. This gave birth to the Third Place, and made those 'staged habitats' become part of the vitality of our cities. People spent their leisure time no longer exclusively at classic entertainment places such as cinemas, football pitches or bowling alleys, but also at the new places of business entertainment, shopping malls, at events and in 'experience' restaurants and bars.

The shoe shop in the travel guide

'You just *have* to see it,' said my then assistant, falling into raptures after returning from New York several years ago. He was not referring to the latest Broadway show but to an over-sized shoe shop, the Nike Town in Manhattan. Needless to say the sneaker producer not only sells shoes at this cult temple. However, their range was not the point of our conversation. There was talk of a huge silver screen being slid into the atrium every 13 minutes, of great video clips and that incredible Dolby surround sound. We talked about that shoe store as we would about a tourist attraction. The truth is that Nike Town can be found in almost any New York City guide – just like the Empire State Building or Central Park.

Many Third Places whose actual function is selling, are simultane-ously marketed as sight-seeing attractions – as is Nike Town. In the eyes of marketing departments such sales places are nothing but 3-D advertising, PR that can be walked into and stepped on. You can place a story with great photography in lifestyle magazines and get many a public discussion going. This also happened when another spectacular flagship store opened in New York. Star architect Rem Koolhaas built a type of over-sized, wooden half-pipe for Prada, and it feels as if the shoes and other accessories are approaching you on a huge flight of steps. The enormous budget and the sheer size of the store immediately prompted a debate as to whether such an ostentatious display of wealth was appropriate after the events of 9/11. Since that day the store has been the talk of the town and packed with customers.

Apart from striking stores it is more and more often the brand lands of industry that develop into first-class travel and tourist destinations. At the new Guinness Storehouse in Dublin we are told in the authentic and emotional atmosphere of a former warehouse about what it means to brew this beer. Just the atrium alone, reminiscent of a giant pint, is enough to draw in the crowds. This is how Guinness managed to make it Ireland's most frequented tourist attraction. Just like the Swarovski

Crystal Worlds in Tyrol. Topped only by Schönbrunn Castle, this chamber of miracles inside a forest giant is the second most visited site in Austria.

Apart from the self-evident added value generated by also qualifying as a tourist attraction, these locations have developed quite a number of additional functions that turn 'places of business' into those vital habitats we experience as Third Places. Hotels are not made for sleeping alone – they are also meeting points for all those who want to identify and reload themselves with their lifestyle. The lobbies of Phillipe Starck hotels, for instance, register a high density of pretty models who come here with their cliques to spend an evening out. Starck's design hotels offer a dramatic entrance like that of a catwalk – at the Delano in Miami Beach it's a deep gorge formed of white, towering tulle curtains spanning the hotel hall – and a host of staged bars, restaurants and gardens.

Waiting at train stations used to be a drag. Today, the new first class lounges of the German Railways (Deutsche Bundesbahn) are among the best in the field of dramatized waiting. In-between places such as lobbies, lounges or museum atriums are noticed with the same attention as the principal places. Museum shops used to be secondary additional facilities. Today some museums look like shopping malls to us. Similar trends towards a multi-functional 'compaction' can be found in restaurants and bars, as well as with other forms of going out or attending trade shows, world expositions, sporting and cultural events or festivals.

Everywhere a core function is complemented by an emotional extra of almost equal value:

▌ Shops double as tourist attractions.
▌ Brand lands double as destinations for family outings.
▌ Hotels double as meeting points with lifestyle.
▌ Museums double as shopping malls and places for energizing.

Ray Oldenburg's world

In Pensacola, Florida, a – no longer that young – sociology professor by the name of Ray Oldenburg has coffee with some friends, policemen in check shirts, every week. His 'coffee with the cops', as he calls it, takes place at the Good Neighbor Coffeeshop, a 'pub round the corner', its name and down-to-earth look with plain wooden tables being inspired by Oldenburg's book *The Great Good Place* (1999). In this book the sociologist rails against the shopping-mall and fast-food society of his country, seen from the perspective of a conservative intellectual American. He calls its places 'non-places' and praises the little barber shop that doubles as the community information centre, the book store where you can enjoy excellent conversations with the bookseller, the pub where everyone knows you. These 'good, old places' where you hang about for hours were called 'Third Places' by Oldenburg as early as the late 1980s. They are emotionally inspiring without being staged, accessible for everyone and situated right around the corner, they exert no social pressure whatsoever, are 'homely' but largely extinct. By way of example for his fellow countrypeople Oldenburg cited the historically grown Third Places in Europe – the Irish pub, the Italian piazza and the Viennese coffee-house.

Shortly before Christmas 2001 it was in the coffee-house capital, Vienna, of all places that a big Starbucks coffee-house opened at a high-street location – right opposite the Vienna State Opera House. It is open from 7 am to 2 pm and has been mercilessly successful from the start despite all prophecies of doom and gloom. Comfy club armchairs grouped around low tables create a lounging atmosphere, and this is by no means a coincidence. With sparkling eyes the Starbucks CEO Howard Schultz, who had travelled all the way just to witness the opening, said: 'Like Viennese coffee-houses our guests all over the world consider the Starbucks Coffee Houses their *third home away from home*, an oasis between home and the workplace where you meet friends.'

Even Ron Lakos, the Head of Marketing Germany for Sony, refers to the Third Place in the PR for Sony's Playstation 2. It says there: 'Free yourself from order and logic and enter into a new place. It is not the workplace. It is not your home. No one has ever spotted it on a map. Nothing is secure. Everything is possible. *Welcome to the third place.*' This slogan refers to the special flair of PS2 video games, their high degree of reality that makes the locations of the games credible as a stand-alone reality, as a third place. Besides that, the slogan is also an allusion to a debate led in the United States, whether the Internet world and other virtual realities are not the genuine third places – temporary places of refuge, accessible to everyone and high on emotion.

Sony and Starbucks explicitly mention in their public relations material what many other companies practise just the same way. They use the emotional added value of a temporary home as a marketing tool. How might Ray Oldenburg feel about that? It is precisely the representatives of the marketing-oriented experience economy he criticized who are now about to recover some elements of the Third Place thought lost. It must be admitted, however, that the personal presence of a bookseller to chat with, or of the bar tender who knows the customers – both of which species are seriously decimated due to globalization – must be replaced with staging measures.

It must be granted that Ray Oldenburg's criticism of the cool calculation and infantility of American marketing arrangements did have something, back then in the era of the fun society. But times have changed. While only a few years ago business entertainment focused on perfectly arranging the refuge into a dream world, now – and not only since September 2001 – a certain thoughtfulness has gained ground.

The successful experience concepts of the present combine the longing for entertainment with true, big feelings, with genuine materials and high-quality design, and help with our problems in everyday life, with quick massage of the soul for stressed-out customers. In a nutshell: the experience society has grown up.

Clear indicators for this development are the changes occurring in Las Vegas, the world capital of stage-set marketing. The new Mandalay Bay Resort, for example, houses a restaurant plus bar named Rumjungle. Only a few years back such a place dedicated to rum, the Caribbean and jungle themes most probably would have featured a computer-controlled pirate figure sitting next to a barrel of rum in front of the restaurant, toasting the guests with a friendly grin. Now people have thought about the ingredients of rum, which seem to have something to do with fire and water, because you enter the place by stepping through a firewall consisting of zillions of gas flames against a black stone backdrop. Inside, almost a dozen jungle waterfalls flow down designed glass slabs that double as partition walls. After 11 pm a strict dress code is applied and guests with sneakers are no longer admitted to the hip bar.

The marketing industry as a whole had to learn that in the past many a well-meaning entertainment venue – in addition to the pressure to consume and the information overflow – exerted an additional pressure on consumers to experience something. Some places suddenly looked like leisure parks for kids – an occasionally disconcerting feel, above all in Europe. Which is why experiences are now used in such a way that they rather subdue the overall impression on the consumer.

In a Vienna supermarket, Austria's biggest supermarket chain Billa has started an interesting experiment. Above the refrigerated racks the wall captivates buyers with an image of a broad sunflower field, projected on to it by means of many linked video beamers (see colour plate section). The resulting video frieze produces astonishing effects. Otherwise hectic buyers stand still, lost in thought, gazing at the sunflowers as they slowly sway – and enjoy this carefully arranged break: this is a massage of the soul in today's hectic everyday life. Here a technical innovation is employed to release the pressure built up during trips to the supermarket. All shopping trolleys are equipped with scanners, allowing shoppers to input the prices of the merchandise themselves. If buyers have a customer card this technology reduces waiting time at the cashier's desk to an incredible 10 seconds.

Such 'convenience entertainment' that makes routine jobs run more smoothly is currently just as popular in the experience industry as the 'mood management' achieved with swaying sunflower fields, allowing consumers to control their mood. Both trends are typical examples of a certain professionalization in business entertainment. Experiences become more adult, authentic, are dosed more carefully than a few years ago. In this respect Ray Oldenburg and his group of friends in flannel shirts were right. They only erred in one point: we will never do without any experiences again. The emotional added value of entertainment in marketing has stood the test of time, both long term as an image-building factor and immediately at the point where things happen; because experiences increase attention levels, residence time and immediately promote sales.

WHY SELL EXPERIENCES?

A commercial promoting the British daily the *Guardian*, which became famous, impressively shows why experiences are so seductive. Like all other quality papers, the *Guardian* makes the advertising claim that it allows its readers to understand and keep track of a complex world. To this end, it shows a dangerous-looking young man who could be a skinhead running down a street, from three different camera angles. In the first shot you can't help thinking of an escape, because the young man starts running while a car appears behind him, with two men – probably cops – watching him; then there's a freeze frame. In the next scene the story suddenly looks quite different. The skinhead-type guy runs immediately at a businessman and without any prior warning grabs his briefcase, which is protectively thrust upwards by its owner. Another freeze frame, and we are firmly convinced that we have just witnessed a robbery. But in the final analysis we have to learn that we were wrong again, because only the third camera perspective reveals that the alleged robber is not after stealing the case but wants to push it along with its owner in the opposite direction. The heavy load of a building crane above the man's head has tipped over, and the skinhead (who isn't really a skinhead) pushes him aside to rescue him from the falling bricks at the last minute. 'It's only when you get the whole picture you can fully understand what's going on' is the message conveyed by the *Guardian.* (See colour plate section.)

The AIME factor

First escape, then robbery and finally rescue: within just 50 seconds spectators figure out three completely different stories and are induced to add the missing pieces of the puzzle themselves. This mental activity has been dubbed the 'amount of invested mental elaboration' (AIME) by psychologist Salomon. If this AIME value is high, spectators have fun and feel alive and kicking in a vibrant way. In this state of heightened attention they eagerly absorb any type of information. Experiences accordingly make consumers open to messages. This is why advertising these days is elaborately produced entertainment, and this is why points of sale are emotionalized.

A place of experience makes consumers check out every possibility and all offers at the point of sale (POS). In the United States this behaviour in stores, museums or at trade show stands is called *browsing.* Consumers want to see it all if possible. In this way their residence time is prolonged and their goodwill for what is presented in that place is increased. Experiences have consistently developed into key marketing tools.

Scripts in our brain

In the case of the *Guardian*, commercial viewers figure out a story. If the signals fit the concept of a robbery we are virtually seduced to finish the story that way. After all, we basically know how a robbery works because we have acquired so-called *brain scripts* for it as well as a multitude of other basic situations in life. Telling a story professionally means triggering these scripts in our brain.

Take five actors who turn their heads left and right in front of a white, neutral wall and then synchronize this with tell-tale 'tock tock' sounds and probably also an off-voice saying things like '15 – love'. No matter who you ask, everyone will tell you this is a tennis match, although you don't see any players, let alone a court or ball. All the signals simply match our tennis brain script.

In most cases, stories at staged places are rather 'emotional' add-ons. A shop window with a wine glass tossed over, red high heels and a piece of lacy underwear – the product that's on sale – and consumers hastily passing by think, 'Oh, what a night'. The story dramatizes the merchandise but the products are still in the foreground. In times where points of sale increasingly turn into temporary habitats for customers, we have seen shop concepts emerge where the range moves to the background and the arranged act of shopping, the story that develops between the customer and the product, moves centre-stage.

How to build a bunny

The most spectacular example of this trend is Build-a-Bear. Cute little cats, teddy bears or bunnies wait in the stores of this US multiple, still unfilled, for their future little owners – or rather for their parents and grandparents. Nowhere else could you see so many grandmas and grandpas with tears in their eyes as they 'build' an animal for their grandchildren at home. From station to station you are more inclined to think you are involved in a process of creation, in a birth. First, you pick the animal – say a cute little bunny with long ears. While you queue up at the filling machine you select a little heart for the animal. A drawer-like bin contains hearts in either red and white checked or bright red material. Some US customers also take a language chip from another drawer. The animal will then say 'I love you', for example. Europeans like myself probably prefer watching the filling material slide through an acrylic glass tube across the whole store and into the colorful filling machine. A young woman sits there, extremely friendly despite her modest pay, and tells you which pedal you have to step on to fill your bunny. Before she machines the final seam, she walks you through the heart ritual. You press the heart to your left eye, then to the right eye, before kissing it and placing it in the animal. This is the moment you are truly moved for the first time.

And it goes on. In a type of compressed-air bathtub you get the bunny's fur into shape. Then the bunny needs an outfit. While the animals as such are quite inexpensive, the accessories can get pretty costly. The bunny first gets underpants with an opening left for its scut. Then denim pants, a jacket, a long red shawl. To be on the safe side, you also buy a few items for summer: sneakers to match an animal size 3, sunglasses and – not forgetting – bathing trunks. All of this costs many times the price of the animal, but you are surrounded by other adults and kids who have fallen victim to a collective buying spree. You swiftly pass over to the computers, where you produce the birth certificate for your animal. Name: 'Honey Bunny' you write, unable to think of a more imaginative name. The computer uses the item code to identify the colour of the fur, eyes and size of the animal. The name of bunny's future owner is still missing. 'Honey Bunny made for Julian from Mama with love', you read, full of emotion, on the computer print-out. At the cashier's desk the animal is completely dressed by another friendly lady although other customers are waiting. Finally, she carefully places the bunny in a little cardboard house for transport. You can still see a piece of bunny's fur showing through a tiny window. And the house says: 'I'm going home'.

A little creature is instilled with life by means of the filling and heart rituals. It is bathed in air, dressed, given a name and birth certificate and finally brought home. To the parent target group of Build-a-Bear this all somehow feels familiar. The *brain script* triggered here in a very subtle yet powerful way produces the emotion that you will remember for a long, long time even after this animal has been ousted by another favourite animal back home. With this concept customers primarily pay for the act of buying, the emotionality of which turns their visit to the store into an experience full of true feelings.

Who let the cows out?

The experience quality of the *Guardian* commercial about the alleged skinhead is not generated by brain scripts alone. While brain scripts tell us what is actually going on there, a second psychological mechanism makes us even enjoy the baffling effect produced by the ad. You have to be quite smart to follow all the turns this story is taking. Escape, robbery and rescue follow each other in quick succession. The plot *turns*, as film people would say. Such an effect is typical in times where many people handle the media and consumption extremely cleverly. They have acquired a high degree of *media literacy*, skills mastered by spectators who grew up with television, the Internet and video games.

Zurich Central Station. I get off the train and can give immediate proof of my media literacy. I am amazed, standing in front of a giant mobile in the station hall. It consists of nothing but painted cow sculptures. The cows practically form this slowly turning mobile. During my walk through town I meet other cows imitating other things or even human beings. A cow in front of the renowned confiserie Sprüngli imitates a chocolate cake complete with fork (in the cow's back) for us. A complete herd of cows approaches me, dressed as soccer players. A single cow greets me as a bellboy in livery as I enter my hotel. When I have dinner that evening, I can't believe my eyes: the front of the (vegetarian) restaurant is covered with greenery and turned into an alpine pasture, including grazing cows that climb up the façade. (See Figure 0.1.)

Figure 0.1   Zurich Cow Culture, Hiltl vegetarian restaurant
© Rolf Hiltl

Such disguising and *trompe-l'oeil* effects attract our attention more efficiently than any other design tools. They are genuine 'eye-catchers', and beyond that make everything seem smart and chic that prompts us to apply our media literacy.

These two properties have made this arranged bafflement into one of the most important city marketing techniques. At present, cities compete for tourists, investors, future inhabitants and taxpayers. Boasting city events laden with wit and humour, the complete city becomes a stage, the baffling mocking effects of which demonstrate to the amazed public what this city has in store for them:

The Zurich Cow Culture of 1998 was among the most successful city events of the past few years. The underlying idea was that companies could purchase one or more of 800 cows in total as unfinished 'standing', 'lying' or 'grazing' styles, then finish them according to their own ideas, turning them into cow sculptures. This campaign not only helped to telegraph the image of the firms involved but also made the city of Zurich a hotspot generating international acclaim. Up to that point, Zurich had always been considered rather serious and a bourgeois place, but certainly not a city with wit. This image is in fact wrong. Freaky stores, bars and an active underground scene have turned Zurich into a hip city over the past few years. With the help of this city event the newly acquired spirit became visible, could be photographed and perceived with all the senses. The campaign was finally so successful that it was copied frequently, by among others Chicago and Salzburg, following the slogan 'The cows are out'. In Berne, Switzerland, bears – in keeping with the city's mascot – populated public spaces according to the same principle, and other animals followed in Germany and other places.

BOOK OF RECIPES FOR NEW EXPERIENCE WORLDS

Experiences – as we have learnt – always form an integral part of a Third Place – not least because they turn every habitat into a sales place in the widest sense of the word. Regardless of whether arranged stories such as in Build-a-Bear come into play, or baffling effects as produced by Zurich's Cow Culture are used, they always activate psychological experience mechanisms like *brain scripts* or *media literacy*.

Experiences are therefore 'designed' following strict guidelines characteristic of all Third Places, and binding for all new experience worlds:

▌ Experience design aims at giving Third Places high exposure, a clean entrance in public life. The external effect they produce must extrovertly manifest their presence, otherwise nobody will enter them – no matter whether these places focus on their consumption aspect or rather wish to be experienced as temporary habitats. So Third Places must become *landmarks*.

▌ Furthermore, experience design aims at making visitors move about the place. If shoppers, visitors to a museum or hotel guests do not 'mall' or stroll when they explore the place, they will not find the merchandise, exhibits or services right for them. Furthermore, they will feel like strangers rather than at home. So Third Places must be designed for *malling*.

▌ Experience design aims at spinning a leitmotif holding all departments and areas of a place together. Third Places require a conceptual line in order to be perceived as a whole. This can be a hidden story, as with the Build-a-Bear idea, or a generally baffling effect as produced by the Zurich Cow Culture. A multitude of dramatizing effects are appropriate as *concept lines* for Third Places.

▌ Finally, experience design aims at arousing the public's curiosity. Third Places must have some kind of magnetic attraction for people, they must feature something you simply *have to* see – they need a *core attraction*.

This 'book of recipes' applies universally – no matter whether it's a brand land like VW Autostadt, an urban entertainment centre such as the casinos in Vegas, a concept store in Soho or a museum with a breathtaking atrium. Nor does size matter. In terms of dramatic arrangement, a mini exhibition stand of a one-person publisher does not differ from a 50 million euro BMW display occupying an entire exhibition hall.

Be a *landmark*, trigger *malling*, feature a *concept line* and draw the crowds with a *core attraction* – these are always the four ingredients of a Third Place. A basic 'cookery course' on the following pages presents some typical and particularly topical applications of this 'recipe'.

1   Landmark

When you stroll through an attractive city these days, you will feel the same liveliness you perceive when watching a well-produced entertainment show. This vitality of public spaces is largely generated by the spectacular external effect produced by Third Places. Their show windows, store fronts and buildings almost radiate, want to be noticed at all costs – they even have to, in order to advertise themselves – and these are the new landmarks of our days. Museums, stores and brand lands virtually call out to us 'come in' and 'photograph me'. If all stores were suddenly forbidden to project these emotional statements externally our cities would instantly turn into barren deserts devoid of any attraction.

As a matter of principle, any type of signalling, each deviation from the norm turns a place into a landmark. This includes the method of upscaling. The London Eye, that new big wheel on the Thames, stands out due to its sheer size and has therefore become one of the landmarks of the year 2000, the millennium year.

A very old and typically European method for producing landmarks is a guild symbol. A large key on a store front used to say 'a locksmith works here'. Guild symbols instantly trigger the *brain script* of a place, its meaning and the activities expected to happen there. The symbol signals what is going on behind the façade. The principle has survived to this day, in the form of the building's *header.* The *header* of an advertising agency in Venice Beach, California in fact acquired cult status. Featuring binoculars large enough to walk into which cover most of the store frontage, this spectacular building by star architect Frank Gehry says: what is going on behind the façade has to do with insight, far-sightedness and forward thinking.

Headers make landmarks

You could even say that headers have transported us into an age of landmarks. Headers are omnipresent today. They are everywhere in public spaces, ranging from the tiny and improvised to the giant and very costly. A clearly visible sailing yacht model placed in the entrance area of a store selling nautical equipment is a small, *temporary header*, which is simply part of the merchandise. At shopping malls around the globe innumerable *headers on store fronts* vie for shoppers' attention. Art World in the UK, for instance, sells art posters and clearly tells us so, with a painting hovering above the entrance door even the most indifferent ignoramus would immediately recognize: Michelangelo's *Creation* from the Sistine Chapel, in which God touches Adam's stretched-out hand with his fingertip.

Another technique – killing two birds with one stone – positions the core attraction in the building interior in such a way that it is clearly visible through a shop window from the outside. At its flagship stores in Seattle and Minneapolis the outdoor sports specialist REI boasts huge free-climbing walls where courageous customers can immediately test their newly acquired gear. Since the spectacularly illuminated rock also stands for the range stocked, it is relayed to the outside through an all-glass façade, thereby turning into the *header of a display façade*. At exhibitions these days many stands look alike. The *exhibition stand as a header*, on the contrary, turns the entire stand into an inimitable statement with unique content. How should an insurance company present itself when it is called Direct Line Insurance and handles all business transactions over the phone? At a UK show this insurance company debuted a stand in the form of a giant red plastic-look kiddy phone the size of a small single-family home, with a white front door for visitors to enter.

Ultimately, some architects even venture to turn complete buildings into a message in stone. Daniel Libeskind, who is currently working on rebuilding Ground Zero in New York, is considered a particularly committed architect dedicated to linking formal solutions with content. A bird's eye view of his Jewish museum in Berlin shows it to look like a gigantic, broken star of David struck by lightning. This message has touched the Berliners so deeply that even long before the museum opened hundreds of thousands came to see the completely empty building. Very much to the surprise of the professional world, this critical, leftist architect is currently busy planning a shopping mall in the Swiss capital of Berne. It consists of many individual buildings forming – together – a huge open hand stretching out from the capital to all of Switzerland. The Migros people who commissioned Libeskind, whom I had the pleasure of advising on this project, mischievously commented that this hand could also be understood as an open hand stretching out for Swiss francs.

A second key method of producing *landmarks* has also caused a stir over the past few years. It is not based on *brain scripts* – the telling of stories and messages – but on human beings' initially outlined ability to deal smartly with life, the media, consumption. This *media literacy* captures our attention faster than any other psychological mechanism. Particularly efficient here is the trick of *replicas*. 'Genuine or not genuine?' was the question posed as early as in the baroque period, when in churches many a column was built, but just as many were only painted hyper-realistically. Visitors approaching the New State Gallery in Stuttgart are surprised to see some sandstone blocks that seem to have just fallen out of the façade and are still lying about in the grass in front of the museum. Of course, this effect is a fake, deceptive impression, but one good enough to make visitors stop and stare. *Replicas* are true eye-catchers that induce passers-by in a hurry to direct their attention to an object for just those few seconds that 'make or break'. Thereby they can turn any place into a striking place.

Replicas make landmarks

Since they are ideal 'fishing nets' to catch passers-by, replicas are predominantly used where consumers are in constant movement and bombarded by stimuli: at public fairs or in busy city-centre shopping areas. At times, you might observe tourists having themselves photographed alongside hyper-realistic *replica figures* sitting on a bench, apparently chilling out enjoying the sun.

Winston Churchill complete with cigar can be found sitting in the same way in a London pedestrian zone. Jeweller Wint and Kidd in London's trendy Notting Hill district and Pleats Please in New York's shopping district SoHo are two stores using exactly the same technique of the *replica shop window* to attract attention. As you approach the display it initially looks hidden by frosted glass. The closer to 90 degrees the angle from which you view the shop windowpane, the more transparent it gets, until you can finally see the merchandise in the shop window crystal clear. As you walk on and look back the shop window closes again. Many people hurrying past and seeing this effect from the corner of their eyes, actually stop after a few metres and walk back in amazement to find out what they have actually just seen.

Replica objects are comparatively inexpensive eye-catchers at exhibitions. While many exhibition stands at the Frankfurt Book Fair look just as boring as their publishers' range, a newcomer with a tight budget really caused a splash some years ago by putting up a simple column of books in the entrance to his stand. All book titles published that year had been pasted one on top of each other to form a physics-defying column that courageously spiralled upwards as an eye-catcher.

2   Malling

Turning into a *landmark* and stopping passers-by in a hurry is one thing, but anyone running a spacious museum or a multi-storey department store knows how difficult it is to get people to move about in the first place. The inertia of motor activity is high. Once the *landmark* has caught the attention of passers-by and they finally enter that place full of promise, many of them first stand rooted to the spot. Yet only those who explore the place without constantly going back to a map, only those who enthusiastically browse a mall will discover the information, exhibits and goods just right for them.

Paco Underhill (1999) and his renowned New York consultancy Environsell found that spontaneous purchases account for the lion's share of POS sales. If people are not strolling about the place being stimulated by the mall in the first place, it certainly will not be possible to guide them to products they had not originally thought of but always wanted anyway. Furthermore, we know now that deliberate malling at store premises can be just as delightful as the actual goods awaiting us there. Intuitive 'searching and finding' is therefore a characteristic feature of all Third Places, and a decisive factor for feeling at home at a place, for perceiving it as a temporary habitat. What you need is not a paper map but rather an internal map that you use with relish.

Cognitive maps

Cognitive psychology has discovered that people principally try to get an internal idea of a place as fast as possible, painting a so-called *cognitive map*. To do so we look for specific reference points. European cities whose histories stretch back to medieval times are excellent examples of psychologically styled places. They always have a main axis, a main street. The intersections of these axes, the large street crossings, are significant *hubs*. They lead to central squares emphasized by a *mnemonic point* – the cathedral, city hall, a plague column or a victory monument. Which finally brings us to the somewhat different nature of residential areas. In times past, these used to be the *districts* of butchers, of craftspeople or the Jewish ghetto. Today they are banking districts, museum miles, red-light districts or areas where wine flows – like Grinzing in Vienna or Sachsenhausen in Frankfurt. *Axes*, *hubs*, *mnemonic points*, *districts* are the four typical features of cognitive maps. Once internalized, these help us to navigate any city, through any grounds with the confidence of a sleep-walker feeling safe and at home. Only cognitive maps turn Third Places into homes from home.

Strolling about pleasantly styled grounds was an activity people discovered early in history. Court pleasances were probably the first Third Places, where entertainment value was primarily achieved by arranged promenading. Even today, since early childhood, all natives of Vienna have used a cognitive map to guide them on their Sunday tour round the gardens of Schönbrunn Castle, and they derive pleasure from this exercise. They simply know that between the castle with its flight of steps and the Gloriette, the Imperial pavilion on the slope opposite, there is the central axis of the grounds, given emphasis by statues set in pruned trees, elaborate flower ornaments and a steep serpentine path that invites sport enthusiasts to take a jog there. Many smaller *axes* run through the park, drawing visitors' attention into the distance. Where they intersect with other *axes* the *hubs* are emphasized by striking fountains, pavilions, a large aviary or imitation Roman ruins. (See Figure 0.2.)

Each walk inevitably leads people along these *axes* to find the major *mnemonic points* of the grounds. They might say they haven't seen the Palmenhaus for ages, or that they have to visit the old maze again, since

Figure 0.2   Entrance map to Schönbrunn Castle, Vienna
© Schönbrunner Tiergarten

it has been extended. Recently, the *mnemonic points* of the park have been scoured by an empire-yellow train on rubber tyres. The size of the castle park enables it to have '*districts*' with completely different functions and atmospheres: the oldest zoological garden in the world, the Tyrol Garden in Alpine style, baroque-inspired free spaces, the area surrounding the orangery, the Hietzinger and the Meidlinger sections.

Baroque castle grounds are the prototype of all staged places. What was developed in the 17th century for the purpose of open-air delights derived from *axes, hubs, mnemonic points* and *districts* is today part and parcel of every indoor experience world, be they shopping malls, urban entertainment centres or brand lands of any type. The elements of the cognitive map, however, do not always have to be arranged with the same intensity. Those who attentively study the picture postcards for sale at Schönbrunn Castle kiosk will immediately identify two methods which obviously constitute the core of strolling.

Emphasized hubs

This method is illustrated best by the picture postcards showing a bird's eye view of how several walks meet dramatically at one hub, where the crossing is marked by a strikingly shaped water basin such as the star-shaped Sternbassin and a fountain statue.

We come across this trick of the *emphasized hub* at practically all central places/squares of experience worlds. Virtually all five-star hotels feature a lavishly arranged bouquet of flowers sitting on top of a table at the precise hub where all paths meet. Many smaller stores feature a circular cashier's desk or information counter in the middle of the room, which is somehow given additional emphasis. At a chic tourist store on the island of Mykonos, for example, this job is performed by a bamboo roof hovering above the centrally located, circular cashier's desk. If a large department store atrium lacks an object hanging precisely at the intersection point where all eyes meet, you can bet the place will be totally deserted from the third floor upwards.

Some years ago, extra large television screens became the latest fashion as visual accents for lifestyle-focused places. At the Meinl am Graben store in Vienna a log fire burns on a large screen like this in winter, warming shoppers in the deli department, at least mentally (see colour plate section). A spectacular example is the huge screen of Toyota's AMLUX building in Tokyo. A screen slides up and down the atrium of the building like a lift, connecting five floors of well-staged cars and transmitting product presentations from other floors or smart video clips. A random generator decides when/whether the screen passes by and where it stops: diversion at its best in the showroom of this Japanese market leader.

The most sensible *emphasized hubs* are those hubs emerging from the dramatic staging of staircases, lifts or escalators – features that are required anyway. Sevens, the designer department store in Düsseldorf, Germany, has a second-to-none solution for this. When you enter the atrium your eye is drawn to a giant egg-shaped screen that hovers high above you. Behind this the glass lifts tempt you with neon-blue light to go upstairs. Looking back into the basement you can see the lounge bar in the form of a ship's stern, attracting everyone's glances to its radiating counter top. The best way to get there is to descend a flight of stairs. Halfway down you step on to a circular platform with tables and chairs – its illuminated floor forever changes colour. All in all the Sevens atrium is a spectacular agglomeration of *emphasized hubs*, promoting delightful promenading and prompting plenty of enchanted tourists to reach for their cameras. The fact that just seconds later bad-mannered young security staff in dark suits pounce, curtly prohibiting them from eternalizing this contemplative delight on celluloid, merely goes to show that some operators have not the faintest idea of how such a dearly acquired experience world should be run: as a vital habitat in the city, as a temporary home.

The suspense axis

Dramatized as they are, all Third Places virtually yearn to be illustrated. This is not only confirmed by the picture postcards showing the Schönbrunn Castle grounds. Alongside *emphasized hubs* impressive, deep perspectives are among the most favoured motifs photographed. Generally they show an alley of trees geometrically pruned in order to direct the eye in an even more focused manner to a target at the end of the path: the castle, the Gloriette, the Roman ruins. Such *suspense axes* make people move, act like rubber bands overcoming the inertia of motor activity. Maybe this is the reason why so many of the locals in Vienna prefer jogging through the Schönbrunn Castle gardens over any other of the city's gardens.

Nine plane hours due west, millions of tourists trek every year along the most impressive suspense axis ever designed as a city marketing and representative tool: the Washington Mall. This axis stretching out from Capitol Hill to the Lincoln Memorial, lined by innumerable fine museums, is two miles long. In-between is the enormous 'needle' of the Washington Monument, the world's highest example of stonemasonry. Regardless of whether you look down from President Lincoln along the axis to Capitol Hill, or from Capitol Hill up to the President, you always use the needle to focus along the suspense axis as a target in the distance. The Washington Mall basically has a 'back and front view', to put it in hunting slang. One element draws the eye into the depths and another keeps it stable on the axis.

This technique is surprisingly also applied in store interior designs. You are standing in front of a medium-sized store – say a mono-label Diesel store – and you look at the back wall of the store, through the front door. The Diesel logotype can be seen both at the end of the axis and above the store entrance. To reproduce this effect the chain store Reiss has recently used blow-ups of its models. In the shop window near the entrance you see a slightly blurred photo of a model wearing something in a distinct colour, red for example. The back wall of the store – the end of the visual axis – features a razor-sharp photo of the same model wearing an outfit in the same colour. The consequence: your eye is constantly drawn back and forth between the foreground and background of this suspense axis, so you really have to take a firm grip on yourself to resist entering the store. (See Figure 0.3.)

Suspense axes make every place a clean entrance: stores, restaurants, hotels. What used to be the red carpet rolled out in front of the Grand Hotel is now the catwalk arrangements that designers of today celebrate in their hotel lobbies. At Yvonne Gold's brand new Le Meridien Hotel in Vienna, guests follow an illuminated stripe on the floor as if being hypnotized. Eyes and feet are led to the suggestively glowing boxes that mark the entrance to the restaurant and change colours several times during the day (see colour plate section). A particularly original example is Philippe Starck's St Martin's Lane hotel in London. First, you wonder about the yellow film that covers the revolving door, making the entrance area look as if it is bathed in sunlight; but once you are past that door you understand why: a beam of sunlight, realistically simulated by recessed ceiling luminaires, crosses the entire lobby and hits the sliding doors of the hotel bar on the opposite side of the lobby,

Figure 0.3   Suspense axis, Reiss, UK
Photo by Dr Christian Mikunda

which are closed during the daytime. In front of the doors is an almost surreal lone chair. Suddenly, some projected clouds drift past or a metre-long goldfish swims across these doors – this is great entertainment achieved through this enhancement of the room.

3   Concept line

On a hot August day in August 2001 Herbert Muschamp, architectural critic of the *New York Times*, goes by taxi from Vienna airport to the city centre. After scarcely five minutes in the cab he sets eyes on four round cylinders in red brickwork, as if electrified. Four star architects have turned these 19th century gasometers into a vibrant urban entertainment centre encompassing flats, a shopping mall, a multiplex cinema and an underground concert hall for rock and pop concerts. A modern extension is leaning on one of the gasometers and looks as if it is about to break in two, thereby delightfully deceiving our senses. This *replica building* designed by the Coop Himmelb(l)au Group of architects is the most prominent *landmark* of the hip Gasometer town. 'Yoo-hoo! Mr Architecture Fan! Over here!' These will be the words

Muschamp later uses in the Sunday issue of the *New York Times* to describe the effect of Vienna's new site (Muschamp, 2001).

A central *suspense axis* connects the four cylinders via glass bridges and leads across squares underneath the domes. Glass ceilings incorporated into the roof of these hubs allow visitors to look up into the inside of the hollowed out gasometers and surmise how people live up there. *Emphasized hubs* are dramatized here with these spectacular insights on the one hand, and through decorations like puppets hanging head down on the other. In conjunction with the axis these carefully arranged places promote *malling*, browsing through an interesting complex. Since you can, of course, never quite see the array of axes and hubs inside the four buildings in its completeness, there are printed plans distributed all over G-Town, helping visitors to capture the cognitive map of the centre at a glance. Such *entrance maps* as you would also find at the cashier's desk in Disneyland or other theme parks with a very large or extensive terrain mean that visitors want to see it all, want to fill every white spot on their inner map. 'Haven't been there yet' is the effect designed to guide customers past every G-Town store and catering establishment. (See Figure 0.4.)

Landmark and *malling* form the arranged basis of each Third Place. The actual sensation of the gasometers, however, is the dramatized contrast between the old and new that you meet wherever you go. There is the contrast between the hyper-modern, curved extension and the time-honoured round buildings. There is the steel and glass of the bridges clashing with the building material of the past – brick walls.

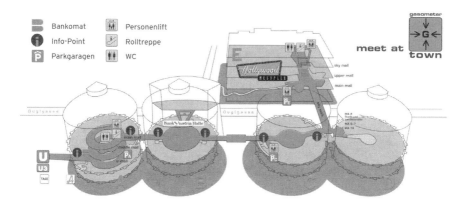

Figure 0.4   Entrance map of G-Town, Vienna
© G-Town

There are the futuristic looking roof structures contrasting with the brick façades and their huge gas dial gauges. And there is the new square cinema complex next door with its gaudy coloured-glass walls making the gasometers look like alien protagonists of a weird sci-fi movie. The *image contrasts* between the old and new are like a leif-motif running through the entire entertainment complex. They serve as the emotional link that blends the different facilities on offer – such as eateries, the cinema, a library, stores and concert hall – into a whole, allowing us to experience the centre in its entirety (see Figure 0.5). The image contrast is the *concept line* of this Third Place.

Figure 0.5   Image contrast, old/new, Gasometer, Vienna
Photo by Alexander Vesely

Image contrasts

While in the United States urban entertainment centres are frequently emotionalized by means of the painstaking use of scenery, artificial thunder and lightning and talking robots, we in Europe get this enticing interplay of contrasts almost for free. This method has stood the test of time. Those who enter the Orsay outlet on Kärntner Strasse in Vienna will experience the delightful contrast between the stucco of the historic atrium and a linear array of blue neon lamps unobtrusively pulsing on to the ceiling.

At the Mango store just across the street a white new-wave tiled wall struggles with classicist columns. At the Zurich hotel Widder – which I consider Europe's finest business hotel – modern furniture contrasts with the exposed frescoes of the Renaissance building, and the hyper-modern steel and glass lift runs through a shaft formed by bulky, heavy stones looking like the inside of a solid rock. At the atrium of the Tate Modern in London many visitors to this 'cathedral of modern art' stretch out on the wide stairs running down the 155-metre-long side wall of this former power plant building. They marvel at the luminous frames hanging high above their heads and the irresistible visual contrast provided by their bright white light against the industrial architecture of this former turbine hall. Vienna, Zurich, London – in many old European cities the *image contrast* between the old and the new was discovered as a key dramatizing link for emotionalizing museums, urban entertainment centres, stores and hotels. Thanks to the new, the old substance of the building seems refreshed, starts to 'glow from within' again and is celebrated. The historic flair of the Renaissance era, the 19th century or early industrial architecture is even more perceivable with this *image contrast.* And conversely, the proximity of the old provides some 'earthing' for the new, tying it to the roots of the place.

How atmosphere emerges

To understand how to produce this effect we need to be aware how the flair of a place emerges. And here the packaging effect comes into play. We all know from our own experience that packaging can make or break a present. It practically makes an image statement, commenting on the wrapped item. '*Inferential beliefs*' is the technical phrase for this mechanism in psychology, meaning that architecture and design trigger a type of prejudice in terms of the image and the atmosphere of a place. A fortified castle with dilapidated walls can have a romantic effect on us without actually being romantic. The flair of a place is merely an idea we get, and in actual fact we construct the product of the image ourselves.

This internal construction is prompted by the effect of the materials used, the style, the sounds at a place, its odours. Bücherbogen, for instance, is a book store in Berlin specializing in architecture and technology, and is located in vaults which stretch right underneath a light-railway train track, of all places. The floor creaks when you go from one room to another, and every other minute a light-rail train clatters across the shoppers' heads. This sound appropriately characterizes the bookstore as a technical place and creates a flair that boosts the image of the range.

The resulting image construct generates the experience felt. Places with a consistent *image contrast* trigger this construct doubly and must have a stronger internal arrangement. They generate bipolar flair that is particularly charming in its contradictoriness. This is how the *image contrast* became an especially successful *concept line* in Europe, creating authentic experience worlds. These places ideally respond to the new need for authenticity and sustainability.

Authenticity-based theming

This need for a great deal of authenticity has also changed a classic *concept line* dramatically: *theming*. Only a few years back 100 per cent scenery-based worlds were still considered the number one technique for producing arranged places, the *concept line per se*. 'Stories to be walked into' were developed for shops, restaurants and hotels, allowing their visitors to escape briefly from everyday life. The optimism of the entertainment industry was so paramount that the omnipresence of themed worlds was even joked about: 'What shall we do once the whole world has been themed?' and so sceneries were eagerly built and the dream world of Hollywood movies was cited as a source of inspiration. There were themed worlds in Wild West, sci-fi and adventure movie style. Visitors to a karaoke bar in Tokyo immersed themselves in an alien-like science fiction world; those who spent the night at a Vegas hotel could watch a burning schooner sink in front of the hotel façade, downed by the pirate ship across the street.

All themed worlds transpose us into a story. Young men, for example, who put on a Stetson at the Wild West section of Disneyland all of a sudden start walking with a rolling gait. Their behaviour corresponds to the scenery. Intuitively they play the inner storyboard that matches the scenery world. Those who make their inner *brain scripts* come true in such a way can lose themselves entirely in that other world, escaping from the here and now to another time and place. Themed worlds were therefore always an escape into a better world; they were escapist. Buyers at trade shows, fed up with inspecting the quality of leather jackets at the stand, took a minute or two to sit down on that Harley-Davidson parked in a scene reminiscent of a 'lonesome old filling station in the Arizona desert', and mutated into easy riders to feel footloose and fancy free.

Suddenly, everything changed. Somehow – under the influence of the recession and imminent millennium – people were fed up with scenery-only themed worlds. Particularly elaborate and authentic theme parks such as Disneyland still boomed, but other themed worlds such as the Planet Hollywood restaurant chain met with trouble. At the same time, it was found that more and more authenticity was incorporated into themed worlds – alongside the scenery. In Disney's new Animal Kingdom, the world's largest arranged zoo, rusted Indian Coca-Cola signs point the way to the refreshments area, where Indian tigers run through rebuilt temples. When you ask one of the young Indian guys on the staff the way, he will answer you in a strong New Delhi taxi driver accent. It seems the operators here chose to recruit for this job Indians just entering the country over those smart third-generation-Indian marketing students. This is why Disney World in Florida exudes an almost consistent Bombay-stic feel.

In Europe planners rely on the authenticity factor even more stringently because this, after all, has always been one of our strong points. Those who fight all the way up through the Tyrol mountains covered with snow until they reach the Haubenrestaurant Hospizalm will be rewarded with an authentic Austrian themed world. Not scenery but largely genuine parts of Alpine culture were used for theming here. On the ground floor of a two-storey atrium there are genuine Tyrolean and southern Tyrolean stone pine parlours lined up like little stages. The year 1888 is carved into the wall of the Montafoner parlour, and we have no reason to disbelieve it. With their hand-painted decorations and wood carvings these parlours transpose guests into another era. Many details nourish this illusion for the rest of the evening. The list of menus looks like a wooden board, and is even bound in wood. The open fireplace in the middle of the room radiates an intense heat we big-city dwellers are no longer familiar with. At this moment a waiter opens a small latch in a wooden wall and serves a glass of heady red wine.

Behind the wall a couple sits in a wooden niche, enjoying the privacy of the tiny room. A cheerful group carouses in the former stables, the initial function of which is still clearly visible. We take a tour of the restaurant. Via a brick slide – quite customary in those days – we reach one of the largest magnum bottle wine cellars, where we pay respects to the two 15 litre Mouton Rothschild 1990s standing beside a tapestry. Each bottle costs €25,000. The tab for our dinner is presented in a little wooden box with wing doors. We open and immediately close it again when we see the price. This place has a themed *concept line*, it carries its guests away and into another world, yet it is doubtlessly European, authentic and – expensive.

Design-based theming

In parallel with authenticity-based theming that always somehow draws on inspirations from the past or nature, an urban version of the authentic flight into dreams has emerged over the past few years: *theming with design*. Here design furniture is not used decoratively – as a styling statement – but it 'beams' us – as usual with *theming* – right into a story. It prompts a *brain script* in which you play a role. The best example of this method is probably Sony Style in New York.

It was found out that many women prevented their husbands from buying the high-quality television systems they had selected with a show-stopper argument: that they did not fit the interior decor. Accordingly, Sony decided to install a lounge for women and families at its flagship store in Manhattan where these expensive toys for grown-ups could be experienced the same way as at home. Potential buyers sink into extremely comfortable designer sofas in front of large-screen televisions. Midnight-blue velvet walls with silver masks, large-format black and white photos of Thirties Hollywood stars and spectacularly illuminated flower bouquets exude an upper-class lounging atmosphere in the immediate vicinity of the sets. We were flabbergasted with the observations we made: the homely atmosphere makes the customers really behave as if they were at home. We saw people fall asleep in front of the television. We observed couples who exchanged not a single word, with nothing to say to each other for a long time. We watched families argue about the choice of programme, although only two were shown alternately. In a word: these customers live the typical *brain script* they have acquired for their individual television-watching behaviour. In other words: these customers do not critically review the sets as they would in a showroom but already use them in the same relaxed way they would at home. Sony has now duplicated this concept, developed by interior designer James Mansour, several times over for, among others, the urban entertainment centre Sony Metreon in San Francisco and the Sony Centre at Berlin's Potsdamer Platz.

Design-based theming lends itself to all applications where planners embark on a new path of style-conscious entertainment. The highest level of aesthetics blends with most discerning demands on entertainment, and is far more than just good design. It therefore does not come as a surprise that this dramatizing method is now also encountered at the new high-quality themed hotels in Las Vegas. 'Noodles' at the Bellagio Hotel is an Asian restaurant themed around pasta. Dozens of pasta types are displayed here in elegant glass cylinders backlighted by a white luminous wall like modern objects of art in a gallery. And guests behave correspondingly. At least with their eyes, or inconspicuously on their way to the toilet, they 'visit' and marvel at the diversity and beauty of the noodles. Only a few metres away in the same hotel, guests at the Japanese sushi bar all share a type of sacred feeling without being able to account for it. Only after a while do they understand. Behind the counter and the sushi chef there is an aquarium-based arrangement that prompts sacred *brain scripts*. The three aquariums seamlessly recessed into the back wall remind us of a three-piece altar picture dating back to medieval times. Fish with a bluish green tinge swim in the left and right 'wing' while golden-yellow jellyfish sparkle in the central aquarium. Live animals become the carriers of design messages here, and unconsciously make us play out a story in our heads whether we like it or not: *theming with authenticity and design* in one.

Image contrast and *theming* are two possibilities to provide experience worlds with a *concept line*. Only if visitors perceive a place in its entirety will this decisive interplay work of core function, that brings us to a place, and add-on function, that makes us stay longer. The exhibition at the museum is one thing – the shopping mall on the premises is another. These shops and restaurants at museums, however, will only seem attractive to us if they are incorporated into the emotional 'context' of the premises.

4   Core attraction

In a skin-tight black cat suit and black gloves she looks like a cat burglar specialized in stealing jewellery from guests at luxury hotels.

Her hands reach out for the steel cable. At the touch of a button the hydraulic winch starts moving. Silently she floats up along the walls of the glass towers passing innumerable, perfectly stored and temperature-controlled bottles of wine. This unusual wine store right in the middle of the restaurant is 17 metres high. The artiste stops at the height of the heady Californian tintos and carefully pulls a Caymus Cabernet Sauvignon 1996 from the rack. Japanese businessmen sit gaping at the bar that surrounds the foot of the tower as they watch this performance. But the bottle of wine served with such panache is not meant for them. It will be taken to a table on the other side of the tower. Over the course of the evening this performance will be repeated over and over again, making many visitors stare in disbelief. Later, they will tell other visitors to Las Vegas about it. In a city like Vegas, 'must see' spectacles like this get about quickly. The wine tower turns the Auréole at the Mandalay Bay Resort into a first-rate sight of the city. It is the *core attraction* of the restaurant, the magnet that draws people in, arousing their curiosity. The baffling *wow effect* that is produced by the performance at the restaurant fully satisfies previously aroused expectations (see colour plate section).

'Wow' effects

While the concept line makes for prolonged visiting time and turns each experience world into a home from home, the *core attraction* generates another, just as typical, added benefit. It turns restaurants, shopping malls, museums into modern attractions for city tourists, into meeting points for the lifestyle-oriented urban community.

The more those things that are necessary anyway are dramatized, the more authenticity is exuded by the central arrangement. A wine cellar is needed at every restaurant serving alcoholic beverages, so why not 'up'-style it into an attraction? Department stores cannot do without lifts and escalators. Why not turn an escalator into a '*wow*' *effect*? This was apparently also the idea of the planners of the Nordstrom department store in San Francisco – which is why they developed circular escalators that have became real head-turners in the atrium. Whoever thinks that this can only take place in America should take time to look at the Billa supermarket at the heart of Vienna's historic old town. In the Singerstrasse right next to the famous Stephansdom cathedral, an unusual escalator for shopping trolleys running along the side of the escalator for shoppers makes for the attraction of the store. It allows easy access to the two-storey market and is well thought out because shoppers actually 'overtake' their own trolleys on the 'people mover', which allows them to pick them up after a relaxed trip.

Psychologically speaking both circular escalators and the tower wine cellar in the centre of the room play with our ability to handle smartly, and marvel at delightfully, such peculiarities of modern life, rather than make a desperate and hasty departure. They address our *media literacy*, an ability we come across repeatedly now. The whole system of the *core attraction* is actually nothing but a correlation of psychological mechanisms revolving around the interplay of suspense and relaxation.

The art of suspense

Everything starts with targeted rumours, with imaginative PR. The audience must be made curious, it must anticipate – literally translated, it must be 'geared to a target'. No one has ever described what this means better than the renowned trainer for screenplay writers, Syd Field (1982). In his seminars he loves to tell a story to show what *anticipation* means.

A travelling salesman arrives at a simple country hotel in the evening. He is tired and goes to bed immediately. But he has lousy luck: at night another guest arrives who is booked into the room above, of all rooms, and who is also pretty drunk. Inconsiderately he drops a heavy boot which hits the floor with a bang, so that our salesman is wide awake. An hour later, still unnerved, he knocks against the ceiling and shouts up: 'Are you ever going to drop your second boot?'

He obviously surmised that this could not be the end of it. Whenever such a presentiment emerges and its fulfilment is delayed you are 'dying' to hear the end of the story; you anticipate, become curious, are motivated to hold on, thereby experiencing a feeling of suspense which is perceived as pleasant for some time in an entertainment environment. But then you want to release the internal suspense called cognitive dissonance and finally experience what was presented to you like a carrot on the stick: the *core attraction*.

Now you decide whether the core attraction lives up to your expectations. There are two basic possibilities for this. Either your expectations are fulfilled with a baffling, so-called 'wow' effect; in which case some type of trick is played on you using your *media literacy*. A wine cellar, for instance, which is usually built top-down into the ground, is basically turned upside down and constructed bottom-up. The baffling change of the viewing angle, additionally dramatized through the artiste climbing this tower, produces the big, flabbergasted 'oh' that releases every expectational suspense.

Or suspense is released by means of a big *show effect* through which this expectational suspense is felt physically. Shows must be 'bigger than life' and trigger our body feeling through additional music, rhythm, great sounds and optical effects that make our eyes fly to the source of this stimulus. This includes rhythm-based cut video clips on the large screen sliding into New York's Nike Town every 13 minutes, surprisingly featuring a different format each time; this includes the fountains in front of the Bellagio Hotel in Las Vegas where water jets dance with the music across a length of 280 metres and spray up 75 metres high. Vegas visitors have tears in their eyes watching the spectacular curtain of water produced by 1,400 nozzles as it majestically closes from both ends, while Andrea Bocelli impressively stays in key for the last note of his song. Finally, this includes the fireworks crowning both large ceremonies and small regional festivities. Light, water and fire – staged larger than life – so that they can be felt physically: they all turn the *core attraction* into a big finale.

Show effects

Classic *show effects* in public spaces also include imaginative neon signs in the entertainment centres of our cities. At London's Piccadilly Circus they were the *core attraction* of the theatre and entertainments district Soho as early as the 1970s. In the Ginza of Tokyo tourists marvel at the light shows produced by large conglomerates; their lights move like on a rollercoaster, producing moving, 3-D light sculptures. At New York's Times Square the hit is huge, high-luminance screens showing racy clips that vie for the attention of the crowds visiting Broadway. Everyone tries to outdo the competition with an even bigger screen. Top of the list in this current screen craze is the seven-storey screen at the Nasdaq MarketSide Tower, which sensationally winds around the cylinder-shaped building.

Show effects aim to trigger body feelings. To this end all light shows bombard us with constantly varying stimuli for the eyes to trigger those so-called *orientation reflexes* (Mikunda, 2002a) in our body. This is an ancient survival mechanism permitting us to respond to fast movements by way of reflexes. Way back in our history when sabre-toothed tigers would jump at us from the undergrowth this reflex allowed us to be gone by the time any tiger had landed by the fireplace we were sitting at. Within fractions of a second all our forces are at our disposal for either escape or attack; we feel how emotions are rising. Racy music videos, modern action movies and advertising make use of this thrilling visual effect. Since we automatically turn towards the source of these stimuli, such effects became a popular method for public neon signs. Planners increasingly discovered the aesthetic value of such arrangements, resulting in the light-centred *core attractions* in London, New York, Las Vegas, Tokyo and Osaka: instruments of city marketing and tourism, meeting points for lovers and night owls, *Third Places* in the city.

Paris, New Year's Eve, 1999. The millennium celebrations reach their climax. The party actually centres on the Champs Elysées but its true *core attraction* is a spectacular *show effect* that moves the Eiffel Tower centre-stage. Everyone is in suspense. The New Year approaches with fireworks of a new dimension, a show of light and fire living up to even the most discerning demands in terms of design and emotionality. Two minutes to midnight and the countdown for the millennium starts. The Eiffel Tower now resembles a rocket about to launch. 20,000 halogen flashlights and never-ending volleys of fireworks slowly work their way up the tower. Finally the clock 'strikes' zero and the magic moment has come. Fireworks now envelop the Eiffel Tower with zillions of floral ornaments. Fans of fire in brilliant white run up and down the tower, in perfect time with the music – like art-deco patterns come to life. Never before has a building been ennobled so emotionally in a live performance as this Paris landmark was on that memorable night. Finally the anchorman of the French station Antenne 2 steps in front of the camera and says: 'The Eiffel Tower has made it' – and the 20,000 mini flashes are left to sparkle alone. Their change of stimulus triggers a multitude of orientation reflexes and produces the aesthetically most beautiful thrill for the human eye ever seen in a public space. All through the year 2000 this effect is repeated hourly after sunset. Even months later tourists still cling to the panes of their sight-seeing buses as their tour guide says emotionally, 'On your left you can now see the Eiffel Tower' and it once again turns into the sparkling *core attraction* of 2000.

SUMMARY

▌ **THIRD PLACES.**

▌ *Following the home and workplace they rank third as staged habitats in the city.*

▌ *These used to be Viennese coffee-houses, Italian piazzas, corner shops.*

▌ *These are now the new marketing places in business such as flagship stores.*

▌ *Brain scripts and other psychological mechanisms make them hyper-attractive.*

▌ *Apart from serving consumption purposes they therefore also recharge us with emotion.*

▌ *It was in this way that shops became sites to see and museums became places for going out.*

▌ *They share the same set-up: pull in, induce malling, provide an all-encompassing idea, arouse curiosity.*

▌ **Landmark.** Third places attract us by featuring landmarks, often in the form of headers which – like medieval guild signs – show people outside what to expect inside.

▌ **Malling.** Third Places make us mall by calling up our cognitive maps using suspense axes and other tricks.

▌ **Concept line.** Third Places have a 'golden thread' running through them providing the different rational functions of a place by means of one all-encompassing emotional idea.

▌ **Core attraction.** Third Places arouse our curiosity with a central attraction that also relieves any remaining suspense when we actually visit it.

▌ *Third Places are experience rooms for business as urban habitats.*

▌ *They are a means of walk-on advertising making people 'browse' in them.*

▌ *They are what the avant-garde of popular culture like rock music or comic strips used to be.*

▌ *They make cities shine the way only palaces and churches did in former times.*

▌ *They give expression to an experience society that has now grown up.*

PART I

VISITS TO BRANDS AND FACTORIES

The leisure park boom has also given rise to the need for experience worlds in Europe. Many people are already used to making their way to emotionally charged places offering delights they previously only knew from movies or the television. Leisure parks, however, are primarily kids' worlds. They tell stories for kids and they correspondingly address families with kids. But where are the stories told for grown-ups, those great stories about the fascination of technology, their passionate inventers, about food and drinks or impressive design?

Today these experiences for grown-ups are offered by fairs and staged brand exhibitions, so-called *brand lands*. Major public fairs such as IFA, the World of Consumer Electronics in Berlin, IAA – the International Automotive Exhibition in Frankfurt – or the CeBIT in Hanover are all places where the staging per se has become almost as important as the actual innovative value of the products on show.

Brand lands – that is, brand exhibitions – have however a number of advantages over staged fairs: one of them indubitably being their budget. When you consider BMW spent some €50 million on the IAA 2001, for a period of just 10 days, you can imagine how difficult it is to finance such large, expensive staged events for such a short period of time.

Brand lands, in contrast to this, can remain unchanged for many years. And they boast another benefit compared with fairs: they are simply more impressive in architectural terms. Most premises for brand lands are new and purpose-built. Many exhibition centres, on the contrary, are developed and grow organically over time, and therefore frequently resemble labyrinths; they hide away the brands in halls so that their attraction can actually only be felt inside that hall but not throughout the entire fair grounds. Brand lands like the VW Autostadt in Wolfsburg can be purpose-built from the outset, meaning that they project an emotionally perceivable picture to the outside. The VW Autostadt, for instance, features a spectacular landmark: two large towers each holding 400 cars waiting to be collected by their owners. (See colour plate section.) The spatial structure is impressive and follows the pre-set principles of the cognitive map. The *entrance map* handed out to visitors depicts a clear separation of different brand worlds arranged like islands in a water world featuring landscaped terrain: there is the 'KonzernForum' area, there is the delivery area, there is the hotel. In contrast to a trade fair, a brand land is easily made visible as an adventure park and all essential brand messages can also become perceivable externally.

For fairs and brand lands the same rule applies: a live experience, the experience one actually gains, has a higher recollective value than simple advertising or conventional PR. When taking a two-day trip to Wolfsburg or the IAA Fair, one makes an excursion and pursues an activity that turns into part of one's own life, one's individual experience: this is visiting the brand or the factory.

1

Brand lands

Charging brands through permanent exhibitions

In the days before the Industrial Revolution the 'making' of products was still immediately accessible for people. They were able to watch the cobbler repairing their shoes and craftspeople making products. This 'presence' created credibility and proximity, and fuelled people's demands for buying something new or their desire to use a service. Then the entire production process was locked up in factories. The craving for new products was safeguarded by advertising, which had just been invented. What was lost in the process, however, was that immediate proximity to production, the credibility and the power of conviction: this function has now been taken over by those permanent exhibitions arranged at corporate locations: the brand lands, the new brand worlds.

A type of fully fledged brand land is the VW Autostadt in Wolfsburg, Germany (see Figure 1.1). On the one hand, it is a *place of understanding* where the brand is 'brought home' to us by way of sensual explanations at the KonzernForum and the Zeithaus. Here a small show makes visitors aware of how solar energy works. In a glass showcase you see little vehicles driving over sand. If you hold the flexible lamps over them, these cars start moving; the moment you tilt the lamp sideways they immediately stop. Seeing is believing. Exactly the same show can be found in the kids' section of the famous Cité des Sciences et de l'Industrie in Paris, a science museum of the new generation. This shows us where the brand land type of approach originally stems from – modern science museums are to be found everywhere these days. This can also be seen inside an installation at the KonzernForum demonstrating to visitors how material testing is done at VW: for example through heat or vibration testing where visitors themselves get 'all shook up'. These are all so-called *hands-on,* interactive installations beamed immediately from the world of science museums to the world of brand lands.

On the other hand, this type of brand lands is a *place of adoration*, of recharging the brand. At the Autostadt this would apply to the brand pavilions of Audi, Seat, Skoda, Bentley and VW that are scattered across the park. They provide no explanations on the brands what-soever – their sole purpose is to recharge the brands with emotion and make their image glow. An example is the Lamborghini building, a black cube reminiscent of the Kaaba in Mecca, featuring a show that merely consists of making a Lamborghini behind bars roar like a wild animal before it is finally released accompanied by smoke and lighting effects. It only clings to the outside wall of the pavilion for seconds before it moves inside again, where the show approaches its grand finale – you immediately feel the force, the savagery, the wild energy of this car. (See colour plate section.)

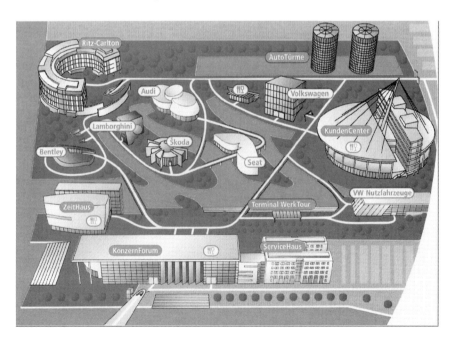

Figure 1.1   Entrance map to Autostadt, Wolfsburg
© Autostadt

Last but not least there are *places of desire*, brand lands where the focus is on the delivery of the merchandise to customers and where the suspense, the longing for the product sensed immediately before it is handed over, is additionally dramatized and staged. At VW this 'staging of suspense' is done by way of the two large car towers that contain the objects of desire, so to speak. Knowing that in three hours' time this large lift will descend with your own car to the delivery hall, you will view these towers with different eyes, a special sense of joyful expectation. This anticipation, this curiosity and thrill is infectious, and transmitted to all other visitors who have come just to see the premises and who are not collecting a car at all.

THE PLACE OF UNDERSTANDING

These *places of understanding* doubtless go back to the guided plant visits so popular in the past. Even at the perfectly styled VW Autostadt you will still spot a collection point marked with a sign saying 'Werksbesichtigung' (guided plant tour). Guided plant tours work along the *looking-over-the-shoulder* principle. They now perform the task that used to come naturally when observing craftspeople. Guided plant tours are offered by all major automotive companies, in Germany especially by VW, Mercedes and Opel. I personally felt the enormous emotional force underlying guided plant tours when I climbed over the building site of the unfinished VW Autostadt, and also when I had the opportunity to visit the plant. There were giant punches cutting metal with such incredible force that the whole concrete floor was shaking. There were the robots – and one of them always slightly lagging behind the others, which was why the VW staff had given it a special nickname. It is simply fun to see these details, and it is authentic: you feel as if you are experiencing live what is really going on there.

This 'being able to watch' is used throughout the world to create proximity to products.

Observing glass blowers in Venice, this looking over their shoulder is a means of direct sales promotion benefiting the factory shop right next door. When you stand on the large spectators' bridge at Riedel Glass in Austria and watch the glass factory at work you are observing part of a brand staging at a plant. When you visit Disney and look over the draughtspersons' shoulders through a glass pane and see with your own eyes how they assemble individual drawings into a real cartoon, or when on the FBI tour in Washington a hidden wall rises and you can watch how a lab team investigates crime scene evidence, the live experience then becomes a calculated competence strategy in a *visitors' centre*, because guided plant tours are increasingly combined with the plant's own visitors' centre. You will find them at national parks, factories and at large industrial companies. At visitors' centres the looking-over-the-shoulder effect produced by guided plant tours can be intensified by additional interactive installations. Hands-on experiences make things easy to 'grasp' in the truest sense of the word. To an increasing extent visitors' centres are installed without a proper plant tour, next to the company premises or at times even completely separate.

The 'seeing is believing' effect

The principle of seeing something with your own eyes is based on a very old dramatic trick. It is all about the persuasive power of appearance, about furnishing evidence to make something credible, about Doubting Thomas. The Bible tells the story of this disciple who was not present when Jesus Christ – dead or resurrected – visited the other disciples. After he returns home the other disciples tell him that Jesus has been there and he says, 'I don't believe it – I have seen with my own eyes how he died.' Some time later Jesus Christ visits his disciples again, and this time Thomas Didimus is present. Jesus approaches him and says, 'Here I am, do you want to touch me?' He shows him authentic details such as the wounds inflicted on the cross, and he urges Thomas to touch these wounds, whereupon Thomas gets down on his knees and believes.

Through the persuasive power of appearance and little authentic details one starts believing things previously only asserted.

Assertion and proof follow each other immediately, that is, the *consumer benefit* that is asserted by a product and the *reason why* this assertion is true. Especially in sectors like the automotive industry where investment volumes are very high, consumers must be given immediate proof of the product benefit – for we live in times where nearly all consumers are Doubting Thomases. Since they spend a lot of money on their cars they say, 'Show me what's so great about this car.' This is why at the A-class brand land by Mercedes in Rastatt consumers can see with their own eyes how the engine block slides underneath the seats in the event of a crash – here simulated at the touch of a button. This is why visitors to VW can witness in person how a lump of clay and other kneadable materials develop into a car model. And why at Toyota's AMLUX (AMLUX is short for Automobile and luxury) car theatre in Tokyo you can compile all the major colours and materials of your dream vehicle and see with your own eyes what your car will look like.

Traffic instructors have used road safety training parks for decades, making children travel round a simulated automotive landscape by bicycle or pedal-car. At the KonzernForum at VW's Autostadt there is a particularly attractive pedal-car track, while the *Toyota E-com Ride* in Tokyo offers an adult version of a road safety training park like this. It features a street that runs through the hall of the brand land and ends up in the outdoor grounds. Every few minutes automatically driven cars pass by – these are concept cars still under development – which you can board and take a ride on. This is great fun and a central attraction to everyone at the brand land, and what's more, it is an original way to fulfil the 'show-me' and 'let's check' need felt by all those Doubting Thomases.

The common rule here is that the competence message must be unique and support the brand image rather than sabotage it. This is what went wrong with Opel Live, the unfortunate brand land built by Opel (Vauxhall/GM) in Rüsselsheim near Frankfurt, which was recently forced to shut down. It did have a number of *hands-on* installations, such as a *competence concept line* where one could, for instance, smell how filters prevent odours from entering the car interior. You could also see how rain affects visibility inside cars. In a vibration simulator you could take a test drive. However, the image effects produced here were disastrous, and actually backfired, because they were completely non-specific to the brand. For one thing, all modern automobiles contain such filter systems these days. And for another, they were counterproductive. After taking a test drive in the vibration simulator many visitors felt that 'if you are shaken up like that in an Opel it can't be the right thing'.

The 'aha' effect

Sony runs a very nice brand land in Tokyo which recently turned 25 years old, making it one of the oldest brand lands in the world. It features a room where all the latest equipment launched by Sony is exhibited in acrylic glass form. Here, for instance, we find a CD player containing 100 CDs. Seeing such a device at a regular Sony showroom may prompt you to think, 'this is quite impressive' but the high-tech image only truly unfolds when you look at the acrylic glass version of the CD changer, where you can actually look into the device and see the 100 CDs lined up ready to play. The same room also contains a professional Sony video camera – the type I frequently saw in my days as a television journalist – which is why I know how carefully such cameras must be placed on the ground to avoid misaligning the target. At Sony I saw the inner workings of this camera for the first time, and the target that produces such disastrous effects when misaligned.

If the true strength of a product hidden beneath the surface is 'exteriorized' by a strategic disclosure, then a so-called aha effect is produced which only makes the actual image core perceptible.

The '*seeing is believing*' effect and the '*aha*' effect taken together form the explanatory *concept line* of each competence-oriented brand land.

Not only can the secrets of a product be revealed and exteriorized by dramatized disclosures, but the secrets of a production process can also be made perceptible in this way. The peculiarities of modern manufacturing also include the principle of 'breathing factories', to name just one. The A-class cars by Mercedes are produced according to this principle. At the A-class brand land in Rastatt, this secret is disclosed by means of Q & A boxes. These consist of metal columns with metal flaps, with a question affixed to them. The question runs, 'What is a breathing factory?' You open the flap and by doing so you disclose the answer. What you see is a photo of the Mercedes member of staff in charge of this department, and he makes a statement on the breathing factory, animated by a chip. The essential point of a breathing factory is that it works where production demands it and stops working if capacity utilization is low. Only the opening of the flap, the peeping underneath and the employee's disclosing statement turn a simple piece of information into an emotional 'aha' effect.

One of the most spectacular 'aha' effects is the disclosure of a corporate image perceived quite differently at first sight. Fujita Vente is an installation in the factory basement of Japan's largest construction company, Fujita. It is a fun basement designed for kids to discover that the electronic controls used in those large, heavy, dusty and noisy construction vehicles can also be used in a very playful way. You can guide one of several robots through the premises, or compose music with a special computer piano. This is how Fujita shows that it is not only a noisy, dirty company, but employs a technology full of adventure and aesthetic appeal, doing something positive for people. To convey this attitude to the outside world there is a tree complete with visible roots freely floating in the entrance hall of the company headquarters, there is an automatic piano playing in the lobby, there is a shark swimming through a fish tank, and there is an atmosphere created that gives a massage to the soul. It conveys lightness, cleanliness and ecology, which has even led to an ecological energy and water supply system so spectacular that it is visited by many experts from all over the world.

Like the 'seeing is believing', the 'aha' effect is also dependent on the message disclosed being individual and unique and having a *USP*, a unique selling proposition. In contrast to Opel Live, the Riedel Sinnfonie brand land is a very neat example of this. Split into three monitor images, the junior boss of the company sits in front of us and shows us what it means to sip red wine from a Riedel glass: how the shape of the glass affects the posture of the head, how it changes and ennobles the taste of the wine. He tells a story – and this is his unique message, his statement, his very personal dramatic disclosure – how his dad several decades ago used blind testing and managed to convince a group of wine critics in London that one and the same wine tastes quite different when drunk from different glasses, and that a glass that perfectly matches the type of wine can clearly enhance its taste.

THE PLACE OF ADORATION

Brand lands of this type are not explanatory: instead they recharge the brand, are designed to make the brand shine.

At the VW Autostadt this type would correspond to the brand pavilions that work along the lines of the aforementioned Lamborghini Pavilion. The image of a brand actually consists of a whole sequence of interrelated image properties generated by the mechanism of *inferential beliefs* described above. What this means is best illustrated by an example: in the past people did not wear colourful spectacles or design 'eyewear', but as is the case today, everyone wearing glasses was automatically considered intelligent – while in fact, wearing spectacles only means a person's vision is somehow impaired. The image is therefore a construction departing from a factual image core, and linked to other associated characteristics that are rather emotional in nature. *Places of understanding* help us to grasp the image core through mechanisms like 'seeing is believing' or the disclosing impact of the 'aha' effect. The *places of adoration* polish this image until it shines, thereby communicating the more irrational aspects of the image.

There are a number of methods to achieve this: allegories, for instance. Allegories are symbols that make something all too abstract immediately visible, thereby 'unlocking the image-sequence'. With VW's brand pavilions the outer appearance is already very striking: it virtually 'speaks', it is self-explanatory. Visible to the outside, the *landmarks* are constructed headlines, *headers* showing everyone from afar the messages being communicated inside the pavilions. In this context there is the roaring animal 'Lamborghini' that turns outwards and hangs spectacularly from the black façade of the pavilion. There is the Bentley pavilion that resembles a racecourse, conveying how Bentley used to be the dominating car make at the famous Le Mans races. There is the VW pavilion with its compelling geometry, comprising a sphere that is 'written' into a cube – cube and sphere being the symbols of perfection.

Allegory

Lamborghini – as VW say themselves – is the *symbol* of masculinity bursting with power and Italian magnificence; it is the danger of an irrepressible animal, it is something bombastic. All image characteristics taken together form the 'image sequence', that is, the image you form about a Lamborghini. The dramatist's method now consists of addressing other elements of this image sequence. The cage holding the car conveys the animal-like features of the Lamborghini; the roaring of the engines, the smoke and fire projections, thunder and lightning signal the power embedded in the cylinders; the special high-tech effect of the car turning to the outside and daringly clinging to the pavilion wall conveys Italian *grandezza* – that grandeur which is so striking about this sports car. Correspondingly, the staging is structured in such a way that each part of it triggers special properties in the sequence. All image properties are summed up in the allegory of the roaring, brilliant animal representative of the Lamborghini. The *inferential belief* mechanism is responsible for making all other properties of the image sequence come to light once one characteristic is addressed, thereby making the brand image shine.

Just a few steps further on at the VW pavilion, lying under a spectacular video projection dome you can watch the story of two girls. They both achieve perfection in their very own way by training and practice. One of them is a violinist, the other a figure skater. This allegory gives us a feeling for the image sequence of an entirely different car, a Volkswagen, where perfection is achieved by hard work and the relentless striving for improvement. To a certain extent this is a very German image – in a thoroughly positive sense: perfection through diligence rather than through grandeur or a special vision.

The 'live' effect

Driving up the mountain at Kitzbühel you invariably end up at the starting hut of the famous and feared Streif ski run. Right there, alongside a video showing the most spectacular downhill scenes of the past few years, you unexpectedly find yourself right where all those daring skiers plunge into the depths. As if by coincidence, two ski sticks are leaning there. Many tourists simply pick up the sticks and intuitively imitate the posture of skiers at the start. At this very moment, in the pit of your stomach you feel exactly what these skiers must be going through only seconds before the start of a run like this, and you feel and experience the emotional situation in a direct, immediate manner. Even those unfamiliar with approaching the start of a downhill race like this will see how the image sequence of the Streif ski run unfolds most convincingly.

Such a dramatized event makes a situation actually separated in terms of space or time into one that is ever present and 'experienceable'.

This is all about playing with the powers of the imagination, playing with *brain scripts*. The point here is to take an idea on face value; like in children's games where they think up stories revolving around their miniature cars or dolls, and actually believe in the presence of these stories as they play.

In an earlier chapter reference was made to the tennis brain script, the script in our brains that is triggered as soon as tell-tale 'tock tock' sounds and other signals associated with a tennis match call up our internal *brain script* for a tennis match. In the tennis departments of

Nike Towns in America or Europe you will hear precisely that tell-tale 'tock tock' sound from concealed loudspeakers. They trigger the tennis brain script and draw our attention to those white tennis socks stocked at the left rear part of the store. In this case, the correlation between the goods and their use is made 'experienceable' and present at the point of sale by triggering the brain script of that product's use/purpose. You are practically teleported into the use situation of the goods emotionally. The brand can be experienced live.

At the AMLUX in Tokyo a special technical effect allows visitors to feel the power of the roaring engines of Toyota cars: they watch a film in a vibration and fragrance cinema, and each time a Toyota car drives off, low-frequency loudspeakers make the shells in which visitors are seated vibrate. But back to the VW Autostadt. Those stepping through the famous four silver rings to enter the Audi pavilion will unexpectedly end up at the home of Max and his family. The famous French scenographer François Confino, who designed this pavilion, welcomes us in a somewhat ironic, self-mocking way. 'You won't believe it,' he makes Max write, 'but I live here with my family.' And then we meet Max again, whose hobby seems to be carving Audi models out of wood. He adores their sensual surfaces, and we come across these models in a workshop that looks more like that of an artist.

What we encounter here is a *themed environment* – an environment that makes visitors to the pavilion become part of the play, and realize some of the *brain scripts* that are triggered here within. And visitors to the pavilion do start sensuously and sensually touching the wooden Audi models that Max has allegedly carved. In the next room we suddenly find ourselves sitting in Max's living room; it is a themed lifestyle living room, a dwelling that stands for typical Audi users as seen by the company: trendy and lifestyle-oriented. Sushi is ready at the kitchen, the whirlpool evokes memories of white sailing yachts projected into the bath tub placed right next to a king-size designer bed. It is a surrealist and ironic world because the next room houses – would you believe – two snowmen discussing the technical features of the new Audi.

In the same way that you feel the lifestyle of the Audi brand by starting to play a role in this themed world, you perceive the divine flair of a very special wine at Opus One, Robert Mondavi's famous wine-growing estate in the Californian Napa Valley. Descending the stairs of the spiral staircase leading to the cellar, you suddenly hit a glass wall overlooking a gigantic ecclesiastical scene. Hundreds of casks holding the famous Cabernet Sauvignon are arranged in a circle. This is King Arthur's Round Table, this is the holy circle of Stonehenge – and in front of them there is a table that again reflects the spherical shape and invites wine connoisseurs to gather around it like King Arthur's faithful followers.

The 'packaging' effect

Back again to the AMLUX by Toyota in Tokyo: it is spring, and the current campaign is designed to communicate the car's proximity to nature, and to stress the close-to-nature properties in the image sequence. Artists have placed ferns on the cars, scattered petals underneath the cars, leaned bamboo sticks and canes against them, thereby bringing an image property to light that would not have been perceptible so clearly without this 'packaging'.

The third method, the third concept line that makes us feel an image, is the classic packaging method, the image-transfer technique, the art of placement. And again the underlying image mechanism applied here is that of *inferential beliefs*. As stated before, we all know that packaging can make or completely break a present.

Packaging always reflects on the image of the packaged goods.

A regular, well-finished, neutral-looking ring lying on a blue velvet mat in a jeweller's shop window looks like something precious, something exquisite, valuable – at least to consumers who only see the ring from the corners of their eyes as they rush by. If you take the same ring and place it on something individual like, let's say, a highly-polished metal sprocket in the window next door, and perhaps illuminate it with a blue spotlight, then the different background against which it is placed, its location, the packaging alone and the inferential belief created by this packaging leaves you with the impression of an individual ring, something artful, something bizarre or extraordinary – at least to a certain extent. The changed background reflects on the image of the object.

At the VW Autostadt it is predominantly the shops, the hotel and the food service that employ this method. Like jewels, sacred objects placed on illuminated pedestals, the vehicle parts are presented at the

Collection, the merchandising store – arranged symmetrically on elevated platforms, as if stacked on altars. At the Ritz-Carlton hotel next door, an absolute deluxe, five-star establishment, a glass designer mantelpiece attracts all visitors' attention in the lobby. It makes a clear image comment on the entire Autostadt premises. It says, 'You are at a place of design, at an extremely high-quality location, a place of modern lifestyle.' This is made clear by the catering alone – no other brand land features more fully decked-out designer wineries like the Chardonnay winery, or restaurants like the Cylinder, where you sit in 1950s car seat shells – a design interpretation on the classic American diner. Even the self-service restaurant, CafeCentral, is a snazzy designer restaurant for hundreds of consumers, priding itself on eight different types of coffee. And in winter a snow ramp is set up right next to the KonzernForum for young people. To the sound of hip hop and rap you can whizz down the snow ramp on car tyres – guided by torches in the darkness of winter.

The classic packaging methods used in the automotive industry include placing cars on *revolving platforms*, thereby putting them on a pedestal. Revolving platforms give even stronger expression to the visual suspense created by the sensual, indeed erotic shape of the car. The constant revolution makes us constantly reconstruct the feeling of the form from all sides. The visual suspense in the shapes becomes even more perceptible in this way. Located right on Paris's Champs Élysées, Peugeot has capped it all. The car exhibited behind the window pane is not only placed on a revolving platform but is also tilted vertically, up and down. This emotional effect is amplified even further by flags kept flying in the air by ventilators.

Image transfer, the art of packaging and placement, is also the method chosen by André Heller to design his big brand lands. At least this is one of the two decisive techniques applied at his Crystal Worlds in the Tyrolean city of Wattens. This is where he conceived a bold brand land for the Swarovski company so successful that it doubled in size in 2002. Famous artists from all over the world have worked with Swarovski crystals, creating work like the crystal-bearing 'Nana' of the famous Swiss artist Niki de Saint Phalle, or the crystal stele of the American graffiti artist Keith Haring. *Art comments on the image* of the crystals, thereby recharging them.

The chamber of miracles

In addition to this – and that is the true *concept line* of the Crystal Worlds – they are modern chambers of miracles.

It is chambers of miracles that transfer us to a place of astonishment and amazement.

Chambers of miracles used to be the most favourite and dear pastime of European dukes and kings in medieval times and the Renaissance. They collected not only valuable artworks but also puzzling, monstrous artefacts. In collections like these you would probably find a precious painting next to a shrunken head or an embryo preserved in paraffin, a monster-like creature with two heads and next to it a mechanical figurine capable of writing or pretending to play chess. Those so-called *media literacy* skills – that is, the skill of perceiving things – are accordingly not only an ability pertaining to our modern age marked by the media and consumerism, but correspond to humanity's essential need for astonishment, for that big 'ooh-aah effect'. André Heller persuaded his commissioners to abstain completely from showing how these crystals are actually cut, and what's more, he even covers up what these crystals consist of. Are they precious stones or simply cut glass? After being recharged in André Heller's chambers of miracles one could not care less about this tiny detail, and will find it hard to resist the temptation of buying some of these little objects in crystal at the store located at the end of a path of 'stations of the cross'.

Astonishment sets in right at the façade of this attraction (see colour plate section): underneath the huge giant's head that serves as a header signalling that you are approaching a legendary place, water jets jump from one bank to the other of an artificial lake. A waterfall doubles as the giant's tongue. In the first room, the large atrium, you are amazed at the world's largest and smallest crystals. From there you reach a crystal theatre, where you are introduced to the creatures inhabiting the crystal planet by way of a 3-D projection. The Swarovski crystals form birds and fish, they amalgamate into various living things, then turn into rain and all perceivable manifestations of nature. *Media literacy*, an effect of amazement and astonishment, is centre-stage here on an emotional level. In chamber after chamber André Heller charges the original product with elements of amazement, until you finally reach a gigantic crystal wall consisting of tons of individual crystals. It runs through the entire building like a recurring theme, and it makes people want to touch it in an attempt to charge themselves up with this emotional packaging, trying to use image-transfer to *massage their souls* so as to transfer some of these awe-inspiring elements on to themselves.

The outdoor area features not only various themed children's playgrounds and a vantage point but also a labyrinth. The centre of the maze is formed by a blue stone shaped like André Heller's left hand though, of course, in gigantic dimensions – rebuilt and simulated with the help of natural resources.

The central attraction of the Crystal Worlds is a *crystal dome*, where the two key *concept lines* for unfolding the image sequence intersect. It is a walk-on kaleidoscope consisting of hundreds of individual mirrors which both perform the image-transfer from the crystals to the visitors and serve as an element of astonishment and amazement. Over and over, mysterious, magic figures, heads and objects appear in these crystals then seem to become transparent before finally freezing into the crystal wall again. After 'passing through the stations' you find yourself in one of the world's largest Swarovski shops, taking a close-up look at the outstanding quality of these glass miniatures through magnifying glasses. The charge is so strong that you can hardly restrain yourself from acquiring one of these pieces.

In the German city of Essen André Heller created a counterpart of the Crystal Worlds – the Meteorit – at the behest of the energy supply group RWE. Surprisingly enough André Heller failed to repeat his success. The RWE Meteorit was a complete failure. It also features an image dome similar to the crystal dome in Wattens; it also features spectacular image-transfer rooms and rooms for amazement like the light cocoon, for example, where 90 kilometres of optical fibres create an amazing, constantly changing sea of colours and light around the visitor. At the Meteorit André Heller tries to produce a similar feeling of adoration like at the crystal worlds, a feeling of adoration through the principles of the chamber of miracles and astonishment. The only problem is that you cannot adore electricity – electricity has become part and parcel of our daily lives and is a mysterious element that should rather be explained; its communication correlations are what the true power, the true nature of electricity and energy is all about.

Electricity is not adorable and this is why André Heller's Meteorit is a place that can only be kept alive with some effort. While the crystal dome in Wattens is an almost divine place of emotional adoration, the image dome at the Meteorit is a place school kids derogatorily call 'the scream room' because the only emotional element that really works convincingly here is the echo when you scream loud enough. This is all the more deplorable as the Meteorit also features several neat details: in the entrance area there is a deep-sea diver who – supported by a projection – practically jumps into the depths of the brand land because the Meteorit structure is spectacularly sunk into the ground. In the final analysis the Meteorit teaches us one thing:

Perfect dramaturgy alone is not decisive for the success of a brand land, it must also fit the product and after all, power/electricity is simply not a suitable product for a place of adoration, or this type of brand land.

THE PLACE OF DESIRE

Thanks to its large, attractive shop the Swarovski Crystal Worlds in Wattens are not only a *place of adoration* but also a *place of desire*. Dr Helmut Braun, the director of the Crystal Worlds, sometimes jokingly says his brand land is nothing but a huge shop with an adjacent little museum. And he is not entirely wrong in saying so, because apart from the big *wow effect*, the major amazement produced by the crystal dome, it is the shops at the end of the path that form the second *core attraction* of the brand land. They do away with the remaining stress by making us buy little items we don't really need but that help us relax in our everyday lives. After visiting the Crystal Worlds you can also board a little train that takes you to the centre of Wattens with its numerous restaurants and pubs – doing away with residual stress for a second time through culinary delights. Underlying each *place of desire* there is the interplay of suspense and relaxation – the *anticipation* that makes one anxious to see something and makes one desire. You always feel that desire when you try to get something at the end that satisfies your expectations emotionally.

Hence, each desire type of brand land is a path of suspense, that starts with a teaser designed to arouse curiosity for the object of desire and ends with a core attraction designed to fulfil the expectation.

Teasers

Sony Wonder in Manhattan is just such a type of brand land. It is located in the same building as the Sony Style Lounge, a place *themed with design* that transports visitors into a lifestyle living room environment and allows them to experience consumer electronics the way they would at home. On the opposite side of the atrium of Sony's US headquarters a brand land was built targeting 7 to 15-year-old children and teens. No wonder we are surrounded by hundreds of school children noisily waiting to be admitted as we queue up at Sony Wonder with a group of European business people. The waiting time is shortened by a teaser: a robot going by the name of 'b b wonderbob'. He looks like a futurist gnome and is obviously capable of talking to the waiting brand land visitors. 'Where do you come from?' he asks a 15-year-old girl from Puerto Rico. 'What a nice red jumper you're wearing,' he flirts with a lady tourist from Norway, and he even manages to upset the board member of a German group of department stores who is accompanying us on our trip to New York with his nosy questions. 'How does the robot do this?' you might wonder, and this is how suspense and anticipation regarding the brand land is slowly built up. This open question must later be solved in the course of the *path of suspense.* First of all, however, you have to log in, speak your name into a camera and are practically 'sworn in' as a trainee volunteer.

Path of suspense

With a personal chip card you now make your way through the Sony brand land. You walk past innumerable hands-on installations that work like *place-of-understanding* type brand lands. There is a television studio where children can work behind the cameras and film the action live, where they can stand in front of the blue-box wall, at the editing or lighting desk. A sound mixing desk in front of a silver screen shows us it is by no means easy to remix a song by Celine Dion, when she suddenly appears before our eyes and welcomes us as trainee sound engineers. We now have the unique opportunity to mix a new song with her – *seeing is believing*. At the end of the way participants receive a diploma printed out with their photo, showing which stations they went through at the brand land.

This is exactly the way that the delivery centres of major automotive companies work. The cylinder-shaped towers of the VW Autostadt customer centre powerfully tower above us and create suspense, leaving us tingling with anticipation as to what will follow. They are the promising teasers marking the start of an exciting path. In Rastatt, Mercedes built a delivery centre for its A-class that also starts off with a teaser. The promising element here is a glass bridge you have to cross to enter the building. Light and sound effects arouse visitors' curiosity and set the scene for the experience. What follows is a *path of stations* packed with hands-on features and explanatory interaction. Here you find the flaps disclosing the breathing factory we already mentioned, and there you pull open drawers containing materials needed for the automobile of the future. Finally you find the design drawings that reveal how a car is planned. The view into the hall where other visitors are already picking up their cars builds expectations and generates excitement as to what is still in store. At a dedicated VIP lounge customers wait for their cars to be handed over. Finally, just minutes before the moment of truth, they are asked to step up in front of a glass pane. Excitement is rising. Finally, the name of the future car owner is called up and you personally feel how your heart starts beating before that magic moment when all expectations are fulfilled – even though you have only come to marvel at this brand land, as visitors, tourists, pensioners or students admiring all those coming to collect their brand new A-class cars here. The frequently hour-long wait for a new car only contributes to the emotional expectation, because *anticipation* requires an element of delay.

This element of delay is achieved perfectly by VW at its Gläserne Manufaktur (transparent factory) in Dresden. Allegedly you are allowed to be present for up to one week while your very own new Phaeton luxury sedan is being built. And you personally witness all those magic moments while your own luxury automobile is being assembled. You are the first to start the engine; you will personally witness the so-called wedding, when the engine block, chassis and body are united. Along the way the hardly bearable suspense is released by little interim elements helping you vent your excitement. You can visit a concert, you can visit the famous Semper Opera or an art gallery, and what's more, you can experience all of this in Dresden, in the centre of the city, so to speak, at a place where the VW staff is dressed in bright white, where nothing is suggestive of a factory, where hydraulic platforms make the highly polished car parts float silently by, where the factory floor consists of a high-quality parquet – reminiscent of a lounge rather than a factory. And finally, the magic moment of the hand-over: the keys to your luxury limousine.

All major brand lands, like VW Autostadt, feature a combination of the three basic types: of understanding, adoration and desire. But in no other brand land are all three types as perfectly planned, emotionally realized and smartly interwoven as they are at Guinness Storehouse in Dublin, the best brand land currently in existence. No other project is so well suited to recall all the factors of such a high-quality experience world for grown-ups, and no other form of expression is better suited to this than that of expertise. Because really, should it only be traditional artworks that are assessed and evaluated?

'Thank you, Mr Guinness'

Those receiving their free pint of beer at Guinness's 360° panorama bar high above the roofs of Dublin are kindly requested by a sign to drink it to Arthur Guinness's health – as the founder of all of this back in 1759. You cannot help but raise your glass a few centimetres before taking the first sip, and are surprised to note that you are even a little moved in the process. How on earth, visitors might ask themselves, has Guinness managed to charge this place and this dark, bitter ale with so much emotion?

The place of desire

Three hours before, you had already spotted from afar the signal-like steel and glass superstructure of the Gravity Bar, which hovers above the neat red brick building of the former warehouse like an eyrie. The bar as a signal, a cue, is the striking *landmark* of this place, and the promise of a relaxing end to one's stay. After all, and this is what our *brain scripts* tell us, each visit to a company producing something to do with food is invariably linked to a culinary give-away. So the bar is also the *core attraction* after passing through the stations. In order to fuel the longing for this cool reward right from the start, visitors are given see-through plastic pebbles with a drop of this black elixir embedded in them as admission tickets. The teaser promises that it will turn into a glass of dark beer in the end.

At the beginning you stand in the atrium and are literally at a loss for words. Like a *déjà-vu* image of an oversized pint, a seven-storey glass building towers up above you. The gigantic *wow effect* is the actual magnet of the place, its *core attraction* that everyone wants to see with their own eyes. Inside the 'abstracted' glass pint there are innumerable escalators intersecting as an *emphasis of the hub* of the atrium, as a central *mnemonic point*. This spaghetti knot of escalators pulls the view upwards so strongly that many visitors simply cannot withstand the pull and thereby miss the spectacular start of the themed ground floor. The *malling* works almost perfectly, and is additionally supported by a durable *entrance map* that links cross-sections of the building with signal-type photos. It features the pebble on the first page, and explains on the last page the view from the Gravity Bar.

The place of understanding

What are the ingredients of Guinness beer, how has it been brewed, shipped and advertised over the centuries? These are just some of the topics explained in this brand land with the greatest degree of sensuality. The start of the tour is marked by an impressive dark room from which you can hear a roaring waterfall from afar. Just minutes later, impressed visitors stand underneath and behind this curtain of water, whose incessantly flowing masses of water are an *allegory* for the incredible amounts of water required by Guinness on a daily basis. In another room you can see with your own eyes how enormous the old barrels were that Guinness used in the past; you can even hear the sound of beer as it ferments: *seeing is believing*. Videos installed in barrels use historic footage to disclose social and working conditions, while swing-out tool shelving with hundreds of tools completely unfamiliar to us makes for *aha effects*. All competence measures taken together plus the emotional quality of the building form the *concept line* of this brand world, its recurring theme.

The place of adoration

The building derives its hypnotic magic from the almost physically perceptible presence of Arthur Guinness. Queuing up for the box office you already step over the original lease contract concluded for the premises of the St James' Gate Brewery. 'This piece of paper is the reason why we are all here today,' the company informs us. A little later our hearts are touched by the *live experience* of sitting at Arthur Guinness's desk, his papers in front of us, next to us his armchair and within us the astonishing realization that in the age of cholera his beer was also an alternative to the undrinkable water and high-proof gin that everyone – including children – turned to. Hence, we raise our glasses to toast the founder of this place at the roof bar. Indians, German tourists and proud Irishmen all sit on the floor in high spirits – since the 50 designer chairs have all been taken long ago. The mood is extraordinary. The Irish call it 'craig' – that inimitably Irish feeling of fun, satisfaction and sense of belonging. And this feeling does arrive – here overlooking the roofs of Dublin. Thank you, Mr Guinness!

SUMMARY

- *Brand lands are permanent exhibitions at corporate locations.*
- *Brand lands give us back the proximity to products.*
- *Brand lands – unlike advertising – allow us to gain a real experience.*
- **Places of understanding.** They explain, often with the help of hands-on activities, what a brand can deliver – its rational aspects. Seeing is believing; the persuasive power of appearance plays a key role here.
- **Places of adoration.** They make the image of the brand shine – its irrational aspects. It is through this that modern allegories emerge, like the car roaring in the cage or those modern 'chambers of miracles' turning simple glass into a crystal treasure.
- **Places of desire.** They are often centres of surrender where the longing for a product is reinforced by staged suspense. Suspense trails close with the act of making a purchase or partaking of food offered to relieve the suspense.

2

Fairs and expos

Curiosity and visitor frustration

Fairs and world expos should actually be the ideal Third Places. They provide plenty of pleasure in viewing plus great experience value. They are urban outing destinations giving people the opportunity to acquire true experiences worth remembering. They are places telling stories for grown-ups. Nevertheless, the question as to whether fairs and world expos have a right to exist has been raised ever more frequently over the past few years.

This does not come as a surprise if you think of the negative coverage about the Expo 2000 in Hanover, and the visitor frustration this world expo is said to have caused. It is known that the people in charge of the Hanover expo had difficulties in communicating the experience quality of the world expo to the public. The Expo theme read 'Man – Nature – Technology' and many Germans thought for a long time it was very difficult and hard to understand. Moreover, this topic was all too random and non-committal. Only at a very late point in time was an advertising agency taken on to produce a commercial with Verona Feldbusch and Peter Ustinov, showing how much fun a visit to the World Expo could be. While, initially, the World Expo had been deserted for months on end, masses crowded in front of the pavilions six weeks before it closed. Then many people started moaning about how tiring the World Expo was, how exhausting the long waiting hours outside the pavilions were, complaining about the information overflow produced by thousands of screens trying to convey their messages. At the same time, the German tabloids started a debate on principles and whether world expos were still valid in our day and age. Isn't there the Internet where everything new appears in real time any way? Isn't humanity more mobile than before? Don't people travel? Don't they see everything strange with their own eyes now they can fly halfway round the world for comparatively little money? Aren't there 35 or more television channels constantly showing what's new around the globe? What should a world expo be good for, if anything new can be seen and experienced elsewhere anyway?

World expos share the problem of uninterrupted over-stimulation and the superficial lack of innovative value with exhibitions and trade fairs. The latest car, the latest mobile phone are all presented on the Internet and in lifestyle magazines long before they are exhibited at the international automobile exhibition IAA in Frankfurt or the CeBIT in Hanover. Furthermore, fairs and exhibitions struggle with another problem: it is simply no fun to explore an exhibition centre. While promenading at a world expo means strolling from one spectacular pavilion to another – that is, the pavilions constitute architectural or scenographic masterpieces – the only thing that often distinguishes one exhibition hall from another is the big number attached to its façade. And the problem lingers on inside the exhibition halls: the problem of the 'all-in long shot' (see Figure 2.1). Many exhibition halls are truly a visual chaos, almost anxious to hide away their highlights someplace.

Nonetheless, it looks as if fairs and expos have found initial solutions to this dilemma. It is precisely the weaknesses causing visitor frustration that hold an opportunity for new staging options. This is how the weaknesses turn into the new strengths of exhibitions and expos offering added experience benefit.

There are the staging measures undertaken against the all-in long shot. There is mood management and massage of the soul to counter over-stimulation. There are well staged corporate icons to counter the innovative weakness of world expos and general-interest fairs.

THE ALL-IN LONG SHOT

I am doing some research with a colleague from ZDF (the second German television channel) at the Berlin World of Consumer

Figure 2.1 All-in long shot at a fair
© Expositions & exhibitions, *Display Designs in Japan 1980–1990* Vol 3, Rikuyo-sha

Electronics. We have been parted for some time and now call each other by mobile to agree on a meeting point. Each one describes to the other a specific corner of the exhibition centre, and we both know exactly where this is. After I've been waiting for 20 minutes my mobile rings again. Each one of us has been waiting in a different place, because the corner we meant exists at several different points – and everything somehow looks the same here. And we suddenly realize:

The problem about exhibitions is not the exhibition stands but the exhibition centre itself!

Today exhibition stands employ the same staging tricks as stores or brand lands. They are absolutely up to date. Next to the classic, escapist theming that probably takes you along on a jungle trip, there is also modern *theming with design*, where automobile accessories are presented like modern artworks, for instance, and this staging triggers a feeling of awe in fair visitors, like in an art gallery.

The problem is the exhibition centre as a holistic experience of space; it is the individual exhibition hall as a perceptible space. Entering modern exhibition halls you often feel overwhelmed with the confusing mass of innumerable visual elements inundating visitors. Their eyes do not know where to look first. In the world of television where I originally come from, you would call this an *all-in long shot*.

When young, inexperienced television movie directors fear their productions are too weak, they often fill the set with hundreds of actors, props and special effects. Some camera operatives are frightened and pan to a shot of the scene so you see everything and nothing. This is the *all-in long shot*, a visual heap of rubbish that does not allow our constantly flitting eyes any hold, thereby preventing any *cognitive map* from forming. If an all-in long shot prevents us from developing a feel for the place, we will also be prevented from moving intuitively through a hall. No need for promenading, malling and strolling through the premises emerges here. But exhibitions and expos want to be experienced like a hiking tour for the whole family because, after all, they are modern, urban outing destinations.

What can you do in order to achieve this? How do you create a *cognitive map* at the exhibition centre featuring mnemonic points, hubs, axes and districts that seduce visitors to stroll around? First of all, it is important to comprehend the need for individual companies to set a spectacular landmark in a hall. An exhibitor installing a huge waterfall that can be walked through creates a mnemonic point that benefits the entire hall. The waterfall could become a key orientation aid for navigating through the hall, a point of reference that all visitors could benefit from.

What else can you do? Remove dead-end aisles that visitors are unexpectedly stranded in; avoid wrong tracks, and emotionalize dead axes by way of staging. While the actual exhibition stands shine out with glamour, their visitors get bogged down in the dullness of boring, endless aisles making their way from one hall to the next. Here trade fair companies could benefit from the methods used by shopping malls, which have long stopped designing stores as stand-alone entities but have also started to theme the semi-public spaces between them. Exhibitions should also draw on inspirations from sporting events and locations like the Roland Garros tennis stadium that hosts the French Open. Those promenading back and forth between the tennis courts pass by honorary statues of sportspeople, eye-catching displays that spectacularly announce the interim results of all the matches, and white marquee cityscapes. This all brings back memories of the campus system of US universities. They feature squares named after famous personalities, statues, striking towers – all in all 'experienceable', perceptible, human premises that you can relate to and that you are inclined to explore. Exhibition centres can thus become emotionally attractive in themselves regardless of the quality of the fairs they host and regardless of the prevailing business climate.

World expos have an easier job by far. The principal course of a world exposition, its *brain script,* lays down from the beginning a specific zoning development so that hubs, axes, mnemonic points and districts, the elements of a *cognitive map,* result naturally. What you need is a central square, a plaza, where the pavilion of the host country is located. You need a second hub for the grand evening show – in most cases this is a lake because the show features water or pyrotechnic effects, and quite apart from this, it provides enough room for people to gather around it. For some years now, the main district of the expo has been a theme park focusing on the general theme of each respective world expo. Then there are the various districts allocated to pavilions which are generally named after their directions – East Pavilions, West Pavilions. These are connected by long axes, alleys lined by trees, by flags of the participating nations and by spectacular design luminaires at night.

There is always a central *landmark* – at the last world expo in Hanover this was a huge, curved wooden roof whose ornate bracing followed a method similar to the legendary Thonet chairs found at Viennese coffee-houses. The unofficial landmark was a pavilion taking the shape of a whale and operated by a non-profit organization. It soon became the visitors' favourite. *Overhead railways* and lookout towers provided visitors with a breathtaking overview of the terrain and helped them, armed with *entrance maps,* to acquaint themselves rapidly with the cognitive map of the premises. *Entrance maps* might ideally feature abstract 3D illustrations of the spectacular individual pavilions. They work like colossal guild symbols exteriorizing the message of the pavilion. They are *headers,* architectural business cards.

This is why the media group Bertelsmann 'landed' a gigantic floating UFO on the Expo Plaza, 'Planet M', glowing at night in different colours thanks to a special lighting system; a UFO to represent the

group's forward looking attitude, a building that I was allowed to coop-
erate on as a consultant to the Berlin scenographer Triad. Also featured
here was the spectacular sandwich building of the Netherlands where
all important Dutch cultural landscapes were stacked one on top of each
other in compact form, even including a 12-metre-high forest growing
on the second floor to symbolize Holland's ecological awareness in
dealing with its resources.

Something in-between a world expo and an exhibition was the
Millennium Dome erected underneath an enormous tent-like roof in the
Greenwich area of London as a year 2000 attraction marking the
millennium. The centre of the Millennium Dome was reserved for a
very large arena show, as the central hub where all paths and views
intersected. This featured a central tower that formed part of the show;
it was surrounded by pavilions, designed as eye-catching *headers*, like
the pavilion on employment whose outer appearance kept changing. A
system of movable louvres made the pavilion look like an oversized
factory first, then like a library and finally like a meadow.

To sum up, it can be said: for each world expo, for each fair or exhibition, experiencing the place proper is the key condition for a
successful event. This forms the basis for any other form of entertainment staged at this place. It fulfils people's longing for designed
habitats; its fulfils their longing for a Sunday walk with the entire
family – though not in the forest but at an exhibition, at an expo.

MASSAGE OF THE SOUL

Which other problems could be turned around, and hence turned into a
staging opportunity? I am invited to the Euro Shop exhibition in
Düsseldorf by a longstanding customer. Suddenly, an interior designer
and author whom I have known for many years rushes on to the stand
and exhaustedly flops down on to one of the sofas. 'Why don't they
provide wellness packages here like they do on so many other fairs?'
she wonders. 'You don't have to have mobile masseurs.' This is when I
remember I actually did see some masseurs giving massages to worn-
out fair visitors at some exhibition stands at the IFA in Berlin some
months ago.

At all exhibitions and expos visitors suffer from the enormous
bombardment of stimuli they are exposed to, a high activation level as

psychologists would put it. There is something flashing and flickering and plunking away all day long. As a result of these noise levels many exhibition visitors look like zombies staggering out of the exhibition halls at the end of the day. The underlying psychological mechanism is the *orientation reflex* we already came across when studying the example of the pleasantly flickering Eiffel Tower. What was a pleasant thrill to the eyes there becomes a torture here, if the orientation reflex hits us in concentrated form, and what is even worse, is triggered by the same unimaginative methods over and over again. It's like a poorly produced music video clip: its racy cut without variation and sophistication fixes our gaze to the screen as if spellbound, without our being emotionally involved in any way. If the stimulation bombardment always remains the same our orientation reflex finally gives the all-clear and the result is the feared zombie effect, where nothing catches your eye unless it wriggles.

Never before in the history of humanity had such a vast number of video screens been installed in one place as at the World Expo 2000 in Hanover. Nevertheless, the most popular pavilions were those with hardly any videos to be seen. Most popular of them all: the Health Pavilion designed by Japanese star architect Toyo Ito. (See colour plate section.) He fully relied on the counter-current to changing stimuli – *mood management*, on massaging the souls of stressed and worn-out expo visitors. The pavilion featured an artificial lake and, arranged around it, numerous cradle beds that started moving and rocking visitors back and forth like babies in a rocker at the touch of a button. This was accompanied by relaxing sounds and a soothing visual environment. On entering the room, visitors were asked by hostesses to only have one go on the beds. But most Expo visitors simply got up after their first go to look around and then surreptitiously sat down two or three chairs further on, to be rocked softly back and forth a second time. Visitors' average time spent at the Pavilion of Health was enormous.

Each type of mood management is backed up by a packaging effect. In the same way as the packaging of a gift reflects on the image of the wrapped item, the emotionality of a room emotionalizes the people entering it. The underlying mechanism is image transfer, *inferential beliefs*: inferring from a place to one's own emotional state of mind. We already made reference to the sunflower frieze projected at the Billa supermarket in Vienna. Here stressed-out shoppers are relaxed by swaying sunflowers while making their purchases.

Massage of the soul is today provided for people everywhere – not only in shops and at exhibitions but wherever lounges, lobbies and atriums are heralding a comeback. Later in this book, I dedicate an entire chapter to staged lounges. I was first struck by this effect in Chicago when I intuitively went to a Nike Town a few years ago to relax there emotionally: in an environment with indirect lighting and sounds that made one feel lighter. The effect was comparable to the tranquillity of a cathedral when the stress of the city becomes overpowering.

Mood management stagings were already particularly popular as early as in 1998 at the Lisbon World Expo. Here we saw a lawn for sunbathing in wave form, allowing visitors lying on the lawn to put their feet up; there were also water sprays that visitors went through to defy the heat in Portugal; there were water-spitting volcanoes and water basins to relax the eye and the soul. The side effects in Lisbon were developed into the principal themes of some spectacular pavilions at the Hanover Expo. Austria, my home country, which usually makes a fool of itself at every world expo, caused a stir in Hanover thanks to a resting landscape designed by the young Austrian star architects Eichinger oder (or) Knechtl. The effect was quite similar to that produced by the wavy lawn in Lisbon. People were lying on the floor with their feet up and surrounded by bird's-eye views of Austria; no information but exclusively emotional signals; floor-recessed loud-speakers reproduced the murmur of a creek or snatches of a poem by Friederike Mayröcker and other Austrian authors. It was 'a floating oasis of relaxation' featuring audio islands and acoustic volcanoes, as the architects themselves phrased it.

Experiencing nature, a slow pace and silence as a feeling – this was also the message of the Swiss pavilion consisting of 3,000 cubic metres of freshly sawn timber beams, arranged by the Swiss star architect Peter Zumtor to form an unusual 55 m wide and 9 m high labyrinth open on all four sides. It was filled by the sounds of a strange group of musicians playing chopping boards on a type of bicycle and moving through the pavilion in slow motion to freeze once per hour – along with all the staff attending the pavilion – to create a minute of silence and reflection at the otherwise so hectic world expo.

The fascination of silence and contemplation was also the theme chosen for the Finnish pavilion. The path leading through the building took visitors across bridges, passing a genuine Finnish birch forest three times. Along the way visitors would stand in an anechoic room whose attraction was absolute silence, and look at a gigantic painting of a Finnish lake district on to which a laser projected an elk, a bird in flight and fish jumping. For the '02 Expo in Switzerland arranged around three lakes in western Switzerland, mood management was immortalized with a monument catching attention worldwide – a walk-on cloud hovering above one of the lakes was invented by the New York architects Elizabeth Diller and Ricardo Scofidio. There, in Iverdon-les-Bains, you were given rainproof gear to struggle along a footbridge into the artificially generated rain cloud and up to the Angel Bar in order to feel the elements and, hence, yourself again. (See colour plate section.)

What applies to world expos also holds true for trade fairs and exhibitions. *Mood management* has been the latest hit at exhibitions open to the public. At the World of Consumer Electronics in Berlin the Panasonic stand was particularly popular – a huge cityscape comprising streets, squares, paths and houses whose façades were converted into an inspiring, relaxing and suggestive water world and colourscape by means of dozens of projectors. In the final analysis, the consumer electronics industry has managed to employ video technology in a completely different manner: not to bother consumers with stimuli but to create *mood management*, a massage of the soul that takes the pressure off stressful places and, hence, conveys all the more emotional experiences.

CORPORATE ICONS

A presenter for a German private television station demonstrates to viewers an innovation from the automotive industry. The idea is a hole in the front passenger's backrest that can be flapped open to allow rear passengers to stretch their legs and feel at ease during the drive. To this end the presenter strips off his shoes and shoves his feet through the hole onto the front seat. '*Demo or die*' used to be the maxim in the past. If you want to launch an innovation on the market you have to demonstrate it or you will perish. Exhibitions are the acid test for innovations, showing whether or not they really work and make sense.

At times where the innovative value of products is low at exhibitions and really exciting news is kept under the counter for selected journalists only, staged exhibition stands focus on principal statements about the corporate culture.

Indeed, it does seem that some exhibition stands are increasingly considered substitutes for non-existent brand lands, and that even world expos are increasingly becoming platforms for making general statements on countries and companies. In terms of dramaturgy, most of these produce 'aha effects', disclosures that bring previously concealed images to light. Who, for instance, would be familiar with all the business units pertaining to the Bertelsmann media group? Who knows that alongside publishing houses and television stations like RTL, Elvis Presley's heritage, current works by thriller author John Grisham, and *the* classic German popular press publication, *Stern*, form part of this group? A Media Gallery was designed to disclose these connections, which had so far been concealed from the public. As in a super-sized display case, 137 installations marked the end of the path at the Bertelsmann pavilion in Hanover. Three hundred windows with special glass at times concealed objects behind frosted glass, and at others unexpectedly revealed them to the puzzled public, thereby disclosing these interrelations by way of photos and artefacts.

Projecting an entirely different image of Germany was the aim pursued on the opposite side of the Expo Plaza. At the 'Ideenwerkstatt Deutschland' (idea workshop) the German pavilion used a 'sculpture-scape' with gypsum torsos – that looked as if they were currently being worked on by a sculptor – to reveal to visitors people who have left a mark on Germany's awareness and identity over the past few decades. The gypsum heads of the stars – some of which were presented here for the first time – were several metres high. They included the teacher Irmela Schramm. Little known by the public previously, she has been fighting xenophobic and discriminatory graffiti for over 15 years. 'Wherever she discovers them in public spaces she takes to acetone, spatula and brush to remove them on her own initiative,' reads the catalogue. Flabbergasted Austrian visitors, however, also learned that Romy Schneider was obviously German because her gypsum head was prominently featured at the sculpture gallery – which bashfully described her as a great European actress. *Corporate icons* should be precise at any price to prevent them from backlash.

All the more spectacular was the disclosure presented by BMW at the 2001 IAA. Spending over €50 million over just 10 days, BMW made a truly powerful statement. It had a purpose-built hall erected for this period, whose aerodynamic shape made visible the void that a BMW leaves through its air displacement when going at high speeds.

Featuring not a single right angle, this unusual space was filled in just as spectacular a way. Luxury automobiles were lined up a mock street and surrounded by a seemingly endless video projection, making us believe that the stationary cars were approaching us at top speed.

Even the Millennium Dome, that striking expo-like staging in London in 2000, was probably more of a general statement on the current state of our world than a presentation of innovations. At the end of the pavilion themed around labour (which was one of the spectacular *mnemonic points* of the Dome thanks to its constantly changing appearance as a factory, meadow and library) visitors really grasped what working as a team means: 'team work' in the truest sense of the phrase. I was accompanying 50 managers from the automotive industry to the Millennium Dome. There was a huge tabletop soccer table which – believe it or not – offered room for 50 players, 25 on each side. A referee in full outfit blowing his whistle was cruising around us on his roller skates. The whistle blew and all 50 car dealers went for the ball. The point here is to stimulate teamwork skills because only teamwork will allow the players to play the match properly and win it. At the end the whistle blew – and the red team won.

SUMMARY

▮ *At today's exhibitions the staging is as important as the innovative value.*

▮ *The problem about exhibitions is not the exhibition stands but the exhibition centre itself.*

▮ **Countering the all-in long shot.**
Only those clearing the 'visual waste heaps' in exhibition halls succeed in making visitors explore the grounds. Spectacular buildings ease orientation; dead axes must be recharged with stagings.

▮ **Countering over-stimulation.**
Only those countering the 'zombie effect' can release the pressure exhibition and expos have come under. Themed experiences of nature and staged relaxing provide a relieving massage of the soul, and that image is transferred to the visitor's psyche.

PART II

GOING OUT AND PARTYING

Going out has always meant first and foremost experiencing something, and maybe also taking in some food, with the outing perhaps built around this experience. People used to go to the theatre and have dinner before the show. People went to the movies and had a drink afterwards. People went to a club to dance and had a drink now and then. The actual target of going out was the theatre building, the cinema, the club and the city centre which – over and above that – provided an extensive food service for before and after. Going out today is still the same mixture of the actual experience and its food add-on, but concentrated in one place, in one entertainment medium that unites all those things on offer at one single location under the same roof.

In summer Europe's most attractive historic squares are used for open-air events. In Vienna, for instance, a music film festival is organized in front of the classic City Hall. The official reason for going there is the projection of *La Bohème* on the big screen; in reality, however, people come because of the atmosphere and the food awaiting them at numerous stalls and stands around the square. Make no mistake – there are hundreds of people visiting the actual screening, but many times that number of people are crowding around the catering establishments on the square. Consequently, the atmosphere and food service are more important than the ostensible reason for coming, therefore making it an excuse to a certain extent. Nevertheless it is wonderful, after having eaten Greek souvlaki, sipped an Italian Chianti and nibbled on a French crêpe, to walk away from the square and stroll through the city, while behind you a wonderful aria or a duet from *La Bohème* rings out, and music is in the air on a mild Viennese summer evening in July or August.

What about those new urban entertainment centres built around theatres and cinemas? Here, too, watching the film is the superficial aim. However, in the final analysis, it is only those movie complexes that deliver a lifestyle experience themed around the moviegoing, and that become genuine urban entertainment centres, that prove successful – as experiences over the past few years have shown. After all, lifestyle is just as important as a visit to the cinema.

There are also spectacular new restaurants with built-in high-quality entertainment. This book has already made reference to the Auréole restaurant in Las Vegas, where the wine waitress climbs a 17 m high glass tower to pick your bottle of red wine. In this context my wife, Denise Mikunda-Schulz, quotes a line from the film *When Harry met Sally* in her book *Das Lokal als Bühne* (Bars and restaurants as stages: Schulz, 2000): 'Restaurants in the 1980s are what theatres used to be in the 1970s.' The truth is that restaurants are reviewed these days just the same way theatre performances are; it goes without saying that critics not only talk about the food but comment on the atmosphere, setting and entertainment, all the more so because such add-ons feature superbly in lifestyle magazines. You could say:

Wherever modern locations for an evening out are concentrated in one place, the add-ons are at least as important as the actual place.

3

City events

Partying in the 'community'

While eating out at hip restaurants or urban entertainment centres is a pastime pursued by couples or groups of people, city events give expression to partying in a larger urban community. 'Panem et circenses' – bread and circuses, as the saying went in Rome – a slogan referring to the social function performed by entertainment in the community. When do people flock to the city in order to experience something jointly? Was it really the presentation ceremony during the Olympic Games that made many thousands of people in Salt Lake City gather at the purpose-built Medal Plaza every evening? Or a freaky party like the Life Ball in Vienna that is taken note of by the entire city and even attended by the Lord Mayor in punk attire? Or the Christmas market next to the Vienna's city square that has long become a tradition in the city and developed into a first-rate tourist attraction?

For the inhabitants of a city semi-public parties like these are an integral part of the feel they have for living in their city.

It is mid-October and my assistant asks me, 'Is the Christmas market open yet?' It is late April and my wife says, 'It should be high time for the Life Ball again.' And since childhood I have known that *Holiday on Ice* plays at the Vienna Stadthalle in winter. I can still remember very well how we got caught in a bad snow storm and how my mother and I, aged five, drove back from the Stadthalle to our house in the suburbs.

Events in the city that always recur are part of our *community feeling*, our feelings for the very specific life we live in a city or region.

Psychologists call this phenomenon the 'generalized consciousness background'. When I read about the plans to extend the U2 metro line beyond the Danube my *cognitive map* of Vienna tells me where it is going to go. When you have to deal with the authorities in Vienna your *brain scripts* tell you how bureaucracy in Vienna ticks and what you should expect.

A Viennese watching a television interview with Vienna's former major knows he is a person inclined to talk too much, but that his liberal political attitude has cost him his left hand – through explosives planted by an insane assailant. The image sequence of *inferential beliefs* keeps the personalities of a community alive within us. *Cognitive maps, brain scripts* and *inferential beliefs* convey a sense of belonging, being at home in a city or region. A whole industry now makes a living on producing city magazines and supplements for dailies that constantly communicate this specific urban life to us, thereby allowing us to apply our *community feeling*, and to feel at home in our 'generalized background of awareness' over and over again. All the events of the city that keep the community together therefore convey a sense of home to us. This is their emotional strength and power.

PLAYED-ON PLACES

It is the year 1756, 15 August and we are in Rome. The two fountains at the Piazza Navona have just been blocked so as to make the water overflow and flood the square. Slowly but surely the Piazza Navona turns into a lake. Quite soon after the rich people will come and line up in their horse-drawn carriages. They will be going round in circles on this artificial lake, circling the fountain over and over again in order to get some refreshment from the burning August heat – observed by thousands of Romans. The square has not only turned into a lake but also into an aqua theatre, a baroque 'spectaculum'. (See colour plate section.) In those days large public spaces all over Europe were refitted as stages or places for evenings out for the community. The Piazza San Marco in Venice, for instance, was fitted with mock buildings and artificial colonnades big enough to house a market many times over.

Up to this very day the staging principle of transformation and disguise is present.

The square in front of Vienna's City Hall has been mentioned several times already. In mid-January this square is transformed into an attractive ice rink in the centre of the city comprising at least two, in some years even three rinks surrounded by catering stalls. (See Figure 3.1.) There is one rink for skating with swing music, a second rink for curling, and sometimes even a third special rink designed as a kind of ski slope with moguls. In July and August the music film festival, as mentioned above, turns the square into an opera house and a cinema. When temperatures drop the city hall windows become an over-sized Advent calendar and the square becomes a wintry marketplace, the Christkindlmarkt (Austrian for Christmas market), while the surrounding park is transformed into an enchanted forest. Many trees are decorated by artists as Christmas trees. The most popular of them is a tree adorned from top to bottom with red glowing luminous hearts – the 'Herzerlbaum' (Little hearts tree) as the Viennese affectionately call it. This astonishing transformation of a familiar place, the *concept line* of the Wiener Adventszauber (Vienna advent marvels) was such a success that it gradually spread to the entire city centre. For New Year's Eve, one of Vienna's landmarks, the Prater big wheel, mutates into a huge watch whose laser-projected hands dramatically approach zero towards midnight – sponsored by the Swatch company (see colour plate section). At the Wiener Graben, the city's largest and most prestigious square, a Baroque fountain doubles as a gigantic Advent wreath. The Secession, Vienna's most renowned exhibition centre dating back to the Art Nouveau period, is given an 'enchanting' human face with a pair of projected eyes (see colour plate section).

This transformation trick is a recurring theme of all staging locations in Vienna, and a classic for dramatizing three-dimensional experience areas, or staged places. In dramatic art this dodge is called *borrowed language*. We came across this trick before in this book when looking at the Zurich Cow Culture. *Borrowed language* is a trick derived from *media literacy*, the skills that allow us humans living in the age of modern media and consumption to address abstract perception ideas playfully but in a smart way. People feel clever and smart also when turning these played-on stage-like places into places full of spirit and pleasure where you revel in the joy of observing. In the Zurich Cow Culture cows became mobile phones; cows served as hotel bell boys, chocolate cakes, a soccer team. Without any transformation effect there is no played-on place with emotional added experience value.

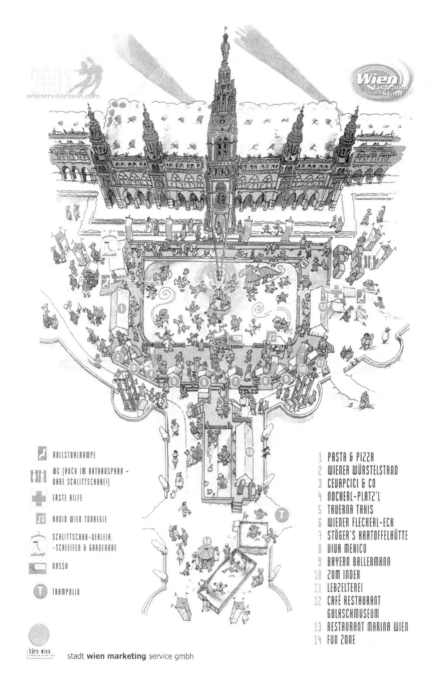

Figure 3.1   Entrance map of Eistraum (Ice Dream), Vienna
© Klaus Pitter

Transformation by means of *borrowed language* can be implemented by a variety of techniques. The Chinese city of Harbin (located in the extreme north-east of the country where temperatures may occasionally drop to –40°C) plays host to a gigantic city of ice from early January to mid-April. Ice is shaped into futurist-looking skyscrapers; ice is transformed into endless, long-columned halls illuminated in green and gold by night. Ice is the building material for clock towers, palaces and pagodas. A completely different kind of artificial world emerges in the heat of the Viennese summer, at both the southern and northern outskirts of the city: this is what the Viennese call 'Strohzeit' (straw time). The attractions of this city event are food, music and large walk-in mazes of straw. From afar a straw puppet lures visitors into the premises, where everything is made of straw: the stage, the table you sit at, the chair you sit on, and naturally the maze you explore.

Compared with these ice and straw worlds, the method chosen by the Linzer Klangwolke (Sound Cloud Linz) is intangible through and through: here the transformation is achieved entirely by a special gigantic PA system. Journalists use the term 'concert hall nature' to describe the thousands of people who gather along the Danube in the evening to watch the live transmission of a classic concert from the Linz Bruckner Haus, which is sometimes assisted by luminous stages floating on the Danube river. The past few years have seen open-air cinemas erected at all sorts of – apt and inapt – locations throughout Vienna. There is the Kino unter Sternen (Cinema beneath the Stars) at the Augartenpark as well as a film festival whose screen stands in Vienna's underground sewage system. As always, the point here is to replace the function of a place with a new function. The company running Berlin's indoor swimming pool complexes, the Berliner Bäder, have come up with a particularly spectacular and successful exchange of functionalities: the project was called LunAquaMarin and transformed various public indoor pools into striking theatres where the pools, diving boards and tower were transformed to become part of the breathtaking scenery.

The transformation effect of *borrowed language* is also the *concept line* of each played-on place. And like each place turned into an experience, all played-on places also feature all the characteristics of a Third Place. Played-on places must be visible from afar, must attract attention and must have exposure in the city. What they need, therefore, is a landmark, a site worth seeing. Vienna's City Hall, for instance, is one of the city's landmarks in its own right. But it is illuminated at night giving it a fairy tale aura, it is transformed by coloured illumination and, during the Ice Dream event, it is even flattered by moving lights swaying to the rhythm of the music. However to my mind, the prize for the most ingenuous *landmark* of a played-on place by day goes to the little town of Haag in Lower Austria. It hosts a theatre festival at its main square in summer. For theatre performances a grandstand is needed, and the Haag grandstand is quite something: it is a striking architectural masterpiece, two storeys high, fitted with a roof and featuring spectacular modern architecture, with a gallery level that looks as if it is ready to take off any minute. The Mayor of Haag was obviously bold enough to permit such a dramatic architectural landmark in his town. This is, of course, not only noticed during the performances themselves, but doubles as the spectacular symbol of the event all summer long and has even become a much admired sight in its own right.

To allow us to find all entertainment and catering options at a played-on place we need a perfect *cognitive map* with all the properties to make us explore the place. The decisive prompter for *malling* (that is, promenading) is an *entrance map*. Adventzauber, Ice Dream and the Music Film Festival all have *entrance maps* that stress the axis of suspense between the City Hall and the Burgtheater, the two landmarks at this location. In actual fact, when promenading around the city square, you are either drawn from the City Hall to the Burgtheater or vice versa. The played-on place basically stretches out between these two landmarks.

Finally, a Third Place naturally requires a *core attraction*, a central attraction that arouses curiosity as a 'must'. The Strohzeit to this end can pride itself on the world's largest labyrinth: featuring as eye-catching aerial views in all advertising and PR publications, as a 3-D illustration on the *entrance maps* and as the world's largest maze labyrinths in the *Guinness Book of Records* – what a *wow effect*! And no Viennese politician would want to miss the great *show core attraction* at the city square when the lights go on at the huge Christmas tree – just like the turning on of the lights at the far bigger Christmas tree in front of the Rockefeller Center in New York, right behind that famous ice rink featured in so many Hollywood movies for heart-warming happy endings.

Played-on places and their events reaffirm our community feeling, our feeling of being at home. But the enormous pleasure derived from watching and caused by those emotional transformation effects has meant that played-on places have now also developed into first-class tourist attractions. Looking for a retreat in a Vienna hotel late last year to work on this book without being disturbed, I discovered all the five-star hotels were fully booked. They were packed with German doctors and lawyers visiting the Adventzauber in Vienna.

SPECTACLES AND EXTRAVAGANZAS

With his face covered in white stage make-up, wearing a powdered wig and with a piqued expression, the courtier raises his cup of cocoa, lifting his little finger in the air as he does so. He seems to be looking right through me and I can't help feeling his wife feels very much the same, sitting opposite him in a glass showcase at Schönbrunn Palace, indulging in this cocoa ritual with this indignant-looking man. Both are part of a spectacle arranged to mark Schönbrunn Palace's designation as an UNESCO World Cultural Heritage Site. Alongside the cocoa ritual are quite a number of events giving the numerous visitors to the festive occasion an insight into everyday life at court. For instance, we see billiards been played in the old-fashioned style and we see court-like dancing, fencing, welcoming receptions and music. All of this is so perfectly staged by Büro Wien, the event organizers, that you gradually start to feel the immediate presence of these long-gone rituals.

This toying with our imagination, with our *brain scripts*, starts to wash over us – the *dramatized event* appears like time travel into the past.

This allows something special, something extravagant to be experienced – something otherwise inaccessible in everyday life.

This opportunity to experience something extraordinary has always been a special incentive for spectacles attracting the crowds. In medieval times during carnivals, law and order was waived for a short period and the masses adopted courtly behaviour while the nobility experienced the thrill of being the servants for once. Back then, toying with a world turned upside down and seeing what it was like in somebody else's shoes performed an important socio-psychological function. It was not only a festival but also a key way to let off steam. Today such spectacles are part and parcel of our modern going-out culture in the urban community. This dramatized event, this toying with an idea we take as real for a short interval, is the recurring theme of each spectacle, its typical *concept line.*

Event acts make for strange encounters

Most festivals of this type are *event acts* involving actors or amateur performers. Throughout Europe medieval 'spectaculi', such as those in the South Tyrolean Bolzano or at Friesach in Kärnten, have become number one tourist attractions and day-out destinations for the whole family. It's not unusual for over 100,000 visitors to come here in as few as two or three days. Here we see merchants in medieval attire selling leather pouches and sheepskins; travelling performers and street ballad singers throng medieval marketplaces with colourful stalls, while knights parade in jousting tournaments.

At exhibitions and congresses we have recently been encountering more and more *event acts*, involving cranky figures pretending to be eccentric congress delegates, and acting out their roles during the entire congress. Just recently I found myself on stage after delivering a talk at a hotel congress in Lucerne and such a figure flung her arms around my neck behaving like the old-maid daughter of a Swiss chalet hotelier. This is the way themed congresses attempt to combine business with a touch of that going-out and leisure culture during the event. In practice, some *event acts* have a little twist about them, a 'displacement of symbols', designed to prevent the actors' disguise from being to obtrusive and apparent. The rococo lady of the court welcoming us visitors to Schönbrunn Palace is compelled to bow down to us because she measures 2.50 m and is walking about on stilts.

Events involving the public make dreams come true

Events involving the public are of particular interest as they turn spectators into actors. The prerequisite for this is a perfect animation that makes the audience live their dreams. On Pleasure Island, the Disney World nightclub isle, New Year's Eve is celebrated 365 days a year. At 20 minutes to midnight actors go about asking, 'Any resolutions for the New Year?' As if responding to a secret signal most of the guests then start drinking champagne straight from the bottle, and offer you a gulp. Then someone on stage starts the countdown 'Ten, nine, eight …' until finally the silver apple comes down, the symbol of the American New

Year, and everyone wishes you a 'Happy New Year' while Mexican confetti cannons sprinkle coloured scraps of paper over the visitors' heads. Ten minutes later everything is over, but the New Year's Eve *brain script* is triggered so precisely that you cannot help but be swept up in that New Year's Eve mood.

The Trafford Centre in Manchester. Like every Thursday afternoon it's time for the tea dance – against the backdrop of a musical paddle steamer, here in the food court of a shopping centre. Coffee, tea and cucumber sandwiches are free. However, the main attraction for the ageing pensioners coming here is the orchestra playing classic English waltzes. To many of them this service to the community provided by the mall is *the* social event and the highlight of the week. You realize just how well this event works when some 50 couples waltz in perfect harmony around the British musical paddle steamer floating in a pool, as if transported into another time, absorbed by the daydream of this event.

A very recent, striking phenomenon is that an increasing number of commercial establishments – shopping malls and smaller stores – are starting to organize *events involving the public* as a service to the community. This is publicity for the sales outlet and a free night or day out for the public. 'Anyone coming to my bakery in pyjamas on a Sunday morning between 10 and 12 will get their breakfast rolls for free,' said Mr Mahl, a baker in a small German town. And he did just what he said. Even families with kids came in their nightwear and joined in the pyjama party – this was the *brain script* of the event. Of course, this was not a 'real' pyjama party, but just enough to make a dream come true for the smallest and youngest members of the family.

The Night of the Thick Books is an *event involving the public* that the very active bookstore owner Irmgard Clausen has been organizing every year for more than 10 years in the German town of Coburg, and the event has risen to international fame. After prior registration up to 15 people are allowed to spend the night inside the bookstore. To this end Mrs Clausen borrows camp beds from the Red Cross in exchange for a donation, provides a nightcap and one night light per bed, and trustingly heads home while her customers are left to their own devices in the closed bookstore. Books are carried to, and stacked beside, beds and delightfully explored by night. At breakfast time the bookseller reappears, relaxed because never ever have any of her books disappeared or been damaged. And why should they? After all, this event makes a very positive, sentimental dream come true, a kind of land of milk and honey for bookworms: endless nocturnal reading in bed and, at the same time, free access to a huge mountain of books.

The Long Nights of the Museums in Berlin and Vienna are similar events for the admirers of painting, art, history and anything else to be found and beheld at museums these days. Buses shuttle between museums, one admission ticket is valid for all, and those otherwise forbidden nocturnal visits to our cities' treasure troves are a special thrill. Extravaganzas of this kind are just one example of the urgently required measures taken by local authorities and municipalities to let us taxpayers share in some of the glamour of the installations financed with our money – and for once outside official opening times and in a more sensual, personalized and experience-focused manner.

OPENINGS AND CEREMONIES

The Winter Olympics at the Mormon centre of Salt Lake City. Usually, two events during the Olympic Games keep hosts on their toes and are watched by virtually billions of people throughout the world: the opening and the closing ceremonies. In my book *Die verbotene Ort oder die inszenierte Verführung* (The forbidden place or staged seduction: Mikunda, 2002b) I describe in detail the dramatic principles followed by ceremonies of this kind. The revolutionary innovation in Salt Lake City was the daily celebration of the award presentation to the winners at the purpose-built Medal Plaza in the centre of the city. This took place against the backdrop of a breathtaking skyline that was *larger than life* in the truest sense of the word.

On the skyscraper façades facing the Medal Plaza organizers had fitted foils with larger-than-life illustrations of winter sports. When sun set during the award presentation these gigantic images dramatically shone into the rolling cameras, becoming the *core attraction* of the event. Furthermore, the stage of the presentation ceremony itself featured prominently. A type of wire mesh formed a stage curtain. At the beginning of the event this opened concentrically from the inside out, accompanied by flashlights and haze. It then retracted to the sides of the stage, serving as an unusual special effect that toyed with visual perception. Both elements taken together became a must every evening for thousands of visitors on site and millions of people at home.

'Do it big, do it right, and give it class' was a slogan used in Hollywood. Seeming *larger than life* is therefore a classic trick applied in entertainment. This *media literacy* trick toys with our media skills and makes people stop and stare, say 'wow', and leaves them wanting to see this *core attraction* with their own eyes at any price. If one takes *larger than life* literally, it actually entails those oversized things like the close-up view on the silver screen or the gigantic images in Salt Lake City. Even the animal kingdom teaches us that ruffling up can cause an amazement. Several years ago a five-storey tower was built to mark the opening of the Vienna Festival Weeks; the lower 'floors' housed the boys of famous Vienna boys' choir, Wiener Sängerknaben, stacked up in lines, while the top floors featured a great video wall showing the choir again. It was one of the main attractions of the opening, and the stacking trick amplified it into a *larger-than-life* experience for the thousands of people attending this ritual at the city square year after year who long to see something amazing there.

For the opening of the 1998 World Cup in France the event designers came up with an entirely new idea. As symbols of the four continents, soccer figures as high as houses were to march into the Place de la Concorde from all four directions. These figures were not on wheels but actually were capable of placing one leg in front of the other, which made them truly *larger-than-life* soccer players. Unfortunately this *core attraction* killed the flow of the opening event, since the figures moved more slowly than anticipated, getting on spectators' nerves. There had been no chance of rehearsing the parade and, hence, the *wow effect* rather turned into an 'oops' effect.

A more successful example was Paris's New Year's Eve party marking the millennium. At an earlier point reference was made to its main attraction, the fireworks at the Eiffel Tower. The second *core attraction* was dozens of big wheels put up on the Champs Élysées. They featured all sorts of aspects typical to France. One wheel featured burning chandeliers – the type one would also find at French châteaux. Another wheel featured video screens playing scenes from French movies depicting the typically French way of life. It was not so much the size of the big wheels that was *larger than life* but rather their number. An endless alley of big wheels showed a total overview of French television.

Larger than life in Hollywood also meant talking about the production expenses, about thousands of extras, millions of props. 'You have to virtually see the money on the screen,' was what media moguls used to say in the past. They would have loved the fireworks watched by millions of people at Sydney Harbour twice in one year: to mark the millennium and the opening of the 2000 Olympics. The millennium saw the longest and most sophisticated fireworks display ever being put on there, featuring the Harbour Bridge as a central attraction. Later, during the opening ceremony of the Olympic Games, the famous fire disk climbed up a wall of water to dizzy heights in order to represent the Olympic fire, and fireworks worked their way back from the stadium to the harbour where they finished in a grand finale.

Consequently, ceremonies are always larger than life. Experiencing a ceremony in one's own community therefore always means sharing an uplifting common experience.

In most cases it is the community landmarks that are dramatized by ceremonies. The uplifting community feeling also forms if the community is not an urban or regional community, but the community within a company and its associates. The inauguration of a new company building is therefore an excellent opportunity for the chosen few to throng to an event.

EON, the energy company, issued invitations to inaugurate its new headquarters in Düsseldorf. After a concert directed by star conductor Daniel Barenboim, one thousand guests strolled along a stage-like axis to the new HQ building. Dancers balanced on long stilts, looking like some kind of children's toy or artefact. Then a roll on the drums – and flying acrobats like those seen at the Cirque du Soleil started floating through the blue illuminated atrium, paying a tribute to its power-packed space by majestically striding across its height.

SUMMARY

▌ *City events are community experiences in public places.*

▌ *City events are an integral part of the way people feel about living in their city.*

▌ *City events dramatize well-known landmarks or create new ones.*

▌ **Played-on places.** Public places are transformed and temporarily given another function. In this way a square becomes a lake or concert hall, or a historical staircase a fashion catwalk. Visitors enjoy this game (media literacy) of 'fancy dress' for familiar places.

▌ **Extravaganzas.** An event makes a situation seem present that is not real. Historical markets show us how people used to live. Visitors explore their own imaginations (brain scripts) and their own 'volition' to accept them as real.

▌ **Ceremonies.** These are openings of events, buildings or commemorative years. Visitors enjoy the 'larger than life' nature of these events, the enhancement of the staging.

4

Urban entertainment centres

The new city centres

It all started in the United States in the 1970s. Back then the appeal of downtown city centres was rapidly dwindling. They were considered criminal and dangerous, and middle-class whites all tried to settle down in the suburbs. They would only go downtown to their office ghettos and then head back home again as fast as they could. What got lost here somewhere along the line was the act of going out in the city, having a drink after work, window shopping, eating out before or after going to the movies or the theatre. This is why 'mock' downtowns were created to replace the real ones. They contain a high density of stores, bars, restaurants and entertainment establishments, thereby imitating the original, organically grown city centres.

Simulated city strolls

The first establishments of this type were erected in locations where the climate promoted outdoor malling. In Florida, for example, this happened at Orlando's Church Street Station. From the beginning one of the characteristics typical of these urban entertainment centres has been the imitation of the 'urban fabric'. Church Street Station, for instance, was created around Orlando's old train station, while the South Street Seaport in Manhattan revitalized New York's old fishing port and created a heavily monitored ghetto for yuppies and tourists not far from Wall Street. Its West Coast counterpart was Fisherman's Wharf in San Francisco. In Los Angeles the Santa Monica Boulevard, a former main street that had degenerated into insignificance, was turned into a magnificent new main street boasting all the typical features of a pedestrian precinct.

An artificial main street, through and through, is the Universal City Walk right outside the Universal Studio Tour in Los Angeles. Like its copy in Orlando it features huge guild symbols in front of shops and restaurants and a plaza with a water world for kids. In the wake of these complexes urban entertainment centres were built throughout the world, comprising urban artefacts. There were streets, squares, canals, bridges, towers, courtyards, market places, arcades and so on everywhere. These architectural imitation cities also paved the way for the imitations of city living. People would stroll through the port, promenade along the streets and explore a city mall. The *brain script* of a city stroll was triggered perfectly, and reproduced the flair formerly lost.

Suspense and relaxation

In Europe the same system was used to instil run-down architectural gems with new life. The Hackeschen Höfe location in East Berlin, with its many enchanting inner courtyards and underground lifestyle, is a brilliant example of this successful real estate development strategy. At the same time, children also altered their attitude towards going out in Europe. The cinema industry suddenly focused on multiplex, multi-screen cinemas, extra large screens and perfect digital surround sound systems – and the blockbusters arrived by the dozen. People started going to the movies again in their droves, but most of these new multiplexes were not located in city centres but next to shopping centres or on other greenfield developments, so pre and post entertainment and catering options had to be created locally. Here urban entertainment centres provided the perfect solution, with their typical city imitations, because the 'city', as such, also always means 'going out and experiencing'.

Moreover, this system puts an end to those never-ending discussions on where to go after the movies. People are already 'on site' and can let off any remaining steam, as it were, by intensifying their social contacts at the principal entertainment location. This system of suspense and relaxation forms an essential part of going out. The anticipation of the major attraction – like the cinema showing – and the subsequent chill-out at a lifestyle bar or the Irish Pub are two sides of the same coin. At urban entertainment centres the functions of 'building up the suspense' and 'relieving the suspense' are linked so closely in terms of space and time that the immediate sensual satisfaction of the need is experienced in an especially intense way.

Simulating urban structures (the first ingredient) and closely coupling major enjoyment and add-on relaxation (the second) make up the recipe for success of urban entertainment centres.

RESORT-BASED ENTERTAINMENT CENTRES

Urban entertainment centres (UECs) are the psycho-active essence of urban feelings and attitudes – and they don't even need a real city anywhere near. You could even build UECs on the moon, and to a certain extent this is what's happening. UECs that include free-climbing walls and skating rinks can be found on cruising vessels; they can be found in the Nevada desert, in the South African savannah or in an archipelago off Dubai. All of these urban entertainment centres share one characteristic – they are temporary resorts and not just hotels.

They are closed-loop, self-contained systems designed to prevent the buying power of their own hotel guests and temporary visitors from flowing away. This is the Las Vegas system of urban entertainment centres.

Landmark: what you see is what you get

All resort-based entertainment centres show only too clearly outside what to expect inside. Their function as a *landmark* is legendary. Those thumbing through the pages of a travel brochure featuring Vegas resorts are to grasp at a glance what awaits them there. Be it an Egyptian pyramid, the Doge's Palace in Venice or the New York skyline, hotel resorts are built in such a way that their themes shine through the archi-tecture. All resort-based entertainment centres are themed, and their architecture is the structural *header* of their respective urban theme: 'You get what you see'.

Having arrived at Las Vegas, holidaymakers have to decide how to budget their time. Hotels fight for the biggest possible chunk of this cake with their promising appearance. Those strolling along the strip opt for a particular type of urban experience inside the resort, based upon the hotel façades. Tourists who allow themselves to be impressed by the elegant water world in front of the Bellagio Hotel will also surely like the lush gardens in its park-like winter garden, the art gallery with its current Impressionist exhibition, the city mall with its Northern Italian feel and the high-end stores stocking the likes of Armani and Gucci inside the resort.

Malling: mazes and super promenades

Nearly all resort-based entertainment centres are primarily casinos. Their main purpose is to make as many people as possible gamble, and keep them at slot machines or roulette tables as long as possible. The access areas to these resorts therefore use a smart dual strategy. If you take a look at just about any ground plan of a typical Vegas hotel you will understand what I mean: the casino area of the resort begins in the immediate vicinity of the reception in most cases, and it is designed with a deliberately incoherent layout. The *cognitive map* of the place is 'disguised' as much as possible. As a result, guests reduce speed drastically. Many a guest armed with a beach bag originally heading for the pool gets stuck at a slot machine while trying to find his or her way – simply because the slot machine is readily at hand and seductive 'ting-ting' sounds can be heard all over the place. Once you reach the actual urban entertainment centre area of the resort with its entertainment establishments, stores and restaurants, this maze all of a sudden turns into a systematically arranged promenade that has perfected the art of seducing visitors to *malling* like nowhere else in the world.

As has already been explained in detail, guests only explore premises if they learn their *cognitive maps* as fast as possible. The reference points they need for this are *axes* to follow, *hubs* where *paths* and views cross, striking *mnemonic points* that ease orientation and differently designed districts. Each urban entertainment centre is about prome-nading in a simulated city centre – which is why all of these reference points have an urban feel about them. The *axes* are historic streets, a *hub* could be a market square or a port, *mnemonic points* would be fountains and bridges, while the *districts* look like residential areas to

us. Let us now look at the tricks used for the ground floor access area of
a typical Las Vegas centre.

The Forum Shops at the Caesar's Palace Hotel are one of the most
successful urban entertainment centres in the world. Under artificial
skies you promenade through a bombastic version of ancient Rome and
can hardly get over your astonishment. The success is essentially also a
result of the perfect malling system, which is so compelling that the
centre has doubled in size.

Today I am back again for the first time after the extension was built,
and my attention is immediately caught by the Super Promenade
system. I am standing next to the large Roman sculpture, Fountain of
the Gods, in the centre of the UEC, where thundering waters tumble
down into a marble basin. I know that the system will first try to drag
me in and accelerate my pace along the long central axis of the centre,
and will then slow me down strategically to prevent me from rushing
past the stores too quickly. To accelerate me my eyes are 'drawn' into
the depth of the Roman main street with its pompous, temple-like
Escada and Louis Vuitton buildings. On the right, towards the exit to
the Strip, this task is performed by the huge decorative figures at the
Disney Store (number 115 on the entrance map: see Figure 4.1). If I
give in to the temptation of this depth I will find that just near the
Disney store the axis bends again, reducing my pace. But just around
the bend is another promise awaiting me: a second marble fountain, the

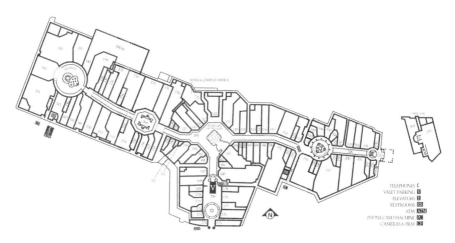

Figure 4.1   Entrance map of Forum Shops, Las Vegas
© Forum Shops

Festival Fountain. Its statues of the gods are instilled with life once an hour using hyper-realistic robots. Seeing this second fountain at the right-hand end of the axis will speed up my pace again after I have passed the bend.

Instead, I now turn left and head for the new district of the Forum Shops where, after a few steps, I see a giant Trojan horse, a sight that attracts me like a magnet. This is the walk-in landmark of the children's toy shop FAO Schwarz. While I approach it in amazement, the horse lowers its head, smoke comes out of its nostrils, a door opens and a little bear appears. 'Girls and Boys, welcome to FAO Schwarz,' he says, addressing the children running up to him. After the square with the horse another bend slows down my pace, but at this very moment I catch sight of three golden columns in the distance; they sit enthroned on a huge fish tank containing rays and sharks. Later, when the Atlantis Show starts, they will sink into the ground – but now they magically draw my gaze into the depth of the suspense axis. Forming a right angle to this major attraction are the smaller suspense axes of the stores, which often feature a video wall on the back wall so that customers' eyes constantly move back and forth between the portal and this point in the distance. The same principle that pulls me along the grand axis of the antique line of houses like a rubber band also drags me into each shop interior. All these features – the bent axis, the hubs in the form of widened squares, the three fountains in the hubs serving as mnemonic points for the centre, and the district division into 'classic Roman' to the right and 'mystical antique' in the Atlantis district – are the elements comprising the Super Promenade of the Forum Shops. The success is ongoing. In 2004 the Forum Shops will open a second extension, featuring a circular escalator as a core attraction.

Concept line: making the urban simulation credible

In my book *Der verbotene Ort oder die inszenierte Verführung* (The forbidden place or staged seduction: Mikunda, 2002b) I analysed several tricks the Forum Shops used some years ago. Back then they were the first to combine a hyper-realistic, painted sky with a lighting system that turns night into day and day into night again in the space of just one hour – from dawn and high noon through to twilight and a romantic sunset. Back then I talked about the importance of this staging for visitors' inner clocks. If time is split up into small units due to the changes in lighting, subjectively this time goes by faster, thereby making our stay at the centre more entertaining. This is classic chrono-technology deployed at a staged location.

However, the lighting atmosphere is also changed for another reason. Each theming needs constant incentives/stimuli to make visitors participate in this artificial world: that is, run free in their *brain scripts* which transpose this escape into another world. Urban enter-tainment centres work with urban artefacts, mostly imitated lines of houses placed indoors.

Without additional signals that allow visitors to get hooked by this simulation, the urban artefacts remain what they are: pieces of scenery.

This is why you walk over the steaming drains so typical of Manhattan when malling between the artificial lines of houses at the food court of the New York, New York hotel. This immediately creates a credible feeling of walking the streets of New York, although the 'roof lining' says something completely different. At the Forum Shops this 'roof lining' is not only painted with a hyper-realistic sky but also comes alive as the time virtually passes by. The Venetian and the Aladdin resorts also try to make believe that indoors is outdoors, although to only varying degrees of success. At the Grand Canal Shops on the second floor of Las Vegas's version of Venice, visitors promenade underneath the usual artificial skies along the Canale Grande, a chlorinated waterway serving as a central malling axis. The water 'comes alive' when 'gondoliere' convey tourists (wearing seat belts) in gondolas and sing (not really a lot worse than the originals). And if a couple happens to be getting married on one of the bridges, a kind of Venice feeling does shine through – even for such dyed-in-the-wool Venice fans like myself who actually got married in the real Venice. (See colour plate section.)

Quite different is the verdict on the Desert Passage of the Aladdin resort. Everything is said to be incredibly authentic there – or at least this is what TrizacHahn (the company that developed it) say. However, the truth is that even the painted skies of the Middle-Eastern scenery from Morocco to Jemen fail to produce the desired effect. Many alleyways are simply too low – compared with the enormously high Forum Shops – for creating a credible sky illusion, and somehow the light is so depressing that you sneak through the streets in oppressive silence rather than join in enthusiastically. The Desert Passage is the most recent of all urban entertainment centres in Las Vegas, and yet it already looks old-fashioned today.

Many urban entertainment centres in Europe imitating the American way share this problem of too low and narrow spaces without sufficient authentic signals that invite visitors to play a role in the game. The unfortunate SI Centrum in Stuttgart housing two Stella Group musical theatres has been suffering from this problem since it opened. Here Las Vegas shows us the European way of theming: *design-based theming*. I wander through the restaurant area of the Mandalay Bay resort with my assistant Alexander Vesely and study the design of an indoor street, a street that is so different from the escapism-based theming we have looked at in centres so far. Left and right of this 'street' you will find some of the world's most spectacular restaurants, which have already been mentioned in this book, like the Auréole with its glass wine tower and the free-climbing waitresses, or the Rumjungle with its firewall and waterfalls crashing down glass walls.

Alex, who I suspect of wanting to administer my estate one day, films me secretly as I take a closer look at this theming. Inside a hall eight famous architects have built eight design houses whose façades hide eight restaurants. Here, the urban 'pieces of scenery' look stylish and futurist. Through the use of state-of-the-art materials like aluminium, back-lit frosted glass, plastic or polished stone visitors feel as if they are in a trendy design district of a metropolis. Portrait-format screens left and right of the monumental entrance door of the new restaurant 3950 display the computer-animated menu. The restaurant is named after its fictitious house number, which features on the façade and on the highly polished black floor by way of an ingenious projection technique.

Opposite, an oblique aluminium roof juts out over the China Grill. On the roof there are spheres radiating light far into the distance – leaving no doubt that this is a design house. Right of the portal I discover an entire village landscape with huts in radiant white and green behind a glass façade. These are the toilets of the China Grill, and Alex and I can't help thinking of the Austrian colloquial term *Häusel* (little houses) for lavatories reminiscent of Alpine-style outhouses. A modern water world, façade reliefs and statues in front of the 'buildings' reinforce this impression of a cityscape. In front of the hip Red Square with its swanky communist front, for instance, we see a headless statue of Lenin – covered with fictitious pigeon excrement. I am particularly impressed with the ceiling design of this district. Stucco elements suspended from the shot black ceiling house luminaires 'alluding' to the ceilings so typical of Vegas hotels, thereby making the entire area look like both indoors and outdoors at the same time. This trick saves the designers the embarrassment of having to simulate an outside world. Everyone knows we are inside a building, and that the urban feeling is a product of our imagination – of the *brain scripts* that were triggered.

Core attraction: valve to let off steam and magnet

The majority of resort-based entertainment centres are basically casinos. Those walking through a large casino hall can almost physically sense the suspense in the air. In resort-based systems entertainment is not only designed to attract gamblers. It is also designed to do away with 'residual stress', to release the tension after gambling so guests are ready for the next round. Tension is released primarily by all those things that trigger physical feelings. This is probably why roller-coasters and flight simulators are booming in Las Vegas. The roller-coaster on the façade of the New York, New York hotel departs from a simulated Coney Island and heads towards the New York skyline, and is hence also embedded into the urban theme.

In general, however, core attractions are simply designed to attract the masses like a magnet, to stimulate a sense of anticipation, arouse their interest and whet their appetite, making sure that people enter this very casino rather than the one next door. This is why in Las Vegas many attractions are located outside, as complimentary façade shows that form part of the *landmark* effect produced by the hotel. The volcano erupting in front of the Mirage Hotel at night was the first in a series of such 'front' shows.

Other core attractions are located inside the resorts, and connected to the mnemonic points of the lobbies, shopping and restaurant areas there. At the Forum Shops three of the four inside *landmarks* are 'played' as core attractions: two fountains and the Trojan horse. These inside attractions primarily aim to prolong the time spent at the resort. When the new Atlantis Show was installed (in which hyper-realistic computer animatronic figures celebrate the fall of the legendary Atlantis with fire, swords and rolling thunder), the pyrotechnic show on the left initially started on the hour, while the water show with Bacchus on the right side commenced on the half hour. On our following visit some months later we found that both shows were now held at the same time – on the hour. The management had realized many visitors rushed over to the second show right after the first one had finished, making it just in time, then leaving the centre afterwards. Now both shows are on at the same time, leaving visitors at least 45 minutes to promenade (and shop) from one side to the other: after all, core attractions should prolong time spent at the resort rather than occupy it.

La Bohème, Act 1, Rudolph's aria and the duet of Rudolph and Mimi. The sounds of 'My tiny hand is frozen' float in Italian across St Mark's Square, and I have to admit I have scarcely heard my favourite passage from Puccini's opera sung with such inspiration as it is here at the Venetian hotel in Las Vegas. Even the seminar delegates from throughout Europe accompanying me here for two days are touched by it. Only one minute before in my introductory talk to the day's agenda I had advocated the trend towards more authenticity here at the world centre of artificiality. In Las Vegas the experience society has grown up too. My group and I agree: such a well rendered performance, a genuinely outstanding piece of achievement, gives the entire centre more credibility. And this is why it is not only concept lines that increasingly feature authenticity and design, but also the sensations, the core attractions of the centres.

Swimming about beneath the robots of the aforementioned Atlantis Show in the fish tank that visitors 'orbit' are colourful fish and little sharks; and in the afternoons a female diver also feeds the fish and explains what they are over an underwater microphone. The Mandalay Bay resort houses a fish tank with many far larger sharks, a shark tunnel and a basin where you can stroke little ray fish. The gallery of the Bellagio hotel has enjoyed great success for many years. This is where I once saw an exhibition featuring the crème de la crème of genuine Impressionist painting – but with the kind of spectacular lighting curators of serious museums would never have allowed. At the same hotel I and a dozen other guests spent an hour sitting on a couch in the lobby in order to marvel at the ceiling covered with a pasture of huge, colourfully lit glass flowers by a renowned Canadian glass artist. The core attraction was so successful that the sofas finally had to be removed simply because fascinated visitors remained sitting there for too long: high-quality design at resort-based entertainment centres.

The big resorts in Las Vegas are like giant laboratories where (on behalf of the rest of the world) they try out what works and what doesn't. They are perfect Third Places that prodigally give away their gifts but get back far more in return for them. They have proven that gambling in conjunction with shopping and high-quality food service can become a completely new species of 'going out' during our holidays. They have taught us that while Japanese tourists might only be prepared to lose a small amount of money on roulette, they will spend all the more at Gucci. They have demonstrated that people travel to a city for a congress but spend just as much time at great restaurants in a quality atmosphere. They have turned a gangster city into America's number one tourist destination, and have created entertainment installations for children (who are not admitted to casinos) that enthuse their parents just as much. They are psycho-technically perfect, self-contained systems that attract, accelerate or decelerate our speed, address our biological clock and arouse our curiosity. In the final analysis, they are city simulations which – thanks to automatic rail cars now connecting 'friendly' hotels with each other, and novel suburb settlements complete with golf courses and artificial lakes – are on the verge of becoming the cities of the future.

SHOW-BASED ENTERTAINMENT CENTRES

Roughly 20 minutes' walk from my flat in Vienna is a medium-sized cinema centre that is currently one of my favourites. Although it is less glamorous than many other movie palaces in Vienna, my wife and I have made a habit of visiting the centre in a very special way. We usually arrive at the Village Cinema some 30 minutes before the showing, and first buy the tickets. Then we head for a mega bookstore housed in the same complex, which is open both in the evenings and at weekends. Luckily the Wien Mitte railway station is located right underneath the multiplex centre, so this bookstore with its extensive CD department falls under the same legal provisions affecting shop opening in Austria as station bookstores do: it is open when we and many other movie goers go out. Denise and I generally stroll through different sections and only meet up again at the check-out where we pay for our booty. Then we queue up for allegedly fresh popcorn and watch our movie. After the showing we spend another half-hour at the book store, Denise browsing through books on bringing up children and I on books on classical music or CDs.

Before the show – after the show

In dramaturgical terms we were not at the movies but at an urban entertainment centre. Before and after the show things happen that turn the cinema into a place where 'going out' is part of the experience. The show is the actual reason for visiting the place. This could be a movie, a musical or a sporting event. Everything happening before and after provides emotional added value. This could be stores where browsing through merchandise is centre stage or it could be the food services offered at the place – these are all increasingly family-friendly variants of the 'good old' gambling hall but without the sex, glorification of violence and the desire to win.

In such a show-based entertainment centre a variety of psychological mechanisms play a role. The aforementioned interplay of suspense and relaxation is in the foreground. You want to see a specific film, a new musical, your curiosity has been aroused by advertising and word of mouth, you *anticipate* the main experience. This suspense is hopefully fulfilled at the cinema or theatre, but smart consumers also let off any remaining tension or 'steam' at the themed Irish Pub, the late-opening bookstores or the bowling alley also located at the centre.

After *anticipation* the second mechanism that warrants observation is our sense of time. Individual perception of time very much depends on the inner structure of our psyche – just like the spatial perception of a place, the flair of a place and the stories that come to our mind at a place. In my book *Der verbotene Ort oder die inszenierte Verführung* (The forbidden place or staged seduction: Mikunda, 2002b) I describe in detail how this perception of time is constructed by means of an inner *time line*. Time at the dentist's may seem like ages while the same amount of time seems to fly by in a heated discussion with a friend. Chrono-technologies describe how to make such time intervals entertaining.

When we have an overview of a time interval, time seems to go by faster than if its end is not foreseeable. One of the techniques applied here is *deadlining*. '50 minutes to go to the beginning of the show' says the sign in Disneyland as we join a queue. At a multiplex cinema this would be a little awkward. This is why you usually kill the time before the beginning of the screening at the store or gambling hall. Diversity is the name of the game that creates an interruption in the flow of time, thereby making the waiting time entertaining.

But what is happening at our end? Until a short while ago our book-store at the cinema centre was open until 10 pm. One day the complete business section was covered with cloth, the video and DVD section was blocked, the children's books and toys were all locked up and the whole store closed as early as 9 pm. The privately employed white-collar workers' union had put an end to the proliferation of such dreadful working conditions. However, Germany and Austria are the only countries (along with Albania) that cannot see that stores of this type have long become part of going out, of tourism, of the leisure facil-ities of a city, and have nothing to do with regular shopping at just any store on any street. I am firmly convinced that many urban enter-tainment centres that have recently gone bust due to 'overscreening' could have survived if they had offered sensible 'before and after' services. Food facilities alone are not enough. The crisis affecting cinema complexes and music theatres in Germany was also caused by restrictive regulations on opening hours. Policy makers and unions have destroyed jobs and investment, and have doubtlessly burdened themselves with guilt.

Metreon

In summer 1999 the Japanese consumer electronics group Sony opened what is currently the world's most exciting show-based entertainment centre in its own four-storey building in the centre of San Francisco. Sony Metreon comprises a multiplex cinema with 15 screens plus an IMAX cinema as the main attraction, as well as lifestyle-oriented stores, flourishing establishments providing a catering experience and family-focused gaming attractions as add-on experiences. The premises were deliberately designed as a meeting point in the city. According to the Sony press release Metreon is an artificial term coined to sound like ancient Greek. Like the English term 'metropolitan', Metreon is to prompt the idea of a buzzing urban environment. Like the Greek 'pantheon' this term is also to 'resonate' with the image of a major meeting place. And Sony Metreon really became a meeting place, a Third Place and city-centre habitat.

The urban artefact selected here was a two-storey arcade with barrel vaulting consisting of white fabric – and the Metreon Gateway running through the centre as its central axis. Beneath this vault, onto which unreal blue light is projected in the evening, we see floating white sails and curved white screens next to blue luminous columns, video screens in portholes and an alley of metal brackets for steel wires that look as if they were designed to hold the lifeboats of a cruising vessel. This urban mall that looks like a ship provides theming by means of high-quality design, and leaves the numerous visitors to the centre longing to promenade – like on the top deck of an ocean liner riding at anchor in the centre of the city.

While my assistant Alexander Vesely films the centre I browse through the stores, and soon notice that I take almost everything on sale there in my hand and touch it. At Sony Style, which has living rooms built around consumer electronics, I spend 10 minutes playing with Sony's computer dog. At Digital Solutions, where gadgets are offered by lifestyle category – like 'Road Warrior' for the latest in laptop accessories – I play with an electronic hourglass. 'Try before you buy' is Sony's PR motto, and the Metreon homepage reveals that the interactivity of the range is the decisive selection criteria at all centre stores.

Urban entertainment centres need as many fun-oriented stores as possible and must give consumers the opportunity to touch, try, and play with the range.

This is the only way to ensure that this shortening in our perception of time before and after the show actually occurs. And by the time you have held five or six goods in your hands and had the chance to play around with them you will be more prone to buy product seven or eight.

Passing the time promotes sales. Incidentally, I acquire a soft lilac automobile for my little son that also doubles as a ball, the digital egg timer and, for Denise, an unusual bag that does not close in the conventional sense but folds like Japanese origami. In Europe, at the G-Town of the Vienna Gasometers, for instance, many stores at the urban entertainment centre are simply too respectable, serious – they fail to understand the task they are to perform in the system as a whole. This is why the gasometers, celebrated for their contrast of old and new at the beginning of the book, are today on the verge of closing down. Their grandiose look is weakened by the all too mediocre stores without any 'residence quality', to such an extent that no one feels like browsing in these shops before going to the movies or visiting a concert. And after the performances they are all closed anyway.

Above and beyond, the Sony Metreon also features attractions as additional magnets and pastimes that come at a price: a two-storey children's playground with *en suite* children's restaurant, a sophisticated gambling hall with a high-quality, attractive range. Strikingly enough, all add-on attractions target families or groups and are packed with options for social interaction.

Going out is not only the interplay of suspense and relaxation in an urban environment; going out is above all also a social experience in a clique, family or circle of friends.

Whatever promotes social exchange works and whatever impedes it fails, even when well conceived. At the Metreon fathers with children are thrilled as they 'act out' the famous American children's book *Where The Wild Things Are* by Maurice Sedak – an attraction where you pull cables to move giants measuring many metres in height and split your sides using soft rubber hammers to club the heads of goblins who cheekily pop out of holes in the ground. At Portal One families with their 10-year-olds and groups of youngsters escape into a dark, futurist Art Deco world whose main gaming attraction is a virtual bowling alley called the Hyper Bowl. Here you bowl in front of huge silver screens where you have to manoeuvre a ball through the virtual streets of San Francisco, for example, to hit the pins standing at the top of a street going uphill while trying to avoid cable car obstacles and the impending fall of the ball down the hill.

A third attraction closed in 2001, two years after it opened. Originally, you sat in a three-screen 3-D cinema to watch the film of the young readers' classic *The Way Things Work* by David Macaulay. The author explains in a very sensual way how complicated technical devices, like a lock on a door, work thanks to 'simple machinery' like an inclined plane. No one wanted to see this fascinating attraction. It simply did not tie in with the going-out system of an urban enter-tainment centre. After all, the Metreon is not a brand land of the Sony Group but a leisure meeting point in the city.

Almost at the same time an attraction in another Sony urban enter-tainment centre also closed its doors: the MusicBox at the Sony Center at Berlin's Potsdamer Platz. There Sony had created an artificial square with the feel of an Italian piazza underneath an eye-catching, gigantic marquee roof – a landmark of the new Berlin. This is surrounded by the usual multiplex cinemas including an IMAX, another Sony Style and other lifestyle-oriented concept stores, plus many restaurants with their open-air terraces clinging to the façades like swallows' nests high above the square. Just as the Spanish Steps in Rome are besieged by thousands of young people and tourists from throughout the world, every evening thousands of people now gather at the Sony Plaza. The huge baroque staircase that makes us stop and stare in Rome stimulates the pleasure we get from observing meeting places, as do the marquee roof in Berlin and the little urban perception games, like the pond floating on a metal platform above a 'hole' in the ground of the square – the windows of the subterranean Berlin Film Museum. This is why in a going-out and getting-together system, an attraction explaining the phenomenon of music was obviously somewhat out of place.

DESTINATION-BASED ENTERTAINMENT CENTRES

These examples of urban entertainment centres show that when the professional design of details within a centre fails to be incorporated into the relevant system as a whole, the details are worth nothing. Alongside self-contained resorts and show-based centres staging the before and after of an event, destination-based centres are the third system. Here an emotionally charged location is centre stage – a destination suitable for going out due to its basic emotionality. What counts here are the entertaining qualities that the place brings to bear. For instance, there are the amusement districts of our cities, known as going-out places to everyone. There is emotionalization through traces from the past perceived at the place of entertainment. Finally, there is the flair of unspoilt nature and originality.

All destination centres share a dense atmosphere that is passed on to the visitor. Mood management, the way a place massages the soul, becomes part of going out, part of the relaxed way we 'breath out' in the city.

The new amusement districts

There have always been specific districts of a city more prone to serving pleasure and distraction purposes. The *cognitive map* of a city allocates a focus on earning money to some districts (like the Frankfurt exhibition and banking area), a focus on culture to other districts (like the museum river bank in Frankfurt) and to yet others, a focus on going out (like Sachsenhausen, where cider flows in abundance). In Vienna this district is the wine area, Grinzing; in Düsseldorf it is the 'longest bar counter in the world' in the Old Town. The *brain script* of how to use a specific area determines the image this area projects on our cognitive map, in our hearts and minds. Recently, these rather organically grown going-out districts were also revamped and professionalized: they were transformed into destination-based entertainment centres with a range of attractions designed to do away with the tension built up by tough city life.

Times Square in Manhattan is probably the most well-known example of this development. It was purged of dirt and prostitution by the Disney Group and the then Mayor of New York, Giuliani. Starting from 42nd Street heading north, it comprises a dense network of cinemas, experience-based food providers, themed stores like the Disney Store, musical stages and attractions like Madame Tussaud's or the Nasdaq Experience. The new levels of safety of a going-out district, the blend of suspense and relaxation and the urban artefacts in the form of giant screens mounted on to building façades (which often do not even house offices any more) have turned Times Square into a meeting place for New Yorkers and tourists alike. People go there to take in the atmosphere, to watch the live baseball transmission on SuperBowl Sunday and to enjoy the glamour. All destination centres – in addition to their central suspense and relaxation aspects and the opportunity they offer for promenading in the city – are also places governed by mood management, massaging of the soul and an image transfer from the place to the visitors. They are exciting in their own right. In summer 1998 when the whole of Times Square was closed to traffic for several days due to the construction problems of a new skyscraper, Denise and I along with thousands of other people flocked to Times Square at night. Here for the first time we could breathe in all that glamour and enjoy it to the full without being bothered by traffic.

The Irish capital of Dublin spent most of its EU grants on construction projects in the new Temple Bar district. Here was built a wide variety of hip design locations, chic hotels and music pubs alongside the traditional pubs. Since then young people in Ireland have been coming here from all over the country in order to release the tension of the apparently tough Irish life with enormous quantities of Guinness and fun. Some years ago, the Disney Group started building artificial, night-time amusement districts outside its theme parks with the same intention but fewer expected alcohol victims. In Paris, Orlando and Los Angeles, the Festival Village and Downtown Disney both now await us right outside the theme park doors. These are whole districts designed for people to let off stream and release their surplus tension after the main park closes. Again we come across the classical elements of urban entertainment centres: multiplex cinemas, experience-based food providers, fun stores and some additional shows like those staged by the Cirque du Soleil, plus a street, urban squares, neon lights and reflections dancing on the tarmac. Tourists flock to this district like none other.

Traces of the past

This version of an emotionalized destination does not bring the established or artificially created *brain script* of a going-out district into the limelight. Instead it focuses on memories of history that still fascinate us today – exuding an atmosphere people enjoy being in, because everything that ever happened at a place becomes an integral part of it and is part of its image. Those returning to their home town today still think they can smell freshly baked bread although a bank moved into the corner bakery long ago. *Brain scripts* of old occurrences cling to the *cognitive map* of a place and become its essence – one that can still be felt today.

Those who did not experience these past events themselves can have them conveyed by means of visible traces of the past. The first time we discovered this staging strategy was at the Ghirardelli urban entertainment centre in San Francisco. It is located on the premises of a former chocolate factory, and allows everyone to imbibe its past by guiding visitors past old chocolate-making machines in the outdoor spaces. Signs explain their function, and kids just love to climb on them and picture what things might have been like back then in the chocolate factory.

Wherever centres exude an air of history, planners apply this method of the *left-behind artefact*: like the Handwerkerhof (craftspeople's court) in Nuremberg where you can shop for olds toys, eat weisswurst sausage and meet a traditional pipe and drum band in medieval castle grounds surrounded by thick walls and embrasures in the city walls; like London's Covent Garden, complete with a museum of tinplate toys, lifestyle shops and restaurants under the roof of a Victorian market hall; and like at the new and trendy Bercy Village district of Paris.

Oops – I almost tripped over the railway tracks left behind here right in the middle of the 'main street' at Bercy Village. These tracks also feature in the old photos hanging everywhere, which show us what it used to look like here. Back then the tracks did not lead up as far as what is now the huge cinema centre that forms the end of Bercy Village. But apart from that, everything else still looks very similar. Even now the same tiny houses with their neat brick walls line the street. The former wine stores of the St Émilion winery have now been converted into shops and restaurants: all of them boast timber-beamed ceilings, and the original house fronts form a consistent visual impression.

Denise, who is generally a lot quicker than I am and who grasps what is so special about any location, points out to me that the interiors of these little houses can come as quite a surprise. Some of the houses, like the olive store with its chandelier made of little olive oil bottles, are as small inside as they look from the outside. Other little houses, however, conceal huge shops inside that extend far back underground or to the back due to hidden annexes. Some little houses – invisible from outside – have been combined to form complexes like the MedWorld of Club Méditerranée, complete with bookstore. This is designed like a hotel lobby and a mega restaurant featuring flying trapeze artists as a dinner show. 'It's like a spectacular play,' says Denise, and only now do I also realize that these constant surprises are a kind of hidden core attraction. It is this 'wow' effect that makes the centre interesting for us. Ultimately, we even discover the pool of a fitness club in one of the little houses. The club is called Waou. Both Parisians and tourists alike sit and relax in the front-yard terraces of restaurants. Even the people spilling out from the nearby metro station after work seem to enjoy the short path they trace through the centre as a 'mini' massage of the soul. As the sun sets, discreet neon lights light up the old house fronts, producing a visual contrast that only adds to the atmosphere of the place. Wherever old masonry has been developed into urban entertainment centres in Europe, this contrast between then and now is a key feature.

At Berlin's Hackeschen Höfe, a suite of inner courtyards in the eastern part of the city, the Art Deco tiled walls of the first courtyard contrast with neon lights and projections. Even the entertainment on site is part of this add-on strategy. Here you watch the colourful artistes of the Chamäleon variety show as they look out of the windows before their performance, and you listen to operatic arias from the restaurant 'l'oxymoron' where waiters regularly metamorphose into opera singers.

And in the United States? Hollywood and Highland shows us how to turn the fascination about a very recent past into a destination centre. The whole world knows Mann's Chinese Theatre, Hollywood's grand old premiere cinema built like a Chinese pagoda, in front of which stars like Marilyn Monroe and Arnold Schwarzenegger have left their hand and foot prints for posterity in concrete. Millions of tourists from all over the world take snapshots here.

When Oscar night was recently scheduled to return from downtown Los Angeles to Hollywood, an urban entertainment centre was built next to and behind this *landmark* to make use of this 'historical' and emotionally charged-up place. A hotel, a street with stores and food providers themed around movies, a monumental Babylonian gate reminiscent of a clichéd historical epic by Cecil B De Mille to stress the central hub, a multiplex cinema and the Kodak theatre – the new home to the Oscar ceremony – are all part and parcel of Hollywood and Highland. Like the actors prior to the award ceremony, visitors enter the premises through a second awe-inspiring gate where the red carpet for the stars is rolled out – and they do so with great respect for the annual historical recurrence of a mythical ritual: the American dream.

Back to nature

With all its strength the little seal tries to hoist itself up on to the floating platform. But some bigger animals seem to disagree. It swims around the raft and tries again on the other side. Its attempts are finally crowned with success, and at least a hundred people watching this incident – children, families, tourists – breathe a sigh of relief. They all stand on a small, improvised grandstand some 10 metres off the seal raft. The backdrop for the seals is the skyline of San Francisco, shrouded in fog that slowly moves its way down here to the sea and is just about to envelop the first few metres of Pier 39. When shops and restaurants were built on this pier some 20 years ago, Fisherman's Wharf was probably the first urban entertainment centre in the world. Today the portfolio of the pier includes not only stores selling funny hats and numerous culinary tourist traps but also an aquarium and a flight simulator.

But the dozens of seals that suddenly appeared one day without warning and never disappeared again steal the show from all of these artificial pleasures. Floating pontoons were built for them, and here they now sleep and enjoy the sun. A simple wooden grandstand was erected so visitors to the pier can watch the animals socialize. While the Motion Ride cinema is suffering from a severe drop in visitor numbers, the seal grandstand is always packed with people.

Fisherman's Wharf has prompted imitators all over the world. In New York, San Diego, Cape Town, Sydney and Barcelona destination entertainment centres were built on the sea where people – apart from shopping and eating out – can above all enjoy one thing: nature, waves, the perfume of the water and the view out to sea. In the meantime, the original in San Francisco had become pretty run down. Despite renovation and investment in entertainment the centre somehow lacked an attraction. But one day, by miracle or smart tactics, a core attraction appeared that was low-cost, natural and authentic, and that corresponded to the new sustainability trend, one that is simply real: the seals of Pier 39. But how long they plan to stay is impossible to say.

SUMMARY

▌ *UECs make for 'one-stop' going out.*

▌ *UECs seduce us to take a stroll in the city by simulated streets and squares – to name but a few.*

▌ *UECs compact the space and time sequence of enjoying various pleasures.*

▌ **Resort-based entertainment centres.** These are casinos with hotels that retain buying power (that is, their guests) inside their own four walls. Outside they look extremely tempting; inside they slow down visitor flows by mazes in the gaming section while accelerating them on the super promenades of their malls. Attractions increase visitors' time spent there allowing them to let off steam away from the system.

▌ **Show-based entertainment centres.** These include cinemas, theatres staging musicals, and sports arenas with stores and food facilities. According to the 'before the show – after the show' principle this environment helps visitors kill time before the show and let off steam afterwards. Within a system like this stores must prompt browsing and allow people to relieve any remaining suspense with the products sold there.

▌ **Destination-based entertainment centres.** These celebrate existing places with special flair – harbour areas, historic court-yards, industrial monuments. Visitors use these places to recharge their batteries, and use them for mood management while enjoying the image transfer of nature or traces of the past. Some centres of this type are entire districts devoted to authentic fun.

5

Hip restaurants and bars

... as a sensation

When times were hard any occasion spent eating out was a luxury, great or small, and therefore a meal plus friendly staff was an event and experience in itself. As prosperity increased and quality consciousness grew, guests were one day no longer satisfied with palatable food and drinks alone. Enjoying the food is almost presupposed, and has become a standard simply taken for granted today. What turns the primary satisfaction of such needs as hunger and thirst into a positive experience are the trappings that go with the food and beverages.

There have always been some special catering formats whose strengths focused on these trappings. The classic pub around the corner was a social meeting point where everybody knew your name rather than a major culinary event. The Italian piazza and its establishments around the square were the stage for adolescent 'showing off' or the place where the village community relayed the latest gossip and scandals. For many writers of literature and other poor blighters, Viennese coffee-houses were heated refuges, offices, extensions to your home, or as one writer whose second home was a café phrased it, a place 'away from home but not in the open air'. Incidentally, even today in my home town Vienna you can still be served a glass of water although you finished your *mélange* coffee ages ago, and the waiter knows you have no intention of leaving.

Pubs next door, Italian piazzas, Viennese coffee-houses and British pubs are the classic Third Places in terms of food providers. All of them were products of a specific social environment and used to be part and parcel of people's everyday lives. They accompanied their lives, were elements of their after-work pursuits or some idle periods in-between, but not really an integral part of a going-out culture.

Going out means linking an attraction like theatre, cinema or music with a food add-on before or after the major event. One thing – the event – is the essence of the evening; the other thing – catering – is the add-on.

Hip restaurants and bars turn the restaurant and bar itself into a show, thereby concentrating the event and the catering environment in one place.

The first ones, the 'establishments causing a surprise', become playgrounds for grown-ups who feel like the protagonists of a smart, urban media society. The latter, the 'new themed establishments', carry their audience off to a dream world, but they do so living up to today's theming culture standards, with a feel for authenticity, high quality and design.

RESTAURANTS AND BARS CAUSING A SURPRISE

In excitement the striking blonde reports to her girlfriend what she has just experienced. 'You just have to see this,' we hear her say. She has just come back downstairs from the first floor, where we suspect the rest rooms are. But what excitement could she have experienced at a designer bar in New York's SoHo district? My wife Denise and I are sitting in Bar 89 after a gruelling day of research, and wonder how anyone can come back with so evident a discussion topic from a visit to the ladies. Equipped with my video camera – just to be on the safe side – I wander off to uncover the secret. You do indeed go upstairs to the rest rooms, a joint facility for Ladies and Gents. Soon I am standing in an antechamber with a bench and a mirror, and stare in disbelief at five completely transparent glass doors in front of three cubicles for ladies and two cubicles for gents. Anyone wanting to 'powder their nose' at Bar 89 has to summon up all their courage. Before the eyes of waiting guests you open the glass door and enter the cubicle. As the door closes, the lights are activated by motion detection, and in that same instant the glass suddenly turns opaque. A piezoelectric impulse controls the change in the transparency of the door. Those returning to their table certainly have something to tell (see colour plate section).

Restaurants and bars turn themselves into shows by giving their guests something to be surprised at, by generating an effect that prompts the *media literacy* of a media-wise, younger rather than older target group with high purchasing power. Those allowed to apply their media-technology consumer skills feel smart and adroit, and experience the place as hip. The effect becomes the 'talk of the town' or, at least, the talk of the establishment. Any necessary part of a restaurant or indeed bar can, without looking artificial, be turned into a gadget like this: the architecture and interior design of the restaurant and bar, its furnishings and furniture, the service and even the food.

Restaurant and bar architecture as a wow effect

A few years ago, the famous French architect Jean Nouvel built a small hotel plus restaurant on a side street of Lucerne, calling it Das Hotel for simplicity's sake. Once you finally find the premises after a long search you are rewarded with a clever special effect on the restaurant façade. The hotel bar and lobby are on the ground floor, the hip Thai design restaurant is in the basement underneath. A shared glazed frontage means that, from the outside, you can see both straight ahead into the lobby and bar and downwards into the restaurant. Hang on what's that? The lobby bar seems to be floating on the restaurant. There is no inter-mediate ceiling to be seen between the floors. Our brain tells us, 'but it must be there', and jump-starts our *media literacy*, which immediately goes in search of an explanation. In actual fact, tilted mirrors and a sophisticated lighting system produce an optical illusion, replicating a 'fake or not fake' effect comparable to the illusion paintings of the baroque era. This mirror effect reminds us that many perception games actually go back to the illusion and mirror effects of magicians and illu-sionists of the 19th century, who wowed audiences even then.

Most architectural games in restaurant and bar interiors are a vari-ation of the *room-in-room principle*. For this trick architects play with the fact that rooms are usually segments of a house but do not stand freely within houses. But this is precisely what is happening in this trick. At Georges, the spectacular roof restaurant of the famous Paris museum Centre Pompidou, five rooms 'grow' out of the floor of the spacious restaurant; fitted with an aluminium jacket these *rooms-in-a-room* look like air bubbles, organic shapes or whales. The young Franco-New Zealand architects, Dominique Jakob and Brendan

MacFarlane, wanted to create a landscape garden within a room, a theatrical spectacle – although the aluminium shapes do have a very profane function. The first houses the cloakroom right at the entrance. What follows is an aluminium cave bar, with a garish yellow interior complete with video screens and avant-garde cartoons. Next is a bright red sort of extra room, with one aluminium hillock for the kitchen and one for the toilets. By deviating from the norm that stipulates that the outer walls of rooms should not normally be visible – and certainly not as spectacle – they turn the interior design of the restaurant into the 'talk of the evening'.

Furnishings as a wow effect

What is the difference between a table and a stool? The question should be an easy one. And yet recently, at the Hudson Bar of the New York hotel of the same name, I spent an entire evening sitting on an acrylic glass shape. Until this day I am still not entirely sure whether it was a stool or really actually a table. The confusion was additionally fuelled by the fact that the roughly 20 managers who had accompanied me here to conclude my annual New York seminar were all sitting on a real tree trunk remodelled into a bench. Next to it was one solitary lady sitting enthroned on a huge 'golden' baroque chair, and what is more, every piece of furniture was placed on a luminous pedestal – the type you would use for sorting slides.

Some years ago, Georg Seesslen called this phenomenon 'semantic disaster' – when in the 1980s telephones looked like cucumbers or Garfield for instance. Today this *playing with the ambiguity* of objects has made its entrance as a wow effect for the furnishing of many restaurants and bars. The famous French designer Philippe Starck, responsible for both the Hudson Bar and the Hudson Hotel, has made this his trademark. At his Delano Hotel in Miami Beach a typical American-style kitchen including kitchen sink protrudes into the timber-panelled lobby at an oblique angle, apparently completely out of place, as if it has fallen out of the sky. Breakfast in this kitchen is excellent, and in the evening you can indulge in oysters, caviar and champagne.

Unusual viewing angles are part of this type of 'wow' furnishing style in catering establishments. In the warmer season the inner courtyard of the Hudson Hotel is a first-class meeting point for New York society. Here you can sprawl on cushions on the ground alongside a 2 metre high sheet metal watering can and enjoy this unusual perspective.

BED in Miami Beach goes one step further. At B(everage) E(ntertainment) D(ining), guests lie on chic low-level divans, eat finger food and sip on cocktails. In the movie *Dead Poets Society*, Robin Williams in the role of a dedicated teacher proved to his students by striding across the tables and chairs in a classroom that a change in perspective can make the world look all new, spectacular and inspiring again.

This is why these *new-view establishments* are first-rate attractions for going-out districts, hotels or indeed brand lands. In Paris it became chic to eat out at Renault on the Champs Elysées. The French automobile manufacturer built a beautiful showroom called Atelier Renault which houses a striking panorama restaurant overlooking the world's most famous street. Here on one of seven bridges arranged at different heights, offering a view both outside and of the other bridges, you see hundreds of guests – like silhouettes against the light – who give you that 'pleasure derived from watching'. Renault thus created a typical Third Place: a car showroom only displaying Formula I cars became what is now the most popular place for lifestyle-oriented business dinners in the restaurant Mecca of Paris.

Food and service as wow effects

Anyway, shouldn't food, drinks and service be the focus of any restaurant or bar? Of course, but for centuries man has tried to turn the core competences of each restaurant into a little sensation to amaze the public. Think of the efforts made in the baroque period, when huge banquets were popular courtly spectacles. Large animals like oxen and pigs were stuffed with smaller animals like hares and pheasants as a show effect, and these – to the amazement and delight of the audience – were in turn stuffed with even smaller animals: *food as a special effect*. Nowadays the West Coast of the United States is an Eldorado for such dazzling restaurant tricks as these. Whenever I am in San Francisco I try to plan an evening at the Stinking Rose, a restaurant that is always packed where everything revolves around the garlic theme. While the restaurant's furnishing features a wonderfully effusive staging of garlic-related kitchen utensils, overly ornate chandeliers and italo-hispanic clichés, the actual sensation of the 'speciality restaurant' is the amazing fact that you can make just about anything using garlic, from hot starters to sweet deserts. What I particularly like is steamed garlic from a copper bowl served before the main course, and the famous garlic ice cream – yes indeed! – as a dessert.

The *cross-over cuisine* found at lifestyle restaurants tries to produce this dazzling effect in a more subtle way through a surprising combination of aromatic elements from different cultures. Eurasian cuisine is already a classic, and now makes it possible for green Japanese *wasabi kren* to feature as an ingredient in something as simple as mashed potatoes.

Initial attempts to make service a dazzling experience occasionally entailed quite strange to embarrassing results in the 1990s. Waiters stumbled about the place on roller skates, burst into song or served on their knees. Most promising are those experiments that seem to be inspired by the old *cooking-machine* and *robot-waiter* dreams of the science fiction world. Right now an 18-metre-long pizza baking line is being installed at Pizza Mania in the new Legoland in the Bavarian city of Günzburg. It allows children, large and small, to watch how their pizza comes into being on its way to the oven. Up to 900 pizzas per hour will be produced this way, as an attraction of the restaurant. The British Yo! Sushi chain offers a self-mocking robot service as a spectacle for a target group that consumes sushi while enjoying loud music and video clips. A fully automatic trolley circles the restaurant, extols the sake at the top of its voice and utters caustic remarks if you take food off the trolley yourself.

THE NEW THEMED RESTAURANTS

A full moon shines down on the coast of northern Greece. The beautiful five-star hotel is called Danai Beach, and its young Greek-German owner experiments with food service stagings. Today the unmistakable voice of Maria Callas rings through the night air. Viewed from the hotel terrace the scene on the beach looks quite unreal. Torches light up the comfortable, softly upholstered wickerwork chairs from the hotel lobby that are now placed on Oriental rugs on the sand. A cigar glows in the darkness, a big balloon glass of select cognac is swayed. The small, portable bar with its foldable mirrors projects a glitter effect on to the softly foaming surf. Now Callas's voice – from the hi-fi – rises to a dramatic pitch, turning the moon, sea and a little boat anchored just a few metres out to sea into the most classic possible Greek scene for a tragedy. Through the temporary theming at this establishment without any pieces of scenery and trumpery I feel transported into another world where my ideas, my *brain scripts* of Greek tragedy come true. The themed world works, the feeling of immersing oneself into another world starts to develop. Themed stagings have always been a particularly effective means of enhancing food into a going-out experience.

It is striking to note that folkloric themes have determined theming from the outset.

The little Italian restaurants that opened in German cities back in the 1960s probably had a lively Italian landlord who said 'buona sera' and lit a candle in a Chianti bottle covered in wax. In the 1970s people went to Greek restaurants with white-washed stone walls and landlords who served ouzos on the house as a token of Greek hospitality. Despite the folkloric kitsch sometimes seen, these early ethnic-theme establishments also exuded the charm of something authentic, and were really able to fill guests with that holiday feeling.

In the 1980s and 1990s theming – under the influence of the United States – took to non-catering-related themes from the movie world, the music scene and glamour. Abundantly garnished, the burger was 'upgraded' – with the devotional objects of famous rock stars at the Hard Rock Café, against the backdrop of movie scenery at Planet Hollywood, complete with impressive motorcycles sometimes even letting off steam at the Harley Davidson Café, and by graceful catwalk models at the Fashion Café. Today, these typically American themes are out of fashion even in America.

Ennobled folklore

Now establishments again focus on folkloric themes – closely related to the dishes served – or to references to art and culture. Here they try to combine the authentic touch of the early years with the spectacular element of escapist stagings. Nowadays, theming is done by means of genuine materials, high-quality design, irony and lifestyle. My introductory chapter featured a description of the Hospizalm in the Tyrol. Here you can take a seat in one of several Tyrolean stone pine parlours from various regions that line up like boxes at a theatre. Design-based theming is also used at Noodles in Las Vegas, another establishment already described. Here noodle shapes are presented against a white luminous wall as at a modern art gallery, and guests can not only sip on their noodle soup but also peruse the noodles it contains.

The new themed establishments tell stories as before but these stories are ennobled and upgraded.

Belly dancing in Turkish and Arab restaurants used to be an embarrassing spectacle for tourists. But at SoHo's chic Casa La Femme, where you sit on the floor in designer tents, are served by perfectly turned-out waiters on their knees who explain the menu, and can visit a palm reader in her tent between courses, the belly dancer dancing for a few minutes in front of each tent somehow exudes the sense of 'dancing before the sultan' rather than of a rip-off spectacle you are forced to sit through. In Berlin's giant Adagio located in the basement of the musical theatre at Potsdamer Platz the romantic clerical scenery is ennobled with genuine Irish choir stalls and an enormous quantity of fresh flowers and fruit every day.

At the Buddha Bar in Paris esoteric cult music provides the musical backdrop for the great golden Buddha at this Far Eastern design location. At the Red Square of the Mandalay Bay Resort in Las Vegas people dine in the ironically cold train station atmosphere of a bad Moscow restaurant. Lenin's head, missing from the statue at the front door, later appears in the form of ice cubes at the restaurant's tiny vodka bar. Guests are wrapped in thick coats since they – along with all the vodka bottles – are chilled down to Siberian temperatures at the bar: the irony of a ritual plus the authentic temperature are thus themed add-on attractions for an award-winning meal out.

Hôtel sans chambres

And this is the latest development: a hotel without rooms – as Christine Ruckendorfer calls her generously spaced catering complex. Her oriental Aux Gazelles in Vienna and Mourad Mazouz's eccentric Sketch in London are the most recent innovations among these new themed bars and restaurants that opened in late 2002.

Both aim to keep guests in their establishment all day long by a multitude of different stimuli, as in a hotel where you find everything you might need during the course of the day. From the breakfast room, seminar and working areas, lunch and dinner, to fitness and wellness, a bar and nightclub, guests are expected to satisfy all their different needs at one single location – all of them with the exception of the overnight accommodation. The Aux Gazelles, for example, houses an oriental café, a 'brasserie' with designer furniture, a little bazaar, a separate seminar lounge, a caviar and oyster bar and a Moorish nightclub where belly dancing meets clubbing. Deep down inside the complex – warm, humid and in semi-darkness – an oriental *hamam* sauna awaits visitors seeking relaxation. It features three different temperature zones, minimalist styling plus its own chill-out room and tea house. Mariah Carey and Sarah Brightman are amongst the illustrious guests already retiring here.

The principle is inspired by Moroccan guest houses, classic Third Places, where you spend a long time or go to on different days with entirely different aims. As is opportune for the new themed bars and restaurants, the layout combines folklore elements with design. This miraculous idea of dramatizing bars and restaurants is also in evidence at bars and restaurants causing a surprise, sporting a spectacular core attraction – such as the designer *hamam* at Aux Gazelles and the incredible rest rooms at Sketch.

An Algerian national, Mazouz has united five different food experiences under one roof at his Sketch establishment. Its two stunning restaurants are the Lecture Room, in a library, and The Gallery, a video art gallery with 360° video projections. All the passageways between the patisserie, the luxury restaurant, the video gallery and the two bars intersect at the featured toilets. One facility is a luminous blue (Gents) or red (Ladies) mirrored treasure trove filled with Swarovski crystals and tunes played from a music box that looks as if a gay maharaja has gone nuts. The other facility plays an even more daring game with *changing perspectives*. It shifts the relationships between the spaces allocated to the bar and the lavatories. The bar is located in a kind of countersunk igloo in a large white room. Left and right flights of stairs lead up on to the igloo roof, where a group of 2-metre-high plastic eggs is positioned – the toilet cubicles that leave many a visitor speechless in surprise. However, the concept of a place with a special ambiance is being completely undermined by Sketch's management. Thus, the Internet is full of angry guests' comments: 'The people who work there are very rude. Because they did not have the main course we ordered, they took the liberty of bringing us a course of their choice! Oh! And don't forget, when you book a table, make sure you eat within two hours, otherwise you don't eat at all. They ask you to move because they have reserved the table for other people. If you book a table for a certain number of people and one of your friends cannot make it, you pay for your friend anyway…' (www.londoneats.com, 20 February 2004). Hôtel sans chambres is doubtlessly the most consistent system within the food sphere where the establishment itself becomes the stage. But a stage without hospitality is definitely not a Third Place. Hence also the business-consequences can read on the Internet: 'Whatever you do – never go to Sketch.' (Halloj on www.londoneats.com, 11 February 2004).

SUMMARY

- *Hip bars and restaurants are part of going out.*
- *This used to mean going to the theatre or movies first and then to the restaurant or bar.*
- *Today hip restaurants and bars incorporate the show into the establishment, making a sensation in themselves.*
- **Restaurants and bars causing a surprise.** These are play-grounds for grown-ups who feel like the protagonists in a smart media culture. 'Wow' effects like crazy toilets, futurist interior designs or cross-over dishes trigger visitors' media literacy, giving them the opportunity to behave smartly and to marvel.
- **The new themed restaurants.** These carry us away into a dream world, call up our brain scripts. But they do so with a feel for high quality and design, ennobling even somewhat more folkloric themes. This is why the feel of adventure at Rumjungle is not exuded by pirate figures and artificial palm trees but by flames reflecting on the slick black outer walls and trendy cascades of water running down walls of glass.

PART III

SHOPPING PLACES AS HIGH-QUALITY ENTERTAINMENT

Paris, not far from the Elysées Palace, home to the French President. Rue du Faubourg St Honoré is one of the world's most expensive shopping avenues. At number 54 a little company sign points the way to a hidden store. Concealed in the second inner courtyard is Comme des Garçons, the Paris flagship store of Japanese fashion designer *Rei Kawabuko*. On the right-hand side of the idyllic courtyard is the design store. To the left, the doors of an unusual room of the shop opposite are wide open. The walls and ceiling are made of bright red plastic. Roughly a dozen dice-shaped stools in the same red colour move about the white floor as if by magic and give off a low buzzing sound. The cameras of Japanese tourists click non-stop; tiny video cameras are rolling. After observing them for some time I notice each stool follows its own movement routine. One always moves a little back and forth. Another one turns in wild circles and additionally wobbles since its axis of rotation is not centred. A third one always moves to the left then to the right. After 10 minutes the Japanese, obviously now charged up, take the store opposite by storm, fiercely determined to shop till it's empty. I stay for some more time in order to reflect on what I have just experienced.

▋ Obviously I have been watching the *core attraction* of a store that aroused curiosity and drew people in like a magnet.

▋ Apparently, I have experienced so-called *shop-o-tainment*, that is, shopping and entertainment in the same place, something that carries customers off into a exhilarated state of emotions which prompt at the actual store to explore the range on offer in high shopping spirits.

▋ This was unquestionably achieved by particularly high-quality and artful design, which goes to show that staged stores can today be the *avant-garde of a new popular culture* like comics, films or rock music were in the past.

▋ What I have experienced here is in any case a *Third Place*, a store that wanted more than a quick sell, one that also wanted to be a place to stay in a strange city, a tourist attraction, a lifestyle to relate to and a cheerful means of massaging the soul.

6

Flagship stores

Business cards for retailers

This new, high-quality and sustainable way of staging sales is a perfect fit for the generously spaced flagship stores in retailing. Beyond the sales-promoting effect produced by experiences at the point of sale, these business cards in the form of architecture aim at producing lasting effects in image building, public relations and brand and corporate advertising.

Flagship stores are therefore walk-in 3-D advertising and must be co-financed by the advertising budgets.

Ideally, they can be featured in travel guides, lifestyle magazines and television shows – at least once from the outside as *landmarks* for the city, and once from inside with their *core attraction*. Furthermore, many flagship stores try to become embassy buildings or *representations* in the city, places that occupy territory within people's everyday realm. You go to Hugo Boss in New York to have coffee. You arrange to meet at Lederleitner at the Vienna Stock Exchange to have lunch in a 19th-century orangery amidst palm trees, British gardening utensils, under vaults and by water fountains (see colour plate section). Flagship stores become such landmarks and fixtures in the city thanks to their emotionalization, the recurrent theme to be found all over the store. There are three typical *concept lines* here:

The store becomes a temple, a cathedral with all the trappings of a sacred, awe-inspiring place. Or the store is like a walk-in lifestyle magazine, the only difference being that you walk rather than thumb through it.

And finally there are those mega stores working like miniature malls: open-plan bookstores, cosmetics stores, sports outfitters.

SACRED STORES

How do you stage awe? Long before the Catholic church had the world monopoly on 'sacred entertainment', the dramatic trick of the *forbidden place* emerged in Egypt in 1400 BC. This trick is based on the reasoning that 'anything that is inaccessible automatically increases in value'. Old Egyptian temples were arranged in such a way that, beyond a pylon (that is, a form of obelisk) watching over the entrance, several inner court-yards followed one after the other so you could see along a central axis all the way down from the first courtyard into the distant sanctuary. But access to the temple was staggered. While all citizens were allowed into the first courtyard, the second was reserved for the Pharaoh and his entourage, the next for the Pharaoh alone, and access to the shrine itself – where a green jade stone mysteriously shone out – was reserved only for priests following initiation rites and drug-induced intoxication.

Selective restriction of access prompts anticipation, curiosity and longing, which charges the place with great suspense.

My last book, *Der verbotene Ort oder die inszenierte Verführung* (The forbidden place or staged seduction: Mikunda, 2002b) bears this dodge in its title, and describes how widespread this trick is in marketing – from staged press conferences to exhibition stands and nightclubs. Three flagship stores in New York impressively illustrate how the *forbidden place* is currently staged in retailing, or – to be more precise – in the luxury segment of retailing, because this is the only sector where it makes sense.

The forbidden place

There is always a suspense axis that pulls consumers into the store. But there is also always some kind of resistance to be overcome first – the store is secluded, a doorman keeps watch, you have to ring the door bell. This is nothing but a 'sanctuary' designed to lure customers in and make them overcome their resistance – as do a 'secret' room within the store, or a particularly spectacular interior design that is not immediately acces-sible. There is always this feeling of *anticipation*, the suspense built as a result of the delay through which the sanctuary can only be accessed step by step; this suspense recharges the place and makes it vibrate.

Finally there is a feeling of satisfaction, of released tension and personal affirmation when you enter a place not accessible to everyone. You can often observe how guests in airport lounges lean back in a particularly relaxed manner when others, full of themselves but without the necessary accreditation, are denied access.

The most spectacular of the three flagship stores in New York is Comme des Garçons in the trendy Chelsea district. No one would expect to find such a store in an area with slaughterhouses and garages. And to top it all, the store even camouflages itself with a wrong company nameplate. What you see is a brick façade, an iron fire escape ladder, a hole in the wall and above it a scruffy sign 'Heavenly Body Works' announcing a car repair shop. Initiated customers are not put off and bravely step into the hole. There they find themselves standing in a metal tunnel with a glass door at the end. But how do you open it – what is the magic 'open sesame' trick? You first have to reach through a hole in the glass door, then the door will revolve around an invisible axis and you practically slip through. (See Figure 6.1.)

Figure 6.1   Façade of Comme des Garçons, New York
© Umdasch Shop-Concept

You carry on through the metal tunnel a few more yards, guided by red recessed floor lights. Then, all of a sudden, you are standing in the middle of the store. A large, all white and surprisingly high space opens up before you – a sacred room. Tall structures in white aluminium stand about the place like white houses in a white village. They serve as goods display stands, changing rooms and partition walls at the same time. Once you have entered the store you are treated in a friendly manner or are just left in peace as long as you do not try to take photographs.

Conversely, Helmut Lang's fragrance store in SoHo at first sight seems to open up towards the outside. It is long and narrow and virtually pulls in customers along its suspense axis. Along this axis neon letters race into the store along a parapet at eye level. This installation features cryptic love poems by the famous performance artist Jenny Holzer, Helmut Lang's long-time companion. But then, inside the actual store, I stop and stand rooted to the spot. What looks like glass distillation apparatus stands on a long counter. Apart from this, the white room is quite empty – with the exception of a sales assistant dressed in black who is looking at me. At this point I would just love to turn round and leave forthwith, but I overcome my unease caused by this Cerberus. There is actually only one perfume sold here, and in most cases there is also only one single flacon in sight, or rather, on display. Passing the 'human watchdog' I try to find my way to that secret room, knowing that it must be here, somewhere. The 'holy of holies' is a little room at the far end of the store: an 'olfactorium' containing more glass apparatus standing on a futurist table. This is where you can – provided you dare – learn how to smell the 'master's' perfume.

The Hugo Boss flagship store on the Upper East Side looks like an oversized glass showcase from outside. Even from the street you can spot the narrow, very steep and endlessly long staircase on the far right-hand side of the store that leads all the way up, taking you past modern paintings as you go. The end of this suspense axis is marked by a mannequin that draws your attention upwards. However there are six bouncers blocking the entrance area, three on the left and three on the right. Well, you may think, after all I am a customer, as you pass these Cerberuses – who, in ancient times, were not without reason called hell-hounds. But where is the spacious sales area we have heard about? The ground floor just houses a medium-sized room. Only gradually do you realize there is an enormous sales area stretching out to the back, hiding behind each of the small landings of the narrow staircase. When you finally reach the top of the stairs and look down on all those levels from a specific point you realize they resemble the levels of a South American housing pyramid, reaching far backwards but in such a staggered array that you are unaware of their existence when standing at the bottom. The sales levels are the 'sanctuaries' for us to discover.

Stores that hide away, suspense axes whose access is restricted by 'open sesame' features or a Cerberus, secret rooms that you want to see nonetheless, and finally a feeling of heightened self-esteem as a result of the added value of Third Places, places that do not only sell but also, as an extra effect, put a specified place in the city at our disposal, a 'sanctuary' – this is what the fascination of the *forbidden place* is all about. The sacred effect produced by this strategy is transferred to the customer. But there are a number of other tricks that also reflect a sacred effect on to the image of goods or the company.

Relics

You can't believe your eyes. A single necktie is lying in an illuminated, pyramid-shaped showcase, well displayed through the shop window. Next to it is a roughly 1.5-metre-high white goods display, which looks like an egg standing upright. The 'belly' of the egg holds jumpers and shirts, the tip supports a valuable necklace reflected in a folding mirror. Behind the egg, suits and dresses hang in bright and shiny wardrobes like mummies in their sarcophagi. All of this can be found at the Armani flagship store of the Bellagio Hotel in Las Vegas. The pyramid, the egg and sarcophagi 'ennoble' the goods, making them relics of the god of consumerism worthy of worship. This principle is tried and tested. Even in the Middle Ages precious relic shrines were used to ennoble bones of saints or splinters of the Golgotha cross, and make them appear worthy of worship. At first glance, some splinters from Saint Sebastian's femur look none too impressive. But once they are 'packaged' along with gold and precious stones, marble and rock crystals in a shrine, the value of this package is inevitably transferred to its content. The reason for this is the psychological mechanism of *inferential beliefs* underlying each packaging and *placement* phenomenon.

When something is packaged so preciously it must be valuable and worthy of worship – this is the image constructed by 'inferential beliefs'.

Many stores feature such *sacred placements* these days. Shoes float on luminous pedestals in showcases. Partition walls in fashion stores are semi-transparent so that the goods only shine through vaguely and thereby seem to be 'ennobled'. Back wall panels in cosmetics stores – thanks to concealed back lighting – become luminous goods displays that surround the products placed in front of them with a special shimmer and brilliance. Even sales assistants touching a product can reflect on the image of the product. The conscious, attentive touching of a piece of jewellery upgrades it and makes you feel the relation between the hand and the gem. A simple touch can become such a *golden touch* if the hand approaches the piece of jewellery slowly, touches it gently, rests on it and – after having retreated from the jewel – pauses for just a little while before the piece is returned to its place. This cautious touch is like a sacred blessing, consecration or anointing. In the age of self-service stores this contact is often only established at the check-out. This is why all the sales assistants working at the check-out of the famous luxury French cosmetics chain Sephora wear a black cotton glove on one hand. Touching the products when packaging continues the enhancement of the goods at the cash desk that started on the luminous display shelving.

Sephora features another striking example of staged image transfer. Young men dressed in radiant white walk about the store to clean it carefully. After all, those who clean a church also proceed with the utmost care. Such staged cleaning struck me for the first time years ago in Japan. In the automotive showrooms there you can watch young ladies in uniforms as they incessantly clean the surfaces of the vehicles on show with huge, fluffy feather dusters. At the stations highly professional teams of cleaners dressed in pink uniforms and equipped with mobile phones wait for the bullet trains to arrive. It only takes them seven minutes to fastidiously scrub the entire train clean, and afterwards they open it up again for the new passengers with obvious pride.

Sacred rooms

I enter a Catholic church somewhere in Europe. It consists of one nave and two symmetrically arranged aisles delimited by the two lines of columns left and right of the central nave. My eyes follow the axis towards the front, where an altarpiece in the distance attracts my attention. Immediately in front of the altar the high room widens into a dome, which reinforces this glorious feeling of grandeur.

I enter the Thierry Mugler flagship store in Paris. A row of luminous columns shining in an unreal blue light – in keeping with the latest

fragrance launch – subdivides the store into a nave and two symmetrically arranged aisles. My eyes wander along the columns to the front,
where a mannequin on a dais in a dress from the latest summer
collection attracts all my attention.

I enter the Versace flagship store in New York and what do I see: on
each floor the end of the axes is marked by an apse with a statue, or a
shop dummy on a raised podium overseeing this floor like a goddess.

I enter the Galéries Lafayette department store in Paris and marvel –
surely for the hundredth time – at the enormous Art Nouveau glass
dome that gives this huge room that feeling of grandeur and magnificence. Underneath the cupola dozens of little temples offer perfumes –
each one of them featuring their inimitable corporate design.

I enter the Japanese Takashimaya department store on Fifth Avenue
in New York and see a golden cupola which is visible from several
levels of the store. On the top floor – where it is bathed in meditative
light and covered with willow sprigs that customers look down on when
they take a break – this cupola exudes a feeling of composure and meditative contemplation.

*I enter a flagship store anywhere and sense – due to the artefacts of
sacred architecture – a feeling of grandeur, of magnitude and meditation which reflects on the range, the image of the company and, last
but not least, on my state of mind.*

Heaven forbid that any shop assistants dare tear me away from this
feeling with their arrogance, thereby destroying the added value of this
Third Place as a sacred retreat in the city. This they will certainly notice
in their sales figures.

The question still remains why so many flagship stores have a sacred
feel about them. It is common knowledge that luxury brands are only
bought for their quality 50 per cent of the time and for their emotional
charge the other 50 per cent. Fashion designers are adored like gurus,
brands enjoy cult status, the sales room is consequently a place of
adoration. But there is also another reason for this phenomenon. As
early as in the 19th century the Church, with its incense spectacles and
processions, increasingly lost its fascination just the way monarchies
and royalty did. The bourgeois middle classes finally moved to the fore.
This is why substitute palaces and cathedrals were erected for the
wealthy citizens within the public rather than the ecclesiastical sphere.
Hotels and department stores featured imperial flights of stairs hitherto
only known from châteaux, and the French 'grands magasins' like

Galéries Lafayette and Au Printemps vied for buyers with enormous stained glass cupolas. 'Cathedrals of consumerism' was what they called these new sites, inspiring awe, glory and adoration. Today, in times where churches are on the verge of losing their last vestige of adoration due to scandals involving paedophile priests, places other than church buildings now fulfil man's deep-rooted need for something sublime. These include the atriums of large museums, which will be covered in great detail later, and the flagship stores of luxury brands.

LIFESTYLE STORES

Sublimity is not the only basic feeling that transforms generously spaced sales areas into the business card of a company. Experiencing the lifestyle that is inextricably linked to the use of a product is just as widespread a strategy for flagship stores today. Glossy magazines have long realized that products are embedded in larger life and pleasure contexts – in lifestyle. This is why magazines like *Vogue* or *Harper's Bazaar* have for decades presented fashion in conjunction with accessories, travel destinations, fine living, hotels and books, movies and design. The single components from fashion to music create a consistent, self-contained world. This world can be projected by means of pieces of scenery featured at the point of sale, or it can simply be instilled with life by offering a consistent range.

Range theming

Those entering the DKNY flagship store in New York will experience an authentic, themed world – the world of Donna Karan and her target group – without the help of any pieces of scenery. Underneath the dresses hung up on display we also find matching shoes; next to these a vase, books flicked open, a designer chair at $5,000 in dazzling colours, while music is played in the store that was produced by DKNY and is only available here. While it is true that books, CDs and shoes are also presented in dedicated departments within the store, seeing them presented here in a home-like context like in real life is more attractive by far. This mix is based on the reasoning that accessories like books or vases are just as much fashion items within lifestyle, and that conversely, dresses or shoes are also indicative of an interior.

Why sell experiences?

Plate 1   An event seen from one point of view gives one impression. Seen from another point of view, it gives quite a different impression. But it's only when you see the whole picture that you can fully understand what's going on.

Source: 'Points of View', television advert for the *Guardian* GB 1988 © BMP DDBL

THE GUARDIAN

Landmarks

Plate 2   Swarovski's Crystal Worlds in Wattens, Tyrol, and the Alligator leather goods store in Vienna. Storefront headers, like medieval guild signs, show people outside what to expect inside.

Crystal Worlds in Wattens designed by André Heller © Swarovski

Alligator leather goods store in Vienna, photo by C Mikunda

Malling

Plate 3 Third Places invite us to 'mall', using suspense axes such as this one in the Le Meridien hotel, Vienna (top), or emphasized hubs as at Meinl am Graben (right).

Le Meridien hotel designed by Yvonne Golds, photo by A Vesely

Meinl am Graben, Vienna, designed by Otto Rau, photo by A Vesely

Concept line

Plate 4   Third Places need a 'golden thread'. At Bluewater shopping mall in Kent, England, you can follow the course of the River Thames on the floor (right) and read the words to a song about the Thames on the wall (top).

Bluewater designed by Eric Kuhne, Lend Lease, photo by C Mikunda

Core attraction

Plate 5   Third Places arouse our curiosity with a central attraction. The wine tower and wine angels create a 'wow' effect at the Aureole restaurant at Mandalay Bay Resort in Las Vegas.

Wine tower designed by Adam D Tihany, photo by Mark Ballogg

Photo of wine angels by Pierre Nierhaus

Brand lands

Plate 6 Places of desire celebrate the act of making a purchase, as at the Volkswagen Autostadt in Wolfsburg, Germany, with its huge car towers (top and left). Places of adoration make the image of the brand shine, as at VW's Lamborghini Pavilion (right).

VW Autostadt 'Car Towers' in Wolfsburg, Germany, designed by Jack Rousse Associates, photo by Laif

VW's Lamborghini Pavilion designed by Bellprat Associates, photo by Marc Oliver Schulz

Exhibitions and expos

Plate 7   The Blur Building designed by Diller and Scofido for the Expo 2002 at Yverdon, and the Pavilion of Health at Expo 2000, designed by Toyo Ito. Experiences of nature and staged relaxing provide relieving massages for the soul.

Blur Building, Expo 2002, Yverdon les Bains, designed by Elizabeth Diller and Ricardo Scofidio, photo by Yves André

Pavilion of Health at Expo 2000, Hannover, photo by C Mikunda

City events

Plate 8 Public places are transformed and temporarily given another function. Rome's Piazza Navona is turned into a lake, Vienna's big ferris wheel becomes a giant watch, and the Vienna Secession building looks like a face.

Piazza Navona, painting by Pannini (1756), photo by Landesgalerie, Hannover

Soulcity at Wiener Riesenrad, Vienna, photo by WIP Marketing

Glass Horizon 2000 at Secession, Vienna, artist Doug Aitken, photo by A Vesely

Urban entertainment centres

Plate 9 UECs persuade us to take a stroll in the city by simulating streets and squares, or even a Venetian 'scuola' and a Grand Canal that runs through the whole shopping mall, as seen at the Venetian resort in Las Vegas.

Entrance map of Venetian Grand Canal Shoppes, Las Vegas © The Venetian Resort designed by Wilson and Associates, photo by Umdasch Shop-Concept

Grand Canal of Venetian Resort designed by WATG, photo by Umdasch Shop-Concept

Hip restaurants and bars

Plate 10 The giant egg toilets of the Sketch restaurant in London, designed by Noé Lawrance, and the 'now I see you, now I don't' toilets designed by Janis Leonard at Bar 89 in New York. Crazy toilets give guests the opportunity to marvel.

Sketch, London, Eat Bar toilets, photo by Umdasch Shop-Concept

Bar 89, photo by C Mikunda

Flagship stores

Plate 11   Lederleitner in Vienna with Leo Doppler's restaurant Hansen – a 19th century orangery with plants, British gardening tools and books. Flagship stores can be like walk-in lifestyle magazines that transport you into a lifestyle and recharge your batteries.

Hansen, Vienna, photo by Hansen restaurant

Lederleitner, Vienna, photos by A Vesely

Concept stores

Plate 12   The Lomo store is based around the product world of the cult Lomo cameras. The entrance door folds out, and the carrier bags are made out of pink lace nighties. This is customer entertainment through smart design and ranges. The store was created by the Egyptian Bibawy sisters, and the bags by Eva Blut.

Lomography Shop designed by Sally Bibawy, Karl Emilio Pircher, photo by A Vesely

Negligee bag, photo by A Vesely

Design malls

Plate 13 Selfridges in Birmingham and London – an impressive landmark on the outside and little sensations inside. There are show acts in the atrium, spectacular changing cubicles and a kid's world with cloud-like goods displays to attract customers.

Optimized places

Plate 14 The SSAWS Skidome in Tokyo – activities only accessible at certain times of the year become available all year round. The NTC in the Austrian Alps – time-consuming and unpleasant elements are removed from the typical skiing routine by a clever ski rental system featuring a robot that prepares skis and pre-warmed ski boots.

SSAWS Skidome, Tokyo, photo by C Mikunda

NTC New Technology Centre, Schruns, Austria, photo by C Mikunda

Lobbies and lounges

Plate 15   Exciting places: Jeunesse Musicale's Colourscape, with its amazing colour showers and emotional interior design.

Relaxing places: the Billa supermarket, which applies 'mood management' to its stressed-out consumers via projected scenes and sounds from nature.

Colourscape, Jeunesse Musicale, Vienna, 1999, photo by A Vesely

Billa supermarket, Purkersdorf, Austria, photo by A Vesely

The new hiking

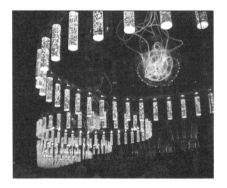

Plate 16 Otto Steiner's Loisium with its spectacular exterior building designed by Steven Holl. The path leads you through the vineyard down to the mystic cellars. Underground cathedrals and attractions like a sunken ballroom with chandeliers make this a unique subterranean hiking experience.

Loisium, Visitors' Centre, Langenlois, Austria, photo by Robert Herbst

Loisium, Cellar World, designed by Steiner Sarnen, photos by Robert Herbst and C Mikunda

Customers stroll through the shop, momentarily feel part of this world, flick the pages of a book, sit down on the expensive designer chair, buy a CD and maybe also a dress. This theming works because it calls up our *brain scripts* and stories of lifestyle and design worlds in the way we know them from those glossy magazines; but unlike with magazines this theming allows customers to play a role in this world.

Flagship stores become walk-in lifestyle magazines, with customers spending a long time in the store.

After all this, and in keeping with the target group, a sushi bar in the centre of the store and two other cafés tempt you to stay and live the DKNY life, and to immerse yourself into its themed world. Lifestyle shops are therefore perfect Third Places to collect your thoughts, charge yourself with emotion in the city, to browse, hang out and use as a meeting point. In the meantime DKNY's dramatic trick of *range theming* has been imitated by many other stores with their own respective lifestyles. Colette in Paris is named after the author of the famous novel *Gigi*, and a more recent, tougher, more underground-like world that follows the motto 'styledesignartfood'. Colette will only stock the most avant-garde styles of all fashion labels, next to Apple's new i-Mac computer, books on the art of piercing, a make-up studio, modern paintings, a water bar in the basement and chic mobiles.

Architectural theming

While lifestyle worlds brought to life by range-based theming are rather immaterial products of our own powers of imagination, products of our ability to 'feel our way', lifestyle-oriented flagship stores have now also emerged, opting for exactly the opposite approach. They achieve theming through physical, architectural measures that occasionally do make you feel as if you have been invited by a fashion designer or lifestyle guru.

Those entering Polo, Ralph Lauren's city base on New York's sophisticated Upper East Side, might easily be forgiven for thinking they have been stranded in the private quarters of the master himself. Surrounded by the finest fashion classics, guests – sorry, customers – stroll from room to room. In each room a fire is blazing in the grate, the exquisite wooden staircase features wood panelling decorated with genuine oil paintings, a saddle is ready waiting for a ride, the 20 sunflowers in the vase are real and the fruit in the basket is fresh. After some time you give up regarding the flagship store as a retail location. You simply enjoy being a guest, and the exquisite atmosphere.

Just a few hundred yards down the road the Frick Collection, housed in an elegant mansion, proves that architectural theming is a dramatic trick and therefore also features in a different context. Here at the founder's house the paintings of this collection still hang where they were exhibited when the millionaire Henry Clay Frick was still alive: not arranged by epoch but the way they are shown to their best advantage within the house. And again it is a staircase that conveys to visitors the feeling they are guests. On the landing they find the biggest organ ever installed in a private home, a neo-classical grandfather clock and a wonderful Renoir dowsed in light.

Ralph Lauren cultivates the aristocratic, classic lifestyle of the polo playing, golfing classes. But, of course, a number of less sophisticated lifestyles can also be made accessible using this principle. At many shops in SoHo the cast-iron columns and other relics of loft architecture are the decisive signals triggering the themed lifestyle world here. The most beautiful example is Anthropology, where a gigantic iron beam juts out all across the store and the themed worlds merely feature in adjacent, open-plan rooms underneath this 'monster': here we find Asian items, junk and bric-a-brac, fashion, candlesticks, home fashion utensils, informal wear that may be a little creased and, to top it all, a cat that sprawls out on the sofa next to us – a sofa which definitely does not require a cover-up.

Again, a completely different approach is taken by the flagship store of Jean Claude Jitrois in the Paris fashion district around the Rue St Honoré. Jitrois, inventor of stretch leather and former psychology professor, had a pretty quirky, psychoanalytically driven world built at his tiny flagship store. A silver foil sky shines over the ground floor; in the basement customers are met by a crazy mirror maze refracting their images a hundred times; next to this you unexpectedly come across underground baroque gardens, golden doors like those at a pasha's place, the madness of an eccentric fashion leather world that makes the likes of Elton John and Celine Dion feel at home.

For all other mere mortals who can at best afford a few souvenirs from the likes of Ralph Lauren or DKNY, lifestyle shops have, to my mind, an irresistible, frequently under-rated cultural and social function. They train our eye for a specific lifestyle even though we just might not be able to afford it yet.

In the same way that the literary salons of the 19th century, the clubs and society circles aimed to convey style awareness to young people, today magazines and lifestyle shops are the new media helping us to feel our way into a style and become style assured.

MEGASTORES

This is a completely different world. Many large stores do not look especially 'sexy' at first sight. Nonetheless, large bookshops or DIY superstores became first-class Third Places. They promote malling and browsing, they allow customers to seek and find objects and – thanks to their vast sales areas – also make it possible to promenade on one and the same level. This is only otherwise possible at shopping malls. The focus is neither on theming nor on lifestyle here, but simply on navigation: malling, the most passionate application of the *cognitive map*.

The pleasure derived from orientation

Often large sales areas, just like museums, suffer from a serious deficiency. They offer the *all-in long shot*. This flaw was described in detail in Chapter 2, focusing on expos and exhibitions. One particular bookstore in Berlin is notorious for visual information overkill of this kind. Here we see dozens of signs with the names of each section, along with advertising, the signs to the rest rooms, plus a host of superfluous information. Customers cannot help but stop and wonder, while rooted to the spot at the pigsty of a store they have come to. Recently, when I described this sales space in one of my talks – without mentioning the store by name – those in the book trade in the audience immediately knew what I was talking about.

The strategy for countering a maze of signs like this is the dramatic trick of the *header* described several times in this book. A large-format picture or three-dimensional fragment of scenery immediately calling up the theme of a department is the super sign that 'triggers' our brain script. In Berlin, Vienna and Berne there are three outstanding bookstores that not only ease orientation for buyers in this way, but also offer a great way of deriving pleasure from doing so.

Top of this list is the Berlin KulturKaufhaus Dussmann (literally, the culture department store), as Professor Wilhelm Kreft, the doyen of shopfitting, calls this book store he planned (Kreft, 2002). Long bright-red axes guide our line of vision into the distance. At the far end of these axes a huge treble clef indicates the classical music department. We see a computer mouse and assume, not without reason, the software department of the store must be located here. An illustration of the blind goddess of justice indicates the department for books specializing in law; and across the entire music department panoramas built by the famous Berlin architect Friedrich Schinkel prompt associations with Berlin. The Jäggi book store in Bern is arranged on two floors around a loop – a bent axis. This curved aisle is lined by a series of open gates with large-format pictures attached to them. Even from afar I spot a door bearing the New York skyline next to five luminous globes, and rightly assume this certainly won't be the place to find cookbooks.

In this way looking for and finding things can be fun and mega stores become the wonderlands of navigation at the point of sale.

So the great expanse at megastores is both their problem and their great opportunity. Exhibitions, concerts, product presentations and cafés contribute to the time visitors spend there. The second opportunity innate to megastores is an immediate result or product of the selling themes of these large specialist markets. Sport items and drug-store goods, consumer electronics and DIY offer an inexhaustible potential for training customers right at the point of sale, to provide them with skills, to make them mature consumers.

Thirst for knowledge

I think I am able to arrange an individual trip around the world for any reader of this book, taking them exclusively to specialist markets and department stores and training them to be experts in their field of interest, because megastores are so spacious they can install sensual 'explanatory' stations which, as in a brand land or science museum, convey know-how on the goods, their manufacturing process, composition, strengths and applications. But unlike in museums these (now skilled) customers buy what they now understand better.

The megastore becomes a place for ongoing education, and hence a Third Place that, beyond its function as a store, offers that fascination of understanding, a new pleasure derived from knowledge.

This brings us to our tour, focusing on hiking, spectacles, cosmetics and sport. Our voyage starts in the Austrian city Lech am Arlberg, continues with a trip aboard the Orient Express to Paris and a flight across the 'pond' to New York, and ends in Seattle on the west coast of the United States. We only arrive at Lech am Arlberg after the sun has set, and yet the first explanatory staging comes into view from the Kaufhaus Strolz department store. Through the shop façade, which reaches all the way down to the basement of this old-established sports department store, we can watch a very special kind of spectacle from the street. Lined up on a wooden bench are some customers, barefoot and holding a glass of beer in their hands. They are obviously in high spirits while foam 'fill-ins' are being stuck on their naked feet. They are waiting for an inverted mould of their feet to be produced, to make what are claimed to be the best ski shoes the world has seen for a long time. These shoes are said to never cause any pressure points. Strolz impressively verifies this claim at the store by way of a demonstration where you can see with your own eyes what is so special about this manufacturing method. The authentic detail of the casting moulds and the chance to watch the cast being made create a credibility that convinces even the last Doubting Thomas among the interested visitors. After all, *seeing is believing*. The persuasive power of seeing with your own eyes is a proven explanatory method, as was described in great detail in Chapter 1 on brand lands; it makes us little experts in ski shoe production. The fact that this demonstration doubles as the *core attraction* of the department store inside and a *landmark* outside is a stroke of genius that truly pulls people into the store.

The next day we board the luxurious Orient Express at the neighbouring village of St Anton am Arlberg, and head off to Paris, where some lectures in perfume-making, spectacle-framing and football-playing await us. We probably learn our first lesson right on arrival, because Sephora on the Champs Elysées is open every day until midnight. Here you can not only experience the sacred *golden touch* with the black gloves, but also learn how fragrances are composed in a 'fragrance theatre'. A red carpet immediately leads customers to a hip-height cylinder display. Inside this cylinder a well-informed lady expects me to point at one of the hundred small bottles that surround her, or ask her if I may smell sandalwood – to name but one scent. She takes a white strip, dips it into a tincture, waves it for the fragrance to unfold and passes it to me. I smell it, and I also smell a number of other essences she proposes to me, only to learn that all those I have smelt, along with the many other fragrances there, are merely the ingredients used to produce this or that perfume. I am impressed and now consider myself an expert in the olfactory trade.

In the immediate vicinity of Sephora we find Grand Optical, the mega opticians and spectacle frame store. Next to the thousands of frames on display here you can read on a white wall which types of visual impairments require which types of glasses, about the visual problems of people aged over 40, and be given a waiting time estimate to the nearest minute for each ophthalmic service. And here it is again: a hole that allows us to look down on to a demonstration, right at the heart of the laboratory (which you can also visit on a guided tour) where someone in a white coat is working on a lens.

On our way to the airport we pop into the new Citadium Sport. The atrium houses a cage inspired by one of Nike's television commercials, where a brutal football match is being played with a steel ball in a cage just like this. Here, in Paris, you stand in front of a life-size television screen placed on end, and try in vain to imitate what the football player is showing you to do: to kick the ball this or that way. Pretty tricky. I think, these professionals really are skilled. And once more the principle applies: *seeing is believing.*

We are on our way to the United States, the home of the two mothers of all point of sale ideas, Nike Town and REI. The REI slogan runs, 'hands-on adventure in a store that celebrates the outdoors'. In the Gore-Tex rain room, for years buyers have been able to see for themselves that garments in this special material really are totally waterproof and do not make you sweat. You enter a kind of glass box, endure tropical rain, remain dry and consequently believe the convincing demonstration.

However, we fly to New York first. At the local Nike Town, the one with the mega screen in the atrium, an expensive hiking outfit is hanging behind an acrylic glass plate with an inscription. The hiking outfit as such appears to be nothing special. Its concealed strengths must be conveyed by means of a dramatic disclosure. Only the inscription shows that this suit is like a machine, with the features it has to offer at the collar, underneath the sleeves, on the trouserlegs and everywhere else. Only now does the image of the merchandise unfold. The *inferential beliefs*, the psychological mechanism also underlying this *seeing is believing*, generate within us the high-quality image appropriate for the outfit.

We fly on to Seattle, the final destination of our journey – where a giant climbing rock behind the display façade of REI triggers the theme of this megastore, where the tropical rainstorm awaits us in the glass box and we can test hiking shoes on different terrains. After many lessons learnt we have become experts on a variety of topics, and it was megastores that taught us these lessons.

SUMMARY

- *Flagship stores are the elaborate business cards of trading brands.*
- *Flagship stores are walk-in advertising.*
- *Flagship stores are also places where customers can find their niche.*
- **Sacred stores.** These are like temples or cathedrals, have altars and naves or at least 'enshrined' relics: sacred placement. This creates a feeling of solemnity transferred to the range, the image of the company and the customer's state of mind.
- **Lifestyle stores.** These are like walk-in lifestyle magazines, which transport you into a lifestyle while you are walking through them. In extreme cases this theming works merely on the interplay of the merchandise and the chairs, garments, books and CDs provided they signal one common fashion culture: range-based theming.
- **Megastores.** These are consumer electronics, book and fragrance stores whose large areas have produced a delightful wonderland for navigation. Explanatory stations also use these areas to educate customers, who gain the pleasure derived from orientation and pleasure derived from being in the know.

7

Concept stores

The shop as a lifestyle gadget

While flagship stores are like awe-inspiring, large-area figureheads of brands and designers, concept stores are the clever shops that aspire to be at least as striking but on a small scale. After all, you have to be aware: *space is not only room, space above all means time.*

Large-area stores automatically lengthen the time spent at them and therefore have more time to conquer customers. They 'breathe' slowly and powerfully. Small shops have no time. They must be effective immediately. So they must 'breathe' quickly and explosively.

In order to win over customers at such speed, small shops must make use of methods that immediately attract people's attention. There is no psychological mechanism that does this faster than *media literacy*, which makes us want to look at all types of tricks, behave as skilfully as possible and feel really smart while doing it. This book has already described a number of dodges that target our media literacy. One of them is what is known as *borrowed language*. At Ted Baker's thoroughly styled store in England the entrance door includes a drawbridge that is actually pulled up when the store is closed. The changing cubicles inside the store look like little houses or huts that you enter when trying on garments. Even large stores such as sOliver in Germany occasionally use such playful effects to create little highlights for the youth and trend segment. The changing cubicles of sOliver look like real shower cabins complete with large shower heads. So lifestyle gadgets in shops become an essential ingredient of the store presentation.

While games like the converted changing cubicles are still isolated, little *core attractions* prompting customers to quietly grin and tell others, genuine concept stores turn gadgets while shopping into the recurring theme of the store, their consistent principle, their *concept line*. Principally, there are two possibilities here. Either the range itself becomes a media-literacy effect comprising *merchandise that is fun*, or the goods displays and the interior design serve as games, thereby creating *stores that are fun*.

MERCHANDISE THAT IS FUN

Lush stores are tiny, and nearly always packed with buyers examining the merchandise with apparent delight. A showcase offers a self-service slice of apple strudel. Right next to it a chunk has already been cut from a typical Dutch barrel of cheese– which is surrounded by chocolate bars in all conceivable colours. A sushi set awaits a buyer. Rather a strange mix, you might think. The apple strudel, cheese, chocolate and sushi here are in fact all soaps, and the *concept line* of Lush consists of passing off soap as food. The dramatic trick of the *borrowed language* transforms the range into a smart, at times ironic game. The face mask for the sophisticated cosmopolitan lady, freshly prepared every day, is presented like caviar at Lush, deliciously arranged in bowls resting on a bed of ice cubes. On display at the store is the brand's customer magazine, where buyers from all over the world tell their stories about Lush products. Most of the anecdotes are told tongue in cheek, culminate in how someone almost took a bite into the soap, and provide 'testimonials' in the form of convincingly staged photos. Pudding and coconut cake soaps are currently selling like hot cakes, says Lush on the Internet. The site also offers vacancies for sales assistants not only able to work under pressure but who also have a good sense of humour. No wonder, since Lush is expanding like mad. Originally from Australia, this concept has now begun its march of triumph throughout the world. In Canada and England there are no 'Lush-free' shopping malls and no high-street locations left uncovered, and from Japan to Croatia and Venice, Lush shops are becoming entertaining city hot spots.

Like any successful concept store, these are urban destinations for those little treats in-between times.

This is the 10 minutes you steal for yourself in everyday life, this is fun for the city's tourists looking for a souvenir or those fleeing from a downpour into the shop. Lush Shops are typical Third Places where all the trappings of the purchase are more important than the functional value of the products. What you buy is the pleasure of purchasing, that delightful moment of micro leisure time, that relief of having found an original, smart souvenir.

Many *concept stores* relying on playful ranges combine this toying with merchandise with an additional aspect. Muji from Japan and Résonances from France lead here. Both publicize their philosophy at the point of sale. 'With us,' says Muji, 'you will find all sorts – from bicycles to notepads, from cabinets to folders – but everything follows the idea of the essential, the minimalist and the functional. Products are black, white, transparent or earth-coloured and so you won't find any gaudy colours at our stores,' they add self-confidently. Résonances somehow reminds us of the Austrian Manufaktum. I spend half an hour browsing at a Résonances store near the Madeleine and end up buying an American incandescent lamp (which looks as if it was just produced by Thomas Edison) and an alum stone (the kind formerly used by barbers to soothe the skin after shaving). This immediately becomes a little humid in my hand and feels refreshing somehow. My wife buys a thalasso-algae milk and a cabinet door handle which is actually very cheap but simply not available anywhere else. The lamp, stone, algae milk and handle are all things reminiscent of the past, just like some of the wellness products. This is the *concept line* at Résonances.

In both shops this range-playing serves to slot each product at the store into the store philosophy, to make customers feel and act smart while making them use their *media literacy*. Anyone not carrying out research like us would do this quite automatically, and would intuitively note how all things correlate. Customers strolling through this type of concept store enjoy being amazed at the sheer variety of unusual objects there, all fitting surprisingly well into this published scheme. Each match detected confirms the customers' skills and the *media literacy* which masterfully guides them through their lives.

STORES THAT ARE FUN

An afternoon spent consulting for an Austrian retail company is drawing to a close. At this point, I am unaware that over the next few years more than 200 stores will be rebuilt according to the basic concept recommended today. Now someone is asking me which architect or shopfitter I would suggest for developing the concrete designs. 'None,' I say, 'use a set designer.' In contrast to the unsophisticated aesthetics of staged scenery, many stores are first-class and these days also serve as walk-in scenery for goods and customers. The smart interior design of *concept stores* has created a situation where complete areas of cities have now become delightful promenading stages for today's trendy consumers. Nowadays you spend a few hours in a shopping area like New York's SoHo and can derive at least the same pleasure from watching, and gain the same insight into the current state of aesthetics, as you would from going to a performance at a renowned Berlin theatre. Just take it from someone with a PhD in theatrical sciences.

In SoHo our usual tour starts at Moss on Greene Street. This used to be a tiny store that was impossibly narrow – just a few metres wide – where both sofas and chairs by world-class designers were sold and presented alongside such small objects as a spider-shaped lemon squeezer designed by Philippe Starck for Alessi. How do you bring goods of such different sizes into line? Moss used the dramatic trick of *changing the viewing angle* to do so. All products, regardless of whether they are sofas or lemon squeezers, are presented 'unusually' at eye level. For this purpose everything stands or lies in showcases hovering about 1.5 m above the ground. It is this unfamiliar perspective that makes designer objects you have seen all too often, like those by Starck, look interesting again, and at the same time as valuable as the designer furniture worth a hundred times more. The unusual viewing angle implies that the goods displays are being played with, and this is what became the Moss store *concept line*. This trick was so successful that the store was finally enhanced to four times its original size.

Denise and I stroll along the street, turn right into Prince Street and walk on to Wooster Street where Tardini, the Italian manufacturer of my wallet, has built its concept store. The staging at this store makes smart use of *déja vu* for the material everything is made of here: leather from skins of various animals. The whole store appears to be an allusion to this material. All goods displays 'arch' out of the floor or walls in a snake-skin look. You can't tell where the wall ends and the display begins. Everything flows into everything else, thereby creating an environment which – playing with our senses – immediately transfixes us and produces a fascinating, walk-on sales sculpture.

Tardini comes from Italy; Camper, the shoe manufacturer on the same street, from Mallorca. All typical Camper stores in the world contain two characteristic features. First, the philosophy of the shoes and the company is presented on one wall of the store, often disguised as graffiti. We are told the shoes were named after '*camper*', the Mallorquin term for farmer, and that they are designed to carry the tradition of comfortable Spanish farming shoes around the globe. We are told we should not hurry around but, with the help of these cool shoes, walk more consciously. Second, all Camper *concept stores* are characterized by an architectural element inside the store that is somehow oversized. In England this is a photo of a Camper shoe several metres high and a 2-metre shoe box in Camper red serving as a bench for customers to try on shoes. Here in SoHo, it is five enormous lampshades by the famous German lighting designer Ingo Maurer which hover above a platform with shoes. This alley of monster lampshades in industrial design can be spotted from the outside, giving the store a spectacular external effect in the battle of SoHo's concept stores that all vie for customers' attention and time spent in the store.

Like Camper, many concept stores are part of a chain. In dramatic terms they therefore resemble television serials, and consequently also use related tricks. All television serials work with characteristic *labels* that make them unique and immediately signal to viewers accidentally tuning in which programme they are watching. In *Ally McBeal*, about the workings of a Boston law firm, the main characters live out their secret thoughts in daydreams. We hear their inner voices, see how tongues grow a metre in length in order to lick a desired object, and at the end of each episode the singer Vonda Sheppard appears singing a soul ballad at the local after-work club. That such *labels* always call up the entirety of messages and emotions is something psychologists call the *contact affect phenomenon*.

In other words: you know immediately what you are looking at. Seeing something extra large I know that I am in for some hip shoes. Seeing T-shirts, blouses and bikinis hanging from the wall sealed in a type of vacuum-packed plastic bag, I know that I am looking at a concept store of Barbara Bui. This type of presentation is absolutely unique. If a style or make can be recognized that unambiguously and at first sight, the store is ripe for multiplication in the form of multiples or shop-in-shop systems. This is why Barbara Bui not only has its own concept stores but also features as shop-in-shops in department stores such as the Galéries Lafayette.

Concept stores are thus versatile, walk-on stages which turn shopping areas into entertainment districts of a city. Concept stores are typical chain stores that, like television serials, use visual labels as a strength of the shop. Concept stores are ultimately places that often form part of the aesthetic avant-garde.

This wrapping trick deployed by Barbara Bui does remind us of contemporary conceptual art like the works of the unconventional artist Christo. No wonder concept stores spring up like mushrooms in the vicinity of large museums. They can be found at the Carousel du Louvre just as they can in Vienna's museum quarter. Here young Egyptian architect Sally Bibawy created an avant-garde store themed around the product world of the cult Lomo cameras that are known to 'shoot from the hip' to capture everyday snapshots. These products come with carrier bags made out of pink lace nighties – an ironic product transformation using *borrowed language*. The slanted entrance door does not open but 'folds' out from the store. However, the real sensation are the goods displays – webs of cheap, polystyrene-like foam with holes cut into them into which the goods are simply inserted. Lomo cameras, rubber boots and strange accessories dangle out of this foam. If the range changes, other holes are simply cut into these unusual, highly flexible displays at the store, or they are clamped to the wall in a different style or bent in all sorts of ways. All of this looks more avant-garde and arty than many of the exhibits displayed at the museums of modern art located in the area (see colour plate section).

SUMMARY

▌ *Concept stores are small, duplicable shops.*
▌ *Concept stores make for those little pleasures in-between.*
▌ *Concept stores turn shopping areas into experience districts.*
▌ **Merchandise that is fun.** If soap looks like cheese or a piece of cake (Lush), the merchandise toys with people's perception and addresses our media literacy. The result: customer entertainment through smart ranges.

▮ **Stores that are fun.** If all garments of a fashion brand, regardless of their type and size, are sealed in see-through plastic bags (Barbara Bui), the presentation of the merchandise is the game addressing our media literacy. The result: customer entertainment through smart goods displays.

8

Design malls

Shopping centres as architectural experiences

Amazed visitors enter the Bluewater mall 25 miles east of London's city centre. Scarcely a few steps inside the place and they are overwhelmed by a flood of colours, styling and design. They are impressed to realize that staging does not end at the entrances here, but is also to be found everywhere in-between. The exquisitely styled aisles, atriums and food courts fuse into a never-ending magnet of design experiences. Everyone wants to experience this magnetism, and this is why thousands of buyers crowd to see the 'Bluewater Experience' as the Australian developers called the mall, this very afternoon. Dressed in a stylish suit and equipped with his half-concealed digital video camera, the researching visitor feels slightly out of place among all these enthusiastic shoppers. That is until he meets the two southern Europeans, also dressed in dark suits, armed with tiny cameras and grinning at their colleague. Nowhere else in the world, he discovers later, is there such a throng of architectural tourists alongside perfectly regular consumers at one single place. All of them are fascinated, all react to the experiences offered by this huge complex.

DESIGN AS A RECURRENT THEME

Gigantic white letters are suspended high up on the wall across the entire length of the axis of the Thames Walk, forming a frieze, forming words. The visitor approaches an elderly lady. She is whispering to herself what all the other visitors cannot help reading either from the corner of their eyes while they walk through this area of the mall: the chorus of a song about Britain's great river. The block capitals here read: 'OLD FATHER THAMES KEEPS ROLLING ALONG, DOWN TO THE MIGHTY SEA'. 'You just read a few words and suddenly this song is ringing in your ears,' the English say. (See colour plate section).

Design-based theming

The floor depicts the Thames in grey granite with its geographical features precisely set into the yellowish stone floor. The visitor starts at the source, promenades along the meandering river, passing many a village shown in golden letters spelling out 'Richmond' or 'Greenwich'. 'Look, this is where I lived for a year,' says my wife. Sail-like structures wave above their heads, designer light fittings on masts vaguely reminiscent of buoys, a clock showing the tides of the Thames – all of this gradually immerses the visitor in the Thames river theme, putting buyers in a 'nautical mood'. (See colour plate section).

In the next district of the mall the strategy is repeated.

Again a theme serves as an all-encompassing bracket for the large space; it evokes stories and is filled with high-quality design. This shapes the free space outside the shops and serves as a concept line of the mall.

'Guildhall' is the name of a district where a two-storey structure features something like a town hall clock: it serves as a meeting place and a landmark for orientation that is visible from afar. Fascinated, the visitor looks upwards. This time, the frieze is composed of sculptures – representing the 106 crafts and guilds in medieval Britannia – and this time it is dramatically illuminated. Time-honoured, cut in stone, the ancestors sit enthroned above us like in a gothic church. The visitor from continental Europe reverentially reads the stone inscriptions underneath the illustrations. 'Basket-makers,' he murmurs looking at the basket being produced. 'Turners,' he says, and the stone turner turns a table leg. 'Stained glass makers' – yes, the Old Masters. 'Hackney carriage drivers' – but what's this? Instead of horse and carriage the stone relief depicts three taxis and one evidently upset driver gesticulating wildly in his classic black cab. This is just as typically British as the irony used here to stage the change in theme at the mall – revealing that the aesthetics of the aisles and plazas is part of a bigger strategy.

Header chains

Those averting their gaze from the spectacularly staged walls of the mall will see the shop façades. One shop rubs shoulders with the next, and even the façades feature a recurring principle, the second *concept line* of the mall.

Each shop states to the outside what hides behind its façade.

Large horns in front of the Just Leather store are a signal already indicating from afar that this shop sells leather goods and saddles. A large white golf ball in front of the Nevada store is a signal indicative of the golf clubs and bags sold inside the shop. The idea is not new. In the shopping streets of past centuries guild symbols on the façades always showed what was on sale inside. The visiting researcher closes his eyes and thinks of the famous Salzburg Getreidegasse in his home country. He sees the wrought-iron, partly gilded signs of shops, workshops and inns – a pretzel for the baker, a large key for the locksmith, a golden deer for a famous hotel and restaurant serving venison specialities. Such 'constructed' headers convey an immediate sense of the meaning of locations, and help outlets to draw attention to themselves over their competitors. In many German malls famous architects issued adamant bans and stringent conditions so as to prevent such trumpery on shop fronts from impairing the perfection of their cool steel and glass architecture.

However, the visitor's eyes are reopened here at Bluewater. One district of the mall shows that it is by all means possible to blend harmoniously high quality with emotional effect. 'The Village' is the urban shopping mall at Bluewater, a tribute to London's famous Burlington Arcade. Visitors are amazed at the precious wooden floor, stroke the timber panelling of the fronts with their fingers, and finally marvel at the avenue of store headers. They are all carved in wood, all attached to the wall on uniform spherical or square metal brackets, and they are all theatrically illuminated. A stack of books made up of five carved wooden books hovers in front of Waterstones, the large British book chain. An arrangement of a globe and rolled-up maps lures visitors into a shop selling old nautical charts and telescopes. A brush plus a stack of paper signals the shop for amateur painting enthusiasts.

On the opposite side we see Thomas Kincade, a chain store for oil paintings which is also represented in the United States. Right behind the portal of the tiny store and clearly visible from outside is a column with a built-in fireplace. Its flickering flames create just the right setting to experience these paintings on the wall. Hence, the fireplace becomes the 'constructed' business card of the shop.

THE SALES PROMENADE

Interested in the architecture of the mall, the visitor sits on a bench to pore over a ground plan of the centre (see Figure 8.1). Bluewater is shaped like a huge isosceles triangle whose contours trace a loop – the round trip through the mall. Its Australian designers have used every trick to make this staged promenade as versatile as possible. You just have to watch children and how they react to the sensual structure of spaces offered here.

A little girl turns the crank at the foot of a kinetic sculpture, thereby moving the wings of a metallic bird that – many metres above and easily visible from both levels of the mall – flaps its wings. A little boy

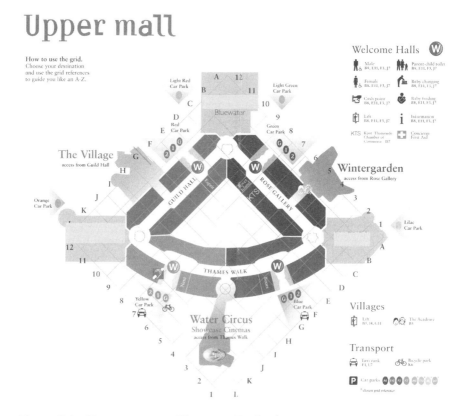

Figure 8.1   Entrance map to Bluewater, England
© Bluewater

climbs over and over again on to the luminous face of the sundial set into the floor underneath the glazed dome of the mall. Bluewater features such landmarks everywhere, providing easy orientation for buyers and a welcome opportunity for children to play. On the 'loop' of the promenade alone 10 spectacular landmarks can be found.

They do not just stand about randomly. Their position contributes to the creation of a cognitive map of the mall and, hence, intuitive navigation – that light-footed searching and finding process at a place where you soon feel at home.

Domes and mnemonic points

Bluewater, for instance, features domes. These are consistently located at the intersections of axes, that is, in the tips of the triangle. They are themed around the sun, moon and stars, and feature a spectacular clock at their centre to emphasize the hub. And wherever there are 'feeder axes' protruding into the triangle from the outside – such as from the food court (Winter Garden), cinema centre (Water Circus) or car parks – these feature statues, towers and fountains that are visible from afar, thereby emphasizing each hub. Each one of these mnemonic features is so high that it can be seen from all levels of the mall. While a wolf stands at the foot of the stone totem at the bottom of the Rose Garden tower, a deer is balanced high up on its tip, telling the story of the mythical garden.

Axes, hubs, districts and mnemonic points are the elements of the *cognitive map* that visitors want to learn by intuition in order to promenade with this map and enjoy *malling*. At Bluewater the axis is the loop of the triangle, which at the same time forms part of three differently themed districts – Thames Walk, Rose Garden and Guild Hall – where sophisticated stories are told using design as a tool. The hubs here are the domes where the axes meet and the flow of customers is redirected into the next district. The mnemonic points are the clocks underneath the domes; the fountains and towers at the intersections of main axis and lateral axis. Bluewater is the epitome of malling systems, both designed and perceived perfectly.

Luxury mile and market square

We are now aboard the privately managed luxury train run by Virgin Railways to Manchester, travelling from the Bluewater Experience to the Trafford Centre. British pensioners meet here for their tea dance against the backdrop of a musical steamer set around the Food Court each Tuesday afternoon (we mentioned this in Chapter 1). Denise and I want to have a closer look at an invention by English architects Chapman Taylor & Partners. At a congress their chief architect rushed towards me after my presentation, saying, 'I have built what you've just described.' So now we want to examine this innovation.

The innovation here: the districts of the mall along the central prom-enade comprise sections for different quality standards.

Everything is subjected to this quality segmentation: the archi-tecture, the design, the furniture, plants, lighting, type and ranges of stores. From the outside the centre, with its dramatic cupolas and colon-nades with giant statues of angels with trombones, is somewhat remi-niscent of St Peter's in Rome. Inside, the sections of the central axis imitate the shopping streets of a metropolis. Like in any city, it features a luxury shopping mile with a correspondingly luxurious atmosphere about it and the presence of major brands. (See Figure 8.2.)

The mall also features middle-class shopping streets, where in England one also tends to find travel agencies. And it features a market square with down-to-earth shops, and niche shops offering items for browsing shoppers.

The main street of the mall is called Regent Crescent in the first of its three sections. Royal palms line the way, adorned with little lamps that

Figure 8.2   Entrance map to Trafford Centre, Manchester, England

light up in the evening. Grand-looking stone benches underneath the palm trees invite visitors to stop for a rest. Brass bowls radiate indirect light, box hedges are pruned to form geometrical baroque shapes, glazed barrel vaulting rises above the main street where lifestyle-oriented shops like Mango and Monsoon can be found. In front of Selfridges, the imitation of London's Regent Street meets a magnificent cupola with frescoes, gilded columns and a lift in highly polished brass.

Then the style of the street changes abruptly. It is called Peel Avenue now, and a middle-class shopping street featuring Marks & Spencer and a megastore of the Boots chemist chain. Instead of royal palms deciduous trees now line the street, and instead of opulent stone benches beautiful yet austere wooden benches await tired shoppers. Twice the avenue passes by little squares with cupolas. A bend in the main avenue, and water jets shoot up to the frescos in the cupolas, slowing down the flow of shoppers. Finally a Portuguese ceramic *azulejo* sign tells us we are now entering the Festival Village. This is where the street ends. Here it widens into a market square where the shops become separate little houses arranged at oblique angles to the square, and are fitted with red and white market-stall awnings. You buy a pair of socks from the Sock Shop, have an iced coffee and marvel at the stencils at the Stencil Store – demonstrating the current wall-decorating trend in England.

Niche products at emotionally relaxing fun stores, something reasonably priced to buy in the mass-market shopping sector, and glamour on the luxury mile – this is the malling strategy pursued by the new design malls. Exactly this grading strategy is also found at Bluewater, at Düsseldorf's Sevens and at CentrO in Oberhausen, where the Bunte Gasse (Variety Walk) – houses a glow-worm shop stocking everything that glows, a wonderful change from the serious designer clothes stores.

THE ART OF 'LITTLE SENSATIONS'

Once an hour the clock at the Festival Village of the Trafford Centre comes alive. Numerous little red lamps start to flicker on the clock, suspended high above the market square, attracting customers' attention for a minute. Alongside the dramatic architectural features that each designer mall aims to include – spectacular domes, or originally designed roofs with futurist glass towers – the clocks of the malls are additional *core attractions* planned to cause that little sensation now and then.

Of clocks and characters

The first attraction of this kind was the 'clock of flowing time' at the Europa Centre in Berlin. Although the centre as such looks run-down today, tourists still stop in front of the workings of the huge clock, staring at the glass tubes and containers in which a bilious green liquid illustrates the passing of time. The highest-quality clock currently installed at any mall is the animal clock at Bluewater. A unicorn pops out of a white wall and supervises other animals – frogs, deer and other forest fauna. Each animal bears one numeral, and they parade past one after the other until finally one of the animals remains visible to display the current hour. The clocks installed in design malls are all 'wow' effects, *core attractions* designed to make us gape in astonishment.

Occasionally, malls also present a bold show effect, mostly linked to characters or people, making visitors grin quietly to themselves. At the Trafford Centre a talking bear drives about in a little car, secretly steered by a type of butler dressed in a red uniform. The two talk to each other all the time, use the lift, give passers-by a fright, flirt with girls and make children laugh. This category of little shows or *core attractions* also includes the numerous dexterity and hands-on games at design malls. In front of Bluewater, for example, model ships can be sailed on a pond. Initially this attraction was designed for children, but in actual fact it is now mostly youths who love to race the ships at high speed.

All 'little sensations' provide the stroll through the mall with an attention peak. These somehow fulfil our expectations without any major effort, and are often part of the anticipation felt, especially for children. In each case they address our inner clock, thereby making our stay a little more entertaining.

The Selfridges system

The greatest innovation in staged retailing undoubtedly originated from London's department store Selfridges, which is thought to be the world's best department store at present. Here an outmoded store meta-morphosed into something that has virtually never existed before. The department store became a design mall without negating its character as an organically grown shopping temple.

It all started with a face-lift operation coordinated by the famous architects Future Systems. The endless aisles of the store were given emphasis by avenues of screens playing video clips featuring the focal points of that shopping month. At the same time, these flat screens clearly contrast with the image of the architecture of this time-honoured store – producing the same effect as the female trapeze artists performing on long white strips of cloth hanging in the atrium or as the DJs playing trendy chill-out tunes in the afternoon.

The core innovation, however, is the rearrangement of the sales areas that derives from turning Selfridges into a landlord, as it were, letting out space to retail outlets. Many of these sales units are cleverly styled as *little sensations* in the process. Nail Heaven on the ground floor, for example, is a steep amphitheatre visible from afar, where female customers sit on the stairs to be manicured and have their nails designed publicly. Likewise, striking merchandise displays have become attractions – such as the Gloves Theatre, where hundreds of gloves are presented in a circle surrounding a column. Trend departments are combined into consistent *image worlds* like the Warehouse, for instance, where many brands are presented in a warehouse loft setting; the attraction of this specific section is the dozens of changing cubicles in bright red metal placed on a gallery that seems to hover above the room. There is a white footwear world for sporty men's shoes, and a black footwear world for elegant to freaky shoes. *Design-based theming* was used to create a futurist world for consumer electronics – 'Technology' – which is reminiscent of a star ship. Since 2003 children have had their own design world, with white plastic goods displays suspended like a low-hanging cloud from the ceiling at child-friendly height. They come in their droves to wander on plush carpet between blue plastic columns on what is currently the most beautiful children's floor in any department store in the world. In this way Selfridges created – apart from the simple shop-in-shops that also exist here – highly versatile units inducing the visitor to mall, as in a city where all districts are sensational landmarks in themselves and variation becomes the name of the spectacular game, thereby becoming the *concept line*. (See colour plate section.) Restaurants and bars add to this impression because they are scattered like 'dew-drops' of colourful precious stones throughout the store, shielded by semi-closed walls and featuring their own lighting and sounds. With their new home at the Bullring Centre, Selfridges even managed to get a spectacular exterior appearance. Like a building from another world, the futuristic department store sits on top of Birmingham's roofs (see colour plate section). Designed by the renowned architecture group Future Systems, it is an expression of a new phenomenon: famous architects are designing points of sale.

The Masters' signature

Why do design malls exist in the first place? Is the crisis of typically American escapism the only reason why now even highly respected designers and architects build shopping malls? Daniel Libeskind, for instance, the famous American architect living in Berlin and until then involved in Jewish museums and similarly monumental projects, suddenly announced in the January 2002 issue of *Architectural Digest*, 'Department stores are cultural complexes. They are places of public activity and it is high time we gave some thought to how we can make better use of their interactivity' (Hosch, 2002). Libeskind has developed a huge design mall for the Swiss Migros group in Berne-Brünnen on the western outskirts of the Swiss capital. The mall, called WESTside, will make Libeskind's artistic signature known to a wider audience. While company headquarters are built by famous architects but are only partially accessible to the public, and while many museums of the 1980s and 1990s face the problem that their buildings are more interesting than their exhibits, the function of shopping malls is plausible to everyone. To architects they are more than shopping centres, they double as publicly accessible stages for their art, and for the public they are also powerful places that massage the soul and recharge our batteries. They are market squares where the community meets; indeed they are *Third Places*.

A year before architects were invited to tender for the Berne-Brünnen project, when I was still working out the concept line for the mall in Berne with those commissioning me, I had no idea how spectacular it would become. I now have the concept drawings in my hands of what will become reality by 2006. Libeskind is the first modern architect to turn his signature radically into the *concept line* of a mall. It dazzles us with a versatile interplay of surprising room heights, it surprisingly moves underground car parks directly into the atrium of the mall, it makes shop windows protrude boldly, it creates a fun indoor pool with terraces that vertiginously stick to the inside walls – in a nutshell, he consistently plays with perception, with penetration, with bold slants and twists on customary perspectives. Never before has an architect made *media literacy* the concept line of a commercial location, and never before has a 'wow' effect been used not only as a singular *core attraction* but as the basic principle of a whole shopping complex. The Swiss consumers coming here will be able to take on a self-image completely different from typical Swiss stereotypes. Visitors coming from abroad will enjoy an urban location in the conservative city of Berne that could just as easily be found in Tokyo, but one which approaches the community in a both friendly and optimistic way.

SUMMARY

- *Design malls make stages not only of their stores but also of the spaces in-between.*
- *Design malls are therefore meeting points for the community.*
- *Design malls are thus increasingly designed by famous architects.*
- **Design as a recurrent theme.** Neither dull aisles with no theming nor cheap American 'scenery' worlds suit the public spaces in up-to-date malls. Instead, any type of high-quality staging is suitable as a recurring theme: an avenue of uniform façade headers, telling everyone what's inside in the stores, as well as design-based theming, or a 'constructed' story.
- **The sales promenade.** The cognitive map of a mall is designed not only to assist orientation and promote malling but also to generate sales. This is why the central promenade of a mall is frequently composed of sections of different quality levels, from luxury to casual.
- **The art of the 'little sensation'.** Tea time for pensioners and sets by DJ for young trendsetters, singing bears and model ships for children, clocks and fountains for all – all these draw a crowd, release tension and make people's stay seem more entertaining.

PART IV

CONVENIENCE ENTERTAINMENT

Some time ago I was commissioned by a bank to deliver a talk on the state of tourism in the Austrian province of Vorarlberg. Embarrassingly enough, I had never been to Austria's most western state in my life. So the bank decided to give me a whistle-stop three-day tour to see everything. I saw lakes, cities, the Bregenz Forest, architecture old and new, lots of hotels and restaurants, and I was carted up to each peak by cable car and on every type of snowmobile imaginable.

At the Hochjoch above Schruns, I – a convinced non-skier – had an enlightening experience. Near the mountain-top funicular station is the New Technology Center, a ski and ski equipment hire shop set in the snowy landscape. The 'new technology' here lies in an ingenious idea: someone really clever analysed a typical day's skiing in the mountains and drew highly profitable conclusions from this. As I see it, you could even take a cable car up the mountain wearing a dark business suit without any heavy skis or cold and damp ski boots – to then have yourself measured from head to toe at the NTC. By your second visit all your data is stored, so all that remains for you to do is select your skiing gear from one of any number of stands. Here we find old-fashioned downhill skis, modern style downhill 'carving' skis, snowboards and even really unusual skiing gear. While selecting you can watch a robot behind a glass wall licking the newly returned skis into shape and bending them again to produce the curve they are said to require. Then you proceed to the next station and receive – dispensed from a well designed rack with sliding walls – your pre-measured ski boots which not only fit you perfectly but are also pre-heated. Finally you take off your suit and slip into the ski suit over your skiing underwear – the only thing you have to take along yourself – and off you go. (See colour plate section).

Children love to go down the slopes on three or four different types of skis on the same day. Being able to compare the skis is part of the fun for them.

Even families with children have not been forgotten. A creche is located right next to the hall. Inside it is themed as the village of singing frogs, outside it features a hillock where children can play and learn to ski next to a baby ski-lift, and where even the smallest can go sledding on shark or Formula 1 shaped toboggans. Once an hour frog characters actually appear to tell their story, dance and sing. But this show, as much as the children may love it and respond to it, is not the great achievement of the New Technology Center.

9

Optimized places

The experience when things run smoothly

The truly outstanding achievement here is the optimization of an everyday routine on the basis of *brain script analysis*. As we have said, these 'scripts in our brains' not only underlie the great stories in movies or theatre, allowing us to figure out the story; they also control routine processes, helping us to get along in life without putting anybody's back up. Those ordering tramezzini or sandwiches at an Italian espresso bar must know how this works. First you say, 'Due tramezzini, per favore,' then you take a voucher to the cash desk where you pay, then you return with the torn voucher to the counter to finally receive your tramezzini. Many a Japanese tourist in Venice fails miserably in this procedure.

Slice of life (SOL) brain scripts is what these concepts conveyed to us by real-life stories are called in strategic dramaturgy. Those seeing through these SOL scripts know about the obstacles in everyday life. Those wanting to create *optimized places* for business can remove the 'barbs', obstacles from the process by way of *brain script analysis*. Minimizing friction in the process means restaging a marketing-relevant situation, ensuring that it is:

RUNNING SMOOTHLY

Humanity has always dreamt of making everyday routine effortless, as if secret forces had moved all stumbling blocks out of the way. As early as in the tale of Aladdin from the *Arabian Nights*, a genie in a bottle appears and builds an entire palace in just minutes, moving mountains and defying gravity on a flying carpet.

Today's dreams of total service come true thanks to convenience entertainment that removes anything complicated, time-consuming or unpleasant from our daily routines.

In tourism, retailing, financial services, in fact wherever the pressure to render perfect services is particularly high, business-focused entertainment emerges which dispenses with the need for great stories or Hollywood flair. The experience here is simply derived from an honest and well-intentioned attempt to improve everyday life. This ranges from the 'location-based services' provided for the new mobile phone generation (where the menu of the nearest pizzeria pops up on the cellphone display for our convenience) to the download of music files from the Internet after store closing time, in conjunction with MP3 recorders capable of storing an incredible 10,000 songs which are then available anytime and anywhere. Especially interesting here are the ideas of …

… Insurance companies

These companies have realized that threatening their customers with the sword of Damocles and pending disaster is too negative a message to retain clients in the long run. Apart from that, they are still fighting the prejudice of us simple folk who assume they would not pay up in the event of a claim anyhow. This is why they use an *SOL brain-script analysis* to remind us of all the eventualities of a disaster. The Help4You insurance package offered by the Austrian Generali insurance company covers not only the loss caused by any burglary at your home but also any extra expenditure incurred, for example for security guards to watch the property over the weekend or until the next working day, the safe-keeping of valuables and even the transportation costs for taking your children from the flat to stay with their aunt. Incidentally this insurance payout is so impressive it would suffice to fly you to Australia if need be. Using packages like this insurance companies show that they wish to offer genuine assistance on a practical level, and that they have understood how we live and what other little problems can crop up in this process. 'Running smoothly' in …

… Tourism

does not only mean arranging a day in the mountains (as was the case at the NTC described above), by the sea or wherever without any obstacles. It also starts with the frequently tedious organization of the trip to the destination, the check-in, baggage collection and dinner on arrival. How many times have I been put up at accommodation near to where my client is located to find nothing to eat either at the hotel or anywhere else in the village? A snack package in my room, indicating an understanding of my needs as a frequent business traveller, would be more to my taste than the breakfast buffet the following morning – which I do not have time to enjoy anyway. In summer airlines increasingly offer kerbside check-in outdoors, in front of the terminal building, so that you can virtually approach the counter by taxi. Austrian state railways, however, still have not got their act together: they recently closed the luggage check-in counters at stations in favour of door-to-door delivery agreements concluded with forwarding agents. Those who realize only at the station that two children plus a suitcase are still too much to handle at once get nowhere – all the more since porters are non-existent at Salzburg station, for instance.

My personal first prize for tourism *convenience entertainment* goes to the ski resort of Oberlech in the Vorarlberg region. This town's PR brochure is impressive proof that someone did their homework here: *SOL brain-script analysis* is definitely at work. 'Oberlech, the sunroof of the Arlberg,' says the PR, 'is located 250 m above Lech and is a car-free city: in winter it is only accessible by a cable car running non-stop from 7 am to 1 pm, connecting Oberlech with the town centre in as little as 4 minutes. By means of a world innovation – a sophisticated system of tunnels – the hotel owners send all supplies to and from Oberlech under-ground.' For this a kilometre-long series of tunnels and 4,000 square metres of subterranean halls were built, equipped with electric cars and a sophisticated communication system. The trip to and from the destination thus becomes a hassle-free experience described in the PR as follows:

While guests park their cars and make their way to their chalets, their suitcases, bags and ski equipment are transported in containers by cable car to the transfer hub near the mountain station. From there they are forwarded in little electric cars through the tunnel system to each house. By the time guests have checked in, their luggage has already arrived in their rooms – and their skis are safely stowed away in the ski store. Over an average winter season some 12,000 containers filled with the

luggage and ski gear of arriving and departing guests are transported in
this way. (See Figure 9.1.)

Impressive, isn't it? And it's just as impressive entering the subterranean
tunnel system. In the hotel I am guided to the basement. I pass through a
bowling alley, a door opens and I stand in an illuminated tunnel where an
electric car buzzes past me. The labyrinth of tunnels and the enormous,
exciting halls somehow transport me into a James Bond movie where
towards the end 007 sends the villain's subterranean HQ up in flames.
The system is only accessible to the guests of the village on the rare occa-
sions when underground events are held. What a shame, I say to myself,
you can't see any of this from outside. Just a short track of the tunnel,
made visible through an acrylic glass tube and impressive nocturnal
lighting would be enough to provide a wonderful *core attraction* for the
town of Oberlech – a 'must-see', as little electric cars are glimpsed
passing through the tunnel while visitors wait in expectation.

Figure 9.1   Oberlech Tunnel System, Austria
© Lech am Arlberg

In any case, the tunnel is the *concept line* of the place, the recurring
theme running through this entire convenience staging. But as you can
see, nearly all *optimized places* also hold the potential for transforming
their facilities into their main attractions. Just like the stagings in …

… Retailing

All Nike Towns, the flagship stores of the American cult sports retail
chain, feature a system of futuristic mini lifts in prominent, central

positions; they transport goods from the underground storage to the different sales floors of these stores. However, they are not bashfully hidden but self-confidently staged as 'wow' effects, as *core attractions*. 'Our developers were inspired by Star Trek,' says the Nike manageress in an advanced state of pregnancy as she presents the system to us in Los Angeles. In see-through acrylic glass capsules, shoes and T-shirts are 'beamed' through the atrium as if by magic. Once they have reached their destination floor, the capsules theatrically slide open in half and the goods are removed.

Originally, the idea was hatched to spare sales assistants the bother of having to leave their customers to fetch shoes in sizes not on display at the spaciously arranged sales area but kept in distant storage. Now, the details of requested shoes are keyed into a hand-held device and just minutes later, at least in theory, the product floats into view. Children (and people like myself) wait in the atrium to watch several capsules meet on their trajectories – because visually this is particularly impressive. The smooth running thereby becomes a *core attraction* in the atrium or, as in Berlin for instance, the attraction of the shop window.

The latest in terms of convenience staged as a 'wow' effect can be found at the Prada store in New York's SoHo district. As we said, the miracle here is the product of the architectural think-tank of famous Dutch designer Rem Koolhaas. Apart from anything else, here we find beautiful flat screens automatically displaying all the fabric and design-related data of any garment you unsuspectingly hold up for closer examination. You have to admit, this is not so far from Aladdin's genie in the bottle.

At first sight, the strategy of optimizing functions and accelerating processes seems like a departure from experience-oriented marketing. The examples presented so far, however, show not only that increased convenience, as such, is an experience but also that many of the techniques underlying those *optimized places* are spectacular. They make us gape in amazement, and the strategies easily become *core attractions* in themselves.

Taken from this angle, each type of convenience entertainment is an example of the new trend towards authenticity and sustainability in staged marketing, rather than a sign of a return to the rational society.

This applies to an even greater extent to a second variant of the *optimized place*. Here several functions that are usually located far apart are combined at one location. In this way stores at train stations and airports became the first places to make products available to us outside restrictive shop opening hours and in places where travellers really needed them. You could say that this made these ranges ...

... EVER READY

When I land with my wife at Vienna Airport after my staff has gone home we always single-mindedly head for an Anker outlet, the Austrian bakery chain, to buy milk and other supplies. This combination of transport hub and shopping centre has been in existence for a long time. What's new here is that some transport facilities are actually now on a par with shopping centres. Victoria Station in London and Union Station in Washington were the pioneers of this development, but the shopping station in Leipzig by far outperforms all of its predecessors. More than 100,000 people stream through it each day, and not only do growing numbers of them buy milk at one of the 140 stores before going home, 20 per cent of them also buy fashion.

Stores at communication hubs

These stores (as marketing expert Reinhard Peneder calls them) are based like all *optimized places* on the *brain-script analysis* of behavioural patterns.

The aim here is not only to make a process run as smoothly as possible by removing any obstacles, but to merge a number of processes that hitherto only occurred separately in such a way that they become a new unit.

Commuters in Leipzig naturally also buy their milk before going home, they also treat themselves to little luxuries at branded product stores. What the inhabitants of Leipzig have here is a city-centre mall open until 10 pm thanks to the station, plus a train station with more security, cleanliness and flair thanks to the mall. Typical station event sequences, or speaking in dramatist's slang, *SOL brain scripts*, and typical shopping-mall event sequences were fused into an *optimized place* here.

Even with this type of optimized place, the method itself is so spectacular that you can hardly believe your eyes. Wow, I thought, when I looked down into the huge hall for the first time as I stood on the second floor of the mall; looking past enormous glazed lift shafts I saw a shopping centre in a historic building and a station with many platforms, the old station clock and trains arriving – all on an equal footing.

This effect of amazement, this idea of the special view, is a recurring theme in all places where different worlds clash.

At the Basle St Jakobs stadium you can watch 2002 Swiss football champions Basel United play, shop at an (actually not so small) mall, eat at a restaurant with an incredible 180-degree view of the stadium, meet in a conference room that seems to hover above the soccer pitch and finally visit the old people's home where a glass bridge offers at least a partial view of the pitch. This view of the pitch where sports events and pop concerts take place is the sensation of the whole premises. The stadium and shops in one sole field of vision, or the 'breath' of a concert starring Céline Dion still hanging over the place, still felt in the conference room, makes this combination of worlds the *core attraction* of the place. The developers' *SOL brain-script analysis* showed – right down to the last detail – which measures were required to make the 'wow' effect work. This included the special video security system, for example, that controls the grandstands so precisely that those annoying barriers between blocks found in every stadium these days could be dispensed with, ensuring an unhindered view from the VIP restaurant holding 1,000 people.

Sport in an unusual location

The above examples present the typical combinations playing a role at these types of *optimized places*. They often involve a transport hub or a throng of spectators, as at the stadium in Basle. Proximity to the sport and its availability are important elements here. This is why the most spectacular *optimized places* of our times revolve around sport.

Some years ago we would occasionally work in Japan, at the SSAWS Ski-dome in Tokyo, for instance. It was here that the first indoor slalom run was built – the original and first of many copies, such as those in the German Ruhr valley built by Luxemburg ski star Marc Girardelli. Outside, the facility in Japan resembles a giant ski jump. Inside, it is mainly snowboarders that race down the two slalom runs while the lighting simulates day and night at hourly intervals. There are snow, ski lifts, cold, sake to drink instead of Obstler at the restaurant and – as a counterpoint – an indoor pool. It is, above all,

Tokyo's young people that enjoy the permanent availability offered by this ski El Dorado in terms of both location and time. Even in mid-July you can go skiing just an hour's drive away – a sensationally short journey by Japanese standards. (See colour plate section.)

The combination of convenience and novelty is spectacular here – the proximity of sports and snow to the urban city environment at any time of year. Recently, a trial project – the Quick Side Park Winter City – opened in Dubai. Here, arranged around a shopping centre, many inhabitants of the city can come and touch snow for the first time in their lives. A simulation of the slalom run is expected to follow in the next few years.

Next to winter sports in summer in the city, water sports in winter anywhere in the world is the second biggest hit in this trend towards the permanent availability of sport. Yet again, Japan pioneered this development. On the most southerly island of Japan you will find the Ocean Dome built right on the sea (see Figure 9.2). A gigantic hall houses a sandy beach, an artificial seascape complete with a perfect wave-

Figure 9.2   Ocean Dome, Japan
© Sheraton Resort Phoenix Seagaia

making machine, very popular among surfers, and a painted diorama replacing the view of the real sea horizon. Why on earth do the Japanese not go swimming in the sea next door? Because it is teeming with poisonous sea snakes, I am told, and because Japanese women are allowed to go to the indoor pool on their own but going to the beach alone would be considered indecent. So in summer the hall roof slides sideways allowing the real sun in. Miniature versions of this idea are the Dutch Centerparks, where people spend their weekend vacation under glazed roofs in a type of Caribbean atmosphere.

Globalization has accordingly also impacted the leisure industry. Those able to jet to the Maldives any time in winter, go skiing on the Austrian glacier in midsummer or shopping at American Christmas stores (where you can buy Christmas decorations even in mid-July) will also want to experience this 'disconnection' with space, climate, time and place right around the corner: at *optimized places* combining convenience and amazement.

SUMMARY

- *Convenience entertainment frees everyday routines from adversities.*
- *Optimized places ensure the smooth running of processes in tourism, retailing and service industries.*
- *This is how entertainment with glamour and story-telling emerges: functional, sustainable.*
- **Running smoothly.** By analysing the brain scripts of everyday routines we detect anything time-consuming, tedious and unpleasant. The optimization of this routine removes the spanner from the works, and is therefore perceived as entertaining. This is how an ideal day spent skiing in the mountains or a special consultation at the bank come into being.
- **Ever ready.** This strategy drastically increases the availability of special offers, thereby producing emotional added value and amazement. To this end, routines usually separated are combined at one single place, at shopping stations or stadium malls. Or activities otherwise only accessible at special times of the year are decoupled from the season – such as ski halls in metropolises.

10

Bricks and clicks

Merging real with virtual rooms

Paris in Summer 2000. She is in her early twenties, wearing inline skates and is standing in front of a rack of shelves with Japanese designer gear. Hovering in front of her is a silver Sony Vaio computer which she carries strapped like a vendor's tray. She moves closer to the shelves and points the Webcam of the multimedia laptop at a Yamamoto suit. While she communicates with a customer at the other end of the world via her keyboard, the bar tender serves New Zealand glacier water. In Melbourne it is midnight, and the owner of an advertising agency is interested in the designer collection of the Printemps department store in Paris.

Of course, each mall, each department store has its home page, making it possible also to shop on the Net. But the girls and boys working here at the original store in Paris, with its spectacular glass dome above the restaurant, represent the world's first fusion of e-commerce with a real point of sale. They are called Webcamers® and they roll back and forth on inline skates between the design departments of the large store in order really to show the products to customers out there on the Internet.

As we all know, one drawback of Internet shopping is the inability to feel the products – something which particularly affects the fashion segment. It was decided therefore to provide customers out there on the net with human agents in the sales area, who answer questions, 'model' the merchandise via Webcam, touch the fabrics and examine the design on behalf of the buyers. The term 'bricks and clicks' has now become established on the scene, meaning that virtual ranges – clicks on the computer – are given a corresponding counterpart in real space – the bricks of a real building.

TELE-PRESENCE

For users out on the Net this means being present at a place without actually having physically to enter it. Users can see, touch and decide. Webcamers® become their eyes, their hands, acting on their behalf and looking after their interests.

Tele-presence is what cyber-culture theoreticians call this phenomenon. What they mean by this is that someone puts his or her hands into a spacesuit at the NASA ground station in Houston, for instance, thereby operating the arms of a robot to repair a space station. Or that a surgeon handles a scalpel in Vienna, making an operation robot in New York execute a decisive incision. In Paris this concept of breaking away from real space actually came true. Interested buyers on the net ask the Webcamer® to hold the suit in such a way that the cut becomes visible, to touch the suit on their behalf, to describe the fabric and tell them the price. They have to know themselves how to best proceed: that is, which SOL brain scripts will be successful to appraise the suit. SOL brain-script analysis thereby permits a process to be disconnected from the physical reality in which this process is executed, and is, therefore, convenience entertainment in the truest sense of the word.

For the first time in the history of humanity we are freed from space and time, able to use our professional skills in places where we are not present.

Some companies have derived emotional added value from the development of teleworking from offices at home and networked offices at various locations, by bringing together their members of staff in virtual rooms by means of *tele-presence*. For this purpose, the American advertising agency Chiat/Day installed the network software Oxygen, which offers all employees a ground plan featuring a billiards room, library, print shop, stairwell, café and so on. Brenda's photo pops up on every employee's screen at the well of the staircase underneath the big company clock. She announces to her creative team that there will be a meeting next Thursday at 10 am in the café. When she subse-quently tries to contact Bob in his simulated office, she only sees the back of his head on her screen. This tells her that he currently does not want to be disturbed. Again the principle applies: *tele-presence* can only work and offer true convenience entertainment at the office if all employees are thoroughly familiar with the proceedings, if they know how life works in this virtual office, and if they comply with the *SOL brain scripts*.

TELEPORTATION

Another type of convenience entertainment in cyberspace has emerged from humanity's deeply rooted need to be able to execute virtual acts in the same real way as physical ones.

If I want to delete a file on my Apple computer I simply click it and dump it into the wastepaper basket that sits at the edge of the screen awaiting new waste. In future, meetings and workshops are to become even more real by means of *teleportation*. The most advanced approach has been taken by the Darmstadt-based GMD-IPSI research institute with its 'i-Land' idea.

Watching the scientists handle their teleportation unit there, you are suddenly quite tempted to believe in the kind of 'beaming up' we know from the likes of *Star Trek*. In an office a file is being prepared for a presentation. It contains text, photos, a video plus sound. Next to the computer there is a bridge, a type of electronic scales. The scientist takes a random object, let's say a bunch of keys, and places it on this cyber bridge. Then he enters the presentation room, places the bunch of keys on the bridge there in front of the giant DynaWall®, and immedi-ately the file pops up on the wall. Without any data carriers in-between, the two networked computers – only triggered by the weight of the bunch of keys – have identified and called up the associated document. Other researchers stand in a circle around the InteracTable®. By merely touching this black high-tech table with its built-in plasma screen they can turn a photo so that everyone can see it. One member of staff moves his arms dramatically through the air and the photo, as if moved by witchcraft, flies up onto the DynaWall® where it is dragged and dropped and embedded into a text. Not without reason the chief developer of the system, Dr Norbert Streitz, is both a physicist and a psychologist. After all, even today the system makes it possible to develop routines previously only possible on the basis of *brain-script analyses*. Beyond its technical component the system imitates real acts such as taking, carrying, placing, shifting, turning and so on through virtual processes.

Both tele-presence and teleportation free real behaviour from the constraints of physical presence and therefore double as perceivable convenience entertainment.

Furthermore, the merging of virtual with real space has produced an independent cyber culture that anticipates a number of imminent technological developments in terms of design. The Webcamers® at Printemps look like urban guerrillas in their high-tech martial-arts-like suits. Special fixtures on their belts and shoulders support the mobile phone establishing a wireless Internet connection and the camera the Webcamer® carries and points at the desired object when required. This somehow reminds us of the imminent cyber suits featuring minicomputers, cell phones, MP3 players and cameras embedded in their fabrics. Large Internet cafés, such as the Bignet in Vienna, even feature special pieces of furniture like surf sofas. From the footrests of these beautiful sofas, flat screens rise up to hover elegantly in front of their users. In future, a wide variety of designer furniture will doubtlessly serve as docking stations for virtual applications.

Convenience furniture, convenience apparel and convenience vehicles will surround us like omnipresent servants in our everyday lives. But technology alone is not enough to give us this convenience experience.

Without skilled handling of routine scripts, without the dramatist's skilled plot development and training, all of these technologies will remain nothing but superficial gadgets.

This is why the last Webcamer® rolled out of Paris's Printemps department store three years on. Unadventurous managers never really understood what the developers and advertising agency had invented in their interests here. When I visited the place with a group of managers from the automotive industry, two ladies in their late fifties tried to get us to buy at least something from the department store. The uniqueness of their futuristic colleagues on skates was completely alien to them.

SUMMARY

▌ *'Bricks and clicks' is synonymous with the amalgamation of real with virtual rooms.*

▌ **Tele-presence.** This means being present at a place – department store or office – without physically entering it, but nevertheless being very much tied to the real place – by a helpful avatar, for example. The convenience entertainment here is produced by freeing a routine from its physical reality while securing it in real life at the same time. What is required here is preparatory brain-script analysis, because even at a virtual office customary habits must be observed.

▌ **Teleportation.** This is the control of virtual routines by real acts such as the shifting of electronic images by means of real hand movements. Here convenience entertainment is the result of one's physically perceivable access to 'non-physical' states.

PART V

MOOD MANAGEMENT

The need to influence one's own state of mind is definitely a mega trend in the grown-up experience society. A look at one of the US trend stores like The Sharper Image, for example, is enough to convince us of this. The hit here is massage chairs where exhausted tourists and business people on their lunch breaks can lounge while they are given a thorough massage. Next to them devices electronically reproduce the sounds of breaking waves, tropical rain forests, rain and waterfalls lulling us into gentle sleep or at least relaxation for a short while. In the CD department Gregorian chants play non-stop. At the cash desk, mood sunglasses dangle from a display in different colours so we can 'tint' our world into rose pink, garish orange or cool blue.

This phenomenon has already been discussed in this book several times – for instance in conjunction with mood management used at locations where the senses are over-stimulated. At the Billa super-market we see a projected field of sunflowers, the blooms swaying in the wind, and at world expos mood-specific pavilions (such as the wet walk-in cloud at Expo 02 in Switzerland or the hall with the cradle beds at Expo 2000 in Hanover) were big hits.

The psychological mechanism underlying mood management was also described. It is the packaging phenomenon of *inferential beliefs* that is essentially responsible for transferring an atmospherically dense surrounding to visitors. The packaging 'rubs off' on the goods packaged, and in mood management we are only too pleased to let ourselves also be 'wrapped up' in a place promising to massage the soul and provide rest, emotional wellbeing or excitement.

This chapter sets out to describe two types of *Third Place* that would not exist without mood management. These include the 'new hiking' phenomenon on themed routes with sensual attractions, which is now replacing traditional weekend outings. They also include the renaissance of lobbies, atria and lounges which are now suddenly moving from the sidelines into the centre of business entertainment.

11

Lobbies and lounges

In-between places become principal places

Train station concourses with their typical station-like atmosphere, fancy company foyers as visible signs of power, musty waiting rooms and endless, dreary passageways all used to be places people wanted to leave as quickly as possible. Few remember that once upon a time flights of stairs on ocean liners or smoking saloons were considered first-class places that gave people an emotional boost. For some years now these in-between places, viewed as 'non-places' for far too long, have increased in importance. For a long time they were considered immaterial because they appeared to play an unproductive role at first sight. But then their potential to massage the soul was rediscovered, and these underestimated in-between places have now turned into new key places for marketing.

To my mind it all started in the early 1980s in New York. At that time people were busy building a new generation of skyscrapers. With great foresight New York's city administration only allowed this on condition that the big corporations gave something back to the New Yorkers in return for the space and light they claimed for themselves. The lower floors of these high-rise buildings were to have publicly accessible atriums which, like Italian piazzas, could become meeting points for the urban community. After initial grumbling, corporations realized that this obligation could be turned into a marketing tool whereupon each tried to outdo the other with staged atriums.

The classic among these staged business atriums is doubtlessly the Chinese bamboo forest at the IBM Building. Monday morning:

outside, New Yorkers rush from appointment to appointment, while here inside, a small group of people whose social and business paths would scarcely cross in their everyday lives take some time out. A banker in a dark suit sits at one of the numerous little tables in the spacious atrium in front of a polystyrene cup of steaming coffee. Next to him is a young tourist, probably a student from Europe, loading a new cassette into his video camera, and an elderly man who evidently has few financial resources at his disposal. None of them pay any attention to the others and yet there is a relaxed atmosphere in the air.

Staged atriums are like neutral territories where nobody feels marginalized as long as they are relatively unobtrusive. In this respect they are typical *Third Places*. This also implies that in most cases there is an obvious main reason for being in the atrium – such as a meeting held in the same building – and also that there are several secondary reasons, such as taking brief, unnoticed little rests in-between times – reasons which are at least as important as the main ones. This is why here at IBM a small kiosk offers coffee and snacks, why Chinese bamboo trees were planted and arranged in groups thereby forming little mini forests and clearings. Being exotic plants, they are the spectacular *landmark* of the atrium, a striking 'monument' for IBM in New York. At the same time, their presence massages the stressed-out souls of those taking a short rest here, and they serve as the *concept line* of the space, constituting the recurring theme of wellness and nature in the concrete jungle of the city. Briefly, the tranquillity is disturbed as a grand piano is rolled in – the place will host to some low-key jazz performances over the weekend, when you might discover modern art amongst the bamboo trees, and when the atrium mutates into an *ad hoc* gallery for chance passers-by.

In-between places turn into principal places of urban vitality and spaciousness. The atriums of corporate HQs, hotel lobbies or VIP lounges are now moving centre-stage for consumers and marketing experts alike. They are ideal places to establish contacts with new target groups or pamper existing customers with emotional give-aways. They show that you as an entrepreneur want to make a positive impact on people's lives through what you are doing. They give expression to your inner attitude.

▌ There are *places for arriving* – trendy hotel lobbies that become places for people to meet in the city, spectacular museum foyers, reception halls at company HQs.

▌ There are *places for waiting* – theatre foyers, lounges at airports and (recently also) at train stations where German state railways, for example, use stylishly designed first-class lounges as image-building tools.

▌ There are *places of transit* – the new 'flying lounges' on intercontinental flights, the transit passageways at airports, the underground walkways in our cities.

▌ Finally, there are *places for pausing* – readers' corners at bookstores, chill-out zones in malls and new mood shops as places of meditation.

Regardless of the area of business where mood-management places emerge, there are always two basic emotions that can be addressed here. Either the place uses every trick in the book to make us feel *relaxed*, or the place makes us feel *excited* and that life is stimulating and thrilling.

RELAXATION

When intellectuals discuss staging or theming it is often automatically equated with action and 'high life'. However, emotionalizing a place through relaxation can be at least as intense. The French fragrance and cosmetics chain Sephora has realized this crystal-clear fact and has tapped into humanity's need for short breaks of the soul to develop an enormously sensual *concept store* by the name of Sephora blanc. The 'white Sephora' is the little brother of the larger Sephora *flagship stores*, where bright red fragrance theatres convert the point of sale into a place of experience, and replaces the older 'black Sephoras', so far only operating with smaller sales areas. Those standing in front of a white Sephora will scarcely be able to resist the temptation of the central axis formed by circular luminaires over the cash desk and goods displays that hypnotically draw shoppers in.

Wellness romantic

Inside the store the story then continues along these lines. White marquee/fabric roofs resting on the luminous hubs of the axis, luminous shelving, a bewitching scent concept and sophisticated esoteric music with oriental undertones relax you after just a few metres. As if in a state of trance you reach out for the products, which are subdivided into Orient and Occident.

Left and right of the axis four tiny booths containing special service ranges open up in the wall. In one booth a lady dressed in oriental clothes waits by an oriental divan alongside a Persian rug and Indian stools, for customers in need of a manicure or pedicure. Opposite, people lounge in comfortable chairs and listen to chill-out music through earphones. Taken together this appeals to our idea of a wellness concept that combines trendy Indian aesthetics with chic design.

Wellness romanticism purposely slows down the arousal zones of the body – our inner 'visceral' vibes of heart frequency, circulation and nervous system make us breathe freely and relax our muscles.

This trend originally came from wellness zones which were intended to relax with water. At the famous baths in Wals built by the Swiss Expo 2000 architect Zumthor, guests swim in a pool awash with fresh rose petals and lie on an atavistic stone that is flushed with warm water. The poolside butlers at the Ritz-Carlton hotel chain pamper their guests with either what they call the Gentleman's Bath (for single businessmen) or the Romantic Bath (a private bath for two, definitely not single). The first combines a bath of tangy herbs and woody forest scents with a glass of cognac, canapés and a cigar, while the latter seduces guests with a bath of patchouli, jasmine and (again) rose petals combined with champagne and strawberries by candlelight. Sephora blanc also tries to slow down your tempo. Here our vibes become harmonious – without water but by means of music, scents, 'floating' light and an oriental feel. At hotels and country clubs in California, stars now relax with bio-feedback, hypnotherapy and oxygen showers. Correspondingly, Sephora is now considering the introduction of booths with light and colour showers after relaxation through music.

Pure nature

Some consultants make stressed-out managers go into the forest and embrace old but living tree trunks. *Irrespective of whether you believe in the effect of such esoteric ideas, the soothing influence of nature on humanity is a fact.*

This effect even works without real nature – like the sunflower fields at the supermarket and the waterfall sounds produced by a sound machine at the gadget store. IBM's bamboo forest is a classic example of this special force of nature for applications in business. While this book was being written the 17 huge royal palms buried under the rubble of the World Trade Center were replanted in the winter garden of the neighbouring World Financial Center in New York. Just as before, they will be covered in thousands of miniature lamps which will light up in the evening to emphasize the feeling of glory emanating from the majestic palm trees and the glazed barrel vaulting above them.

In hotels, nature has a special meaning for stressed-out travellers who jet around the globe, at times almost desperately on the look-out for something authentic at all those airports and business locations. Philippe Starck, the French design guru and architect of a now impressive total of seven hotels, employs green apples at all his design strongholds. For instance, at the Delano in Miami Beach Denise and I love the silver hand protruding from the wall. This features right next to a door presenting a green apple, with the comment, 'An apple a day keeps the doctor away.' André Putman, Starck's famous architect colleague from France, recently opened the Pershing Hall Hotel in Paris. Here a kind of floral waterfall (a term taken from the *Architectural Digest*) flows down the originally bare wall of the inner courtyard. To achieve this the roots of the little trees were anchored in felt bags, and a luminous cable was installed to contrast this nature with at least some design.

Putman combines image transfer to the soul with a playful perception of the forest which is 'hung' in portrait format: authenticity and smartness at a glance.

This combination of design and nature is typical of modern mood management. It also incorporates the use of water in hotels, where it is integrated so frequently that you hardly believe your eyes. At hotels in San Francisco, Singapore and Osaka we marvelled at such water stagings and experienced them as 'mood adjustments' of the soul. At the Royal Hotel in Osaka a creek flows through the lobby, and you cross it by carefully balancing over a number of Japanese bridges. The creek flows into the hotel lobby from an outdoor pond, which in turn is fed by a waterfall that you see but cannot hear through a spectacular 180-degree window.

A leap to Europe. Here they discovered that people are about as fond of going to banks as they are to hospitals. Even people with money dislike going to their banker. This is why a flower tower rises several storeys high at the headquarters of the Bank Austria in Vienna, and this is why a miniature forest in the atrium was proposed for the headquarters of the Düsseldorf municipal savings bank, which has now reopened under the name Finanzkaufhaus (financial department store) Düsseldorf. Unfortunately, two or three trees are all that is left of this initial idea. But while other highlights of the Finanzkaufhaus such as the food establishments went largely unnoticed, visitors huddle together under those few trees in the café. At times it is nice to see that end users have understood an idea better than the architects and building proprietor.

Lounging

These days when flicking through journals featuring new restaurants and bars, you will find that nine out of ten articles deal with lounge-style establishments. These new hip places look like over-sized living rooms with designer furniture. People say '*lounging*', and by that they mean that the style of relaxing airport lounges can be found everywhere today in the form of high-quality mood management: in catering, but also at exhibition stands, bookstores, shopping malls, in the VIP areas of hotels, cosy offices, and even aboard planes and in luxury limousines.

Lounging means that a high-quality private atmosphere is linked with extremely relaxing add-ons.

The relaxation you experience when you curl up on the couch at home is transferred to a semi-public place of business, a *Third Place*. While it is true you might be pursuing another activity at this place – such as reading a book or travelling – this activity is pursued in a relaxed, sprawling posture, and is probably also sweetened by some sort of food and drink and upgraded by beautiful design that flatters your soul and ego.

British Airways, Europe's largest airline, has undergone some impressive developments over the past few years. The airline's First Class and subsequently its Business Class were restyled as 'flying lounges'. The basic idea here was to do away with the awfully rigid row arrangement of seats and introduce reclining seats with panels allowing more privacy and other kinds of extras (see Figure 11.1). Here cabin space is completely redefined, becoming a 'Lounge in the Sky', as BA calls its Club World – the business class for long-haul flights. *Convenience entertainment* and *mood management* determine the functions and arrangement of these cabins to an equal extent.

Figure 11.1   British Airways' 'Lounge in the Sky'
© British Airways

Those travelling alone can fold out their privacy screens while working or snoozing, thereby ensuring maximum privacy and their own territory on board. This implies that many of the seats are arranged back to back: that is, one passenger faces in the direction of the flight while his or her neighbour faces in the opposite direction. If you feel like chatting with your neighbour you can simply fold down the screen. Large screens can be swivelled down in front of you for in-flight entertainment. Right in front of your seat is a kind of stool anchored to the ground. This forms part of your bed when the seat is horizontally reclined. It also doubles as a chair if someone comes to chat with you from another area of the cabin or from Economy Class.

Maximum reclining comfort and privacy are what the mood management of Club World is all about, maximum flexibility of convenience entertainment in the sky.

Lounging in transit and transport will increase in importance over the next few years. There are a number of indications of this. In DaimlerChrysler's new Maybach luxury limousine you stretch your legs as you sit on the leather back seat. Like on a plane, the seat is equipped with automatically extending leg and foot rests – made possible by the 6 metres of overall car length. In the meantime the first class lounges of the German state railways feature lampshades from 1960s-style living rooms, elegant sofas, free drinks and a relaxed view of the platforms.

Lounging at exhibitions and in offices shows that people now also want to see work in a more relaxed, less dogged light. In a nutshell, they want to see it harmoniously embedded in life. At Euroshop 2002, the big shopfitting trade fair, the company Decoprojekt surpassed everyone with its lounge fair stand; the centre comprised a type of piazza surrounded by a circular 'bubble' containing the conference rooms and a lounge in the then 'hip' 1970s style. On a video I filmed there you can watch a visitor to the fair in a dark suit gently doze off on an incredibly comfortable wall-side bench underneath the video projections, relaxed by jazz music, films showing shots from nature, a mirror wall making everything look even bigger, and real, strikingly illuminated flowers.

Meanwhile, many companies also want to use the mood-management lounging of their atriums to improve the working climate of their offices and now offer their employees a living-room-like working environment.

Lounging in stores and shopping malls releases the pressure to consume at retail places; it offers customers a time-out and is a true customer service. Hugendubel in Frankfurt-on-Main is a book store that always stocks my books. It was also the place where I met my current publishers, the meeting point where this book was discussed and its details finalized. A great deal could be said about Hugendubel: about its central stairwell with its temple-like structure, its spectacular bridges and allusions to a large library, about its café, about its layout. But the great innovation at Hugendubel is without doubt its spacious reading lounges in the form of bright red square balconies with comfy benches hovering above the scene. This is where bookworms, families and business people on their lunch break lounge as if in swallows' nests that cling to a steep coastline overlooking the world.

Even today, the sales area is all about releasing pressure, offering scope of movement, being generous in 'not having to sell' – and therefore 'selling' particularly successfully.

Meanwhile, a two-hour flight west takes us to the Bluewater Experience near London, where dozens of customers used to lounge underneath the *mood-management dome* of the Water Circus – the access area of the multiplex cinema of this, the epitome of design malls. Here a globe of blue illuminated glass measuring several metres hovered high above an enormously thick, blue carpet perfectly set into the floor. Kids aged from zero to seven romped around here, enjoying the fleecy playground. Encircling them, their parents sprawled, exhausted but happy, on numerous leather chairs with their full shopping bags parked left and right of them and their undone shoes in front of them. The sheer amount of high-quality seating was incredible. Back-to-backs, 'chaises longue', 'fauteuils', sofas, chairs with high rests, all of them made of high-quality leather, were arranged in a circle around the carpet and the glass globe, facing the unobtrusive water projections on the inside of the dome. While outside the mall each shop tries to outdo the other on an extremely high arousal level, while even the neutral promenades are themed from the Thames to Rose Garden, while consumers are exposed to enormous pressure to experience and to buy something everywhere, they used to find a neutral place for taking some time out here underneath the dome, a place that reduced the pressure, slowed down the arousal pace again and allowed them to regain their strength. Today, several years after the opening, this lounging landscape has had to give way to an extension of the cramped food service establishments in the mall. Although this decision seems justified and reasonable, Bluewater has clearly lost one of its emotional fixtures, and this is a crying shame.

EXCITEMENT

We all know what effect a sunny spring day can have on our mood, when the first rays of sunlight appear after a long period of darkness and cold. This effect can be attributed to our physiological system which allows us to perceive light and colours. The image popping up on our retina is transmitted to our brain by three different nerve channels. There is a channel for blue and yellow, one for red and green, and one for black and white, or the level of brightness. 'Antagonistic transmission of stimuli' is what a system like this is called – which usually transmits a medium level of stimuli if the brightness levels are medium and the colours are mixed. If, however, very high brightness levels follow a period of subdued light – the first sunny day after cloudy weather – or a single one of the basic colours is seen purely as a luminous or shocking colour, the system suddenly peaks in one direction only and the nerve channels practically start to glow. This is noted by the whole body, which steps up the arousal. Bright light and pure colours produce this effect. This is why red rooms seem to be warmer than blue rooms, and glowing red appears somehow sensual to us.

Colour showers

In Russia luminous, so-called 'bright light energy' columns are currently the latest thing, as their bright bath of light helps to fight the winter blues, that depressing phase in the darker period of the year. In Germany the furniture producer Interlübke launched 'eo', a mood-management cabinet, whose glass wall can be set to bilious lemon green, over-ornate red or cool midnight blue: colour therapy within our own four walls.

'Light can be woven into curtains and cushions, it can make tiles and wallpaper glow fluorescently, it can make bath tubs shine in semi-transparency and it can make new veneering materials radiate in an expansive and disembodied way,' reports Rolf Mecke in the *Architektur und Wohnen* magazine.

While the relaxing effects of lobbies and lounges make us all relaxed, any type of colour shower makes us feel stimulated, and even excited.

A multitude of *Third Places* is fitted with such stimulating mood-makers, offering the public colour therapy in a semi-public space. The American light artist Keith Sonnier was the first to realize humanity's need for stimulating *colour showers* at airports. He created neon installations for the Chicago and Los Angeles airports which filled otherwise 'dead' areas like those endless transit aisles with life. A particularly striking example is his 1,000 metre long underground light corridor at Munich Airport. Stress caused by hectic travelling causes a kind of muscular tension, which is appropriately described by the Austrian idiom *einkrampfen*. Literally translated, Austrians say people are 'cramping in' when they are doggedly determined to achieve something. Sonnier's *light showers* that produce ever new and surprising patterns by means of endless horizontal and vertical colour bars counteract this cramping effect, causing a physical body state which makes even dogged travellers find themselves again.

Colour and light have always been part and parcel of entertainment. In Gothic cathedrals the intense focus of colour provided by stained glass windows set into stone was used to heighten the effect of the Mass and sacred music. This was also the basic idea underlying Colourscape (see colour plates), the cave-like labyrinth of plastic components used by Jeunesse Musicale as a venue for jazz and classical music events. In this cave system – where taking off your shoes in the entrance area is obligatory – you experience life music in honeycomb-type chambers, aisles, bubbles and holes bathed in garish colours by the sunlight shining through the fabric walls. Each type of music is thereby enhanced. The idea here is to make it easy for children and young people to open up to a sensual, active music listening experience. Quite apart from this, once set up at Vienna's Rathausplatz the place was a huge playground for young and old, and for clambering around in generally.

Philippe Starck and Jean Nouvel

'Ding' goes the lift stopping on the ground floor. We enter and have the colour shock of our lives. Immersed in bilious green we make our ascent. As experienced long-time guests of Starck Hotels in London, New York and Miami Beach, and as lovers of his restaurants in Madrid, Tokyo and Paris, Denise and I know that Philippe Starck would not dream of letting us wander through his world without being emotionalized.

It all began with the Teatriz restaurant in Madrid, where the master placed a luminous onyx bar counter in a former children's theatre. It was frequently copied and even 'cited' by Starck himself at the rooms of his St Martin's Lane Hotel in London. There you switch on not only the normal room lights but also a yellow, luminous onyx table placed in the centre of the room as a desk. As if this was not enough, a metal disc beside the bed allows you gradually to set the lighting atmosphere of the room. From sultry red and wan white to sun-bathed yellow, a variety of colour moods can be created and used strategically as a message to your fellow guest. The effects produced by such pure spectral colours can be observed at the luminous bar on the ground floor. There lovers are so intensely bathed in stimulating light by the colour showers that one of my business partners recently complained bitterly about the indecent behaviour of some kissing couples.

In the lobby in front of the bar the emotional sensuality is continued by other means. All hotel lobbies, gardens, bars and restaurants designed by Philippe Starck are popular meeting points for models, advertising people, actors and other beautiful people. This is due to a trick that stimulates us like the colour showers, but does so by other means.

Philippe Starck styles smart hotel lobbies full of visual sophistication. His compatriot and famous architect Jean Nouvel specializes in equally smart foyers of operas and concert halls.

In a photo my young son, hardly a year old back then, sits on a large golden throne in the lobby of St Martin's Lane. Next to him is an almost 4-metre-high aluminium vase with flowers and a gigantic chessboard, the larger-than-life type you would only usually find in parks. Behind him the giant goldfish projected on to the doors of the luminous bar (closed during the day) swim past. Playing with unusual sizes and perspectives is part of Starck's signature style, which he uses to 'tickle' as it were our *media literacy*, and to turn all of his lobbies into places tingling with pleasure derived from watching. Philippe Starck stimulates all of our perception skills in order to make hotel lobbies a feast for the eyes of today's smart visual generation.

The escalator takes us through a green glowing well up to the lobby of the Hudson Hotel in New York, making us marvel at the *replica effect* produced by an old chandelier whose burning lights are holograms of incandescent lamps. Similarly striking is the Delano in Miami Beach. You drive up in a limousine and are puzzled by the oversized living-room luminaires standing on the terrace in front of the entrance. In the lobby this *playing with viewing angles* and perspectives is repeated. A never-ending aisle with white tulle over-drapes flying in the wind protrudes into the panelled hall at an oblique angle and pulls flabbergasted visitors into the garden, where the similar drapes of the garden suites are just being closed so the beds can be turned down. However, this does not happen *inside* the rooms, as would be expected, but outside since the over-drapes surprisingly hang from the façade of the building.

Jean Nouvel also uses this form of stimulating *mood management* through visual tricks. Reference was already made to his hotel in Lucerne with the original name The Hotel. But the focus of his work is museums, operas and concert halls. In Lucerne, the Culture and Congress Centre Lucerne or KKL is located just a five-minute walk from his hotel; it houses one of the world's most beautiful modern concert rooms. Its doors close without a sound as if by magic before the concert starts, and its lights in the white room then take on the shimmer of candlelight.

The foyers of KKL play an ironic game with their windows. Some of them are huge, reaching down to the floor, others are like narrow, horizontal embrasures. All of them overlook the lake, the mountains and the lake promenade of Lucerne. Nouvel has oriented the windows so precisely that the view out of each window produces an incredibly kitsch picture-postcard panorama. You could say that he uses the windows like postcards, thereby playing with the dramatist's trick of the *borrowed language*, as in many of his buildings.

He rose to fame with a comparable effect at his Institut du Monde Arabe in Paris. There, an entire glazed façade is covered in iris diaphragms that open and close depending on the light levels, working like a camera shutter and resembling oriental ornaments in the semi-darkness of the museum. In Lucerne Nouvel 'makes picture postcards' out of windows, and the citizens of Lucerne visiting the famous music festival do not know whether to be embarrassed, amused or proud.

Up on the roof Nouvel employs the *borrowed language* trick a second time. The curved wall seems to us like the resonating body of a cello, so that one practically looks down on the 'lid' of the room when standing up here in the galleries. Many a concert-goer strokes this 'instrument' in fascination in a seemingly unobserved moment – thinking he or she can still feel the vibrations of the music that has now faded away.

SUMMARY

▌ *Wellness has long left the area of bathing and spas behind.*
▌ *Wellness worlds feature public spaces where the pressure is particularly high.*
▌ *This mood management is an image transfer from places to the state of mind.*
▌ **Relaxing places.** These are environments using natural elements, measures to relax muscle tension, and sensory impressions like fragrances and sounds to slow down our body's arousal. Masseurs at fairs, the revival of lounges at stations, and areas in

retail spaces that reduce the pressure to consume, therefore contribute to decelerating our lives.

▌ **Exciting places.** These are environments using colour showers and emotional interior designs filled with perception games to relax our muscles. This is how designer hotel lobbies and the publicly accessible atriums of museums have become internationally noted meeting points in the city.

12

The new hiking – experience attractions

Exciting experiences with nature and history

Back in the days before trendy hotels, relaxation domes in shopping malls or walk-in clouds at world expos were discovered as places for massaging the soul, mood management meant a walk in the country, hiking or at the least going off on a little Sunday excursion. This regular Sunday outing of our childhood was often associated with a certain degree of pressure. What was seen as relaxing by grown-ups was often a boring chore for children. The typical behaviour pattern observed on these walks was that the children would run back and forth, hide behind trees, gather sticks and take detours – in a nutshell, just about anything to inject some action into the walk they saw as so dreary. The end of the excursion would be marked by an obligatory reward in the form of a little treat at a restaurant or pastry shop and maybe a round of mini-golf.

In dramatists' terms an excursion of this kind is a 'trail of suspense' with a tension-releasing reward at the end but little that is sensational in-between.

Adults would relax, enjoying this image transfer of nature to their souls. This image transfer, however, remained largely an obscure secret to the kids unless they were hiking in sensationally high mountains or maybe in a deep gorge complete with raging rapids. Consequently, hiking gradually started to change.

Themed hiking paths were invented, linking the need for experiencing nature with all types of little sensations in-between which, in addition to all this, fulfilled the need for authenticity.

'New hiking' makes us walk over humid moss, distinguish herbs by their different smells, discover old mills, follow in the footsteps of cheesemakers, migrate with animals or discover ancient Roman stone relics. I was recently the judge in a contest for the best Austrian themed hiking path, looking at over 350 entries.

Another aspect of Sunday excursions that children disliked has changed in a similar way – visits to museums. Not only are conventional museums increasingly being dusted down and turned into first-class destinations for tourists and families, new additional attractions have also come into being, where a variety of exhibits are on display that focus on experience. Most of these attractions give us immediate, sensual experiences on one topic or theme. You virtually conduct an orchestra at the Haus der Musik (House of Music), or visit memorials staged in such a way that the atmosphere of the past can be felt close up. In dramatic terms these attractions have a dazzling similarity with the new hiking trails. *They also work along a suspense curve (though in most cases inside buildings), they include event stages that allow us to obtain authentic experiences, and they end with a tension-releasing gift: the museum shop at the end of the trip. Instead of nature you charge yourself with a sensual theme – with wine, music – and the act of choosing from these also gives expression to mood management.*

Seen from this angle, these rather urban attractions also form part of new hiking, above all if the attraction doubles as a memorial where events occurring in the past are conveyed to us now.

Both forms of *new hiking* – themed hiking paths and attractions – feature all the properties characteristic of *Third Places*. Through a staged external effect, the *landmark*, through the 'malling' in a promenade (which takes us forward, with the recurring theme of a *concept line* and sensations big and small in-between) and through the *core attractions*, all the way down to releasing the tension at the end of the trail, new hiking is the condensed form of what experiencing nature or exploring a subject has always been about.

Through its professionalization, new hiking in nature and in cities has become a decisive factor for regional tourism marketing.

Winter resorts use it to combat their summer slump and formerly sleepy destinations gain unforeseen appeal as hiking villages.

As far as tourism in cities is concerned, new attractions are winning back the younger generation who may show little interest in classic sites but who do find it hip to climb down into Vienna's sewage canals to experience the return of the *Third Man* or climb up to the Reichstag in Berlin to wander about in its glass dome.

Landmarks

The Reichstag building by Sir Norman Foster with its walk-in cupola is a typical example of the new attractions whose strengths lie in their external effect.

Anyone seeing the hyper-modern steel and glass dome as it sits enthroned on top of the Reichstag, contrasting with the old National Socialist architecture, cannot help wanting to go up there. There is nothing wrong or strange about this because people have always wanted to climb up the landmarks of the city – its church towers, the Leaning Tower of Pisa – or go for a ride on Vienna's big wheel, or now on the London Eye on the Thames. Foster has taken this need into account by designing a spiral-shaped walkway inside the cupola, ultimately turning the simple landmark into a genuine Third Place. Inside, you head up to a vantage point from which you can look down on to the plenary room of the German federal parliament, the Bundestag; what you see there is a cone with its tip menacingly pointing downwards at the parliamentarians. You virtually feel the central message of democracy, 'All power emanates from the people.'

Other attractions are merely based upon their external effect. Very often these are memorials telling a story. In Washington every good American visits the Lincoln Memorial, the Vietnam Veterans' Memorial, the Korean War Veterans' Memorial. Here soldiers are shown plodding over slippery steps, in danger of slipping in the mud. A situation is practically caught in a freeze frame and made accessible to posterity as a *built event.*

The past can also be experienced as presence at the Globe Theatre in London. The replica of the famous Shakespearean theatre building is a 'fake memorial' because the original building not only burnt down long ago, it was also located a few blocks down the road (and just a plaque marks its former location). But what you experience at the Globe today has not changed since those days, since here spectators watch Shakespeare plays standing up while commenting on the performance as it is played out. This famous building, known to schoolchildren around the world, is a spectacular *replica landmark* – you can scarcely believe your eyes. Like a statue long lost and yet known to everyone suddenly reappearing before you in the flesh, the Globe is an attraction where the resurrection of the building, and hence its outside impact as a landmark, are more important than the plays staged or the well-equipped shop selling Shakespearean merchandise inside.

In most cases, however, the landmark of 'new hiking' is simply the start of the tour.

At the starting point of a visit to an *attraction* or a hiking trail you are supposed to feel that this marks the beginning of an undertaking that will lead you along a certain path to a climax. This should at least be a plaque that depicts the overall course of the path. During the hike proper this should best be a three-dimensional sign which is driven into the ground like a flag. Many of the new hiking trails start off at a gate set in the landscape that hikers are to walk through, for example a beautiful wooden gate made of two slightly curved trunks with a board on top that says, 'Nationalpark Hohe Tauern, Naturlehrweg Gradental' (National Nature Reserve, Hohe Tavern, Nature Learning Trail), or a large stone chair whose legs form the gate. And *header landmarks* even telegraph the message of a path. At the departure point of the Kärntner Friedensweg (Corinthian Path of Peace) which traces the First World War front high up in the Alps, barbed wire wrapped round a dead tree trunk warns hikers about the consequences of violence against man and nature.

Malling

It all began with the natural, still un-staged perception of one's natural surroundings. A tree rises on the horizon and attracts our attention. A narrow path meanders over the hill to end at a little church in the distance. Wherever you look, the need emerges to strive for a destination beyond this visual axis.

Hiking trails are trails of suspense.

Therefore, they link two psychological mechanisms: *cognitive maps* and *anticipation*. This can best be explained using a concrete example. Figure 12.1 shows the entrance map of the First Austrian Nature and Environment Learning Trail for Children, which was created in the Ramsau region at Dachstein as early as 10 years ago, and has been extended continuously since. It was recently awarded the title of Austria's best themed hiking trail from a total of 350 entries.

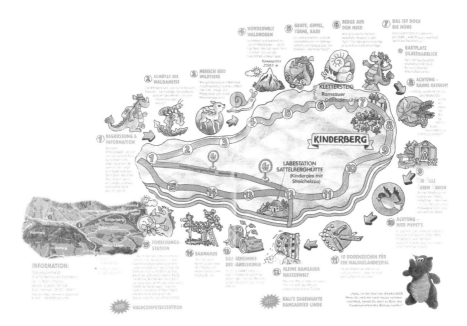

Figure 12.1   First Austrian Nature and Environment Experience Trail for Children, Ramsau
© Tourismusverband Ramsau

The approximately 4 km forest trail is a classic loop, a round trip that leads up a children's mountain and back down again by another route. The loop also forms the axis of the *cognitive map* visitors follow. It starts with the official welcome by 'Kali the Ramsaurier' (Kali the Ramsaur), the (dinosaur) mascot of the trail, and is basically made up of two sections: the way up to the peak and the way back down to 'base camp' where the research station is located. What immediately strikes you is that the path is strongly segmented. The developers did not rely on the variety of the terrain alone, which includes forest, clearings, rock towers and a mountain col, but planned 15 stops, making the trail extremely varied.

The axis, otherwise empty in the eyes of many kids, is filled with attractive experience points. These are the mnemonic points of the cognitive map that will be remembered later – for instance where the climbing trail or the waterworld were.

For a change of scene let's look at an attraction in the city centre of Lucerne and compare its spatial structures. Figure 12.2 shows that the

Figure 12.2   Entrance map of Gletschergarten (Glacier Garden), Lucerne, Switzerland
© Gletschergarten

same principle also applies here at the Gletschergarten (Glacier Garden), which is arranged around a series of glacial crevasses from the Ice Age. You enter the grounds (incidentally redeveloped according to one of my concepts) along an alley of steles that all announce the highlights in advance, and you walk right through the little box-office building into the *attraction* itself. Then you wander along a loop with the crevasses on your right until you reach the museum building. Leaving this on one side you then ascend the mountain, where you pass mountain stages like an alpine hut which offers a simulated view of a glacier. At the end you enter a mirror maze.

As we can see, the grounds are clearly segmented: they feature a spectacular roof structure – similar to the roof of the Munich Olympic stadium – built to house the 20,000 year-old rock crevasses. It features a museum built in nostalgic Swiss marquetry style, a Tower Walk leading up to the lookout tower and finally a maze that teleports us to Granada's Alhambra – a coincidental left-over of a historic world exposition. At the Gletschergarten, too, this principle applies: new hiking needs a *cognitive map* marked by individual stops and broken down into clearly distinguishable sections. This is what produces *malling*, this feel of a lively exploration of the grounds.

At the same time, visitors and hikers are 'pulled' along the trail by their desire to reach a destination with a sense of anticipation due to this build-up of excitement. In this case the destination might be a small peak offering the best and most beautiful view, what is known as the Silberklarblick (crystal clear view) at Ramsau. Or is it the lookout tower at the Glacier Garden that nigh on every visitor wants to climb so as to look down on Lucerne from there? In between, each stop is 'anticipated' as a mnemonic point on the entrance map, thereby becoming a little in-between destination. In the end the remaining suspense is released. On the Ramsau hiking trail this is achieved by a research station that answers any remaining questions. At the Glacier Garden it is the 'wow' effect produced by the maze, where you wander about accompanied by atmospheric music and theatrical lighting, searching and finding, laughing and marvelling.

Concept line

What has been the all-encompassing idea for hiking trails since people started hiking? Man has always been interested in two things: the histories to be found along the way, the secrets of nature and any other mysteries that need unravelling.

Accordingly, theming and sensual explanations are the two concept lines used most frequently, often even in parallel. They use interactive games and are brought to life by hands-on activities.

At the Ramsau children's hiking trail you clear forest pests and environmental polluters from your path like skittles (Stage 9), pass some revealing 'wow' effects like titmice that can stay awake for 18 hours without getting tired (Stage 10), or discover the secret of tree rings on trees cut open (Stage 13). At the Gletschergarten you pass a display of a huge, petrified fern leaf. Over this you can fold a real fern leaf embedded in an acrylic film that features an explanation on the back.

Next to the leaf, the sound of breaking waves filters out from hidden loudspeakers, and warm lighting conjures up an atmosphere of the South Seas. In actual fact, Lucerne was once a tropical beach by the sea, and the fern dates from those times – which visitors are teleported back to by way of theming effects. Right next to this, ice can be heard crunching away ominously. The sound projected over the crevasses gives you an idea of what it must have felt like in the Ice Age when these crevasses in the rocks, a global geological sensation, were formed by the forces of nature.

Being transported to another era, having one's *brain scripts* triggered, fulfils that need for an authentic story to be told while hiking and at attractions. Since the Ramsau hiking trail predominantly targets children, the escapist world themed around Kali, the dinosaur, is certainly an empathetic concept. And even here the escapist, child-like style is complemented with a selection of games attempting to transport kids into another world by means of authenticity. They can play the forest cross-country game (Stage 11) or become scouts reading tracks in the soil.

Many themed hiking trails pick up on traces from the past and guide visitors past the relics of long lost worlds, like the prize-winning Erlebniswelt Mendlingtal – Auf dem Holzweg (Experience World Mendlingtal – Following in the Tracks of Wood). Exciting log cabins at the waterside, utensils, winches, photos of rafts, even the occasional real-life raft made of tree trunks tied together floating by revive memories of times past.

The need for the highest possible degree of authenticity in theming has predominantly benefited (the now ever greater number of) memorials over the past few years.

The United States Holocaust Memorial Museum in Washington is probably the most famous of these. As I embark upon this round trip I am given an ID pass with the number 1434. The first page features the photo of my designated (and now personally identified-with) victim of the Holocaust. It is Wilhelm Kusserow, born on 4 September 1914 in Bochum. As I slowly make my way round the permanent exhibition along with thousands of other people I look at the pass now and again and read something about him. I am told not to open the last page until I reach the end of the exhibition. Finally, I find myself standing in a cattle truck, just like millions of Jews who embarked on their final voyage this way. A young man from Israel can scarcely hold back his tears. Then I finally reach the wall on which I look for my personal victim of the mass murder. Now I open the last page of the passport and learn about how the conscientious objector was executed.

'The Return of the *Third Man*' is an occasional event, an attraction, that takes visitors down into Vienna's sewers during the summer months. This is where in 1949 the famous movie *The Third Man* featuring Orson Welles in the leading role – a mysterious tale of smuggling and the black market – was filmed. Even the famous chase in Vienna's underground and the famous zither theme were shot here.

What's so special about this attraction is that it is acted out by real sewage cleaning workers. Two of them, talking in broad Viennese dialect and oozing with local charm, dress expectant visitors in protective jackets and off they go, down the steep spiral staircase. Here we are chased under various pretexts from one sewage canal to the next, and stand a hair's breadth away from approaching waste water while dramatic lighting sets the scene. Something dangerously hisses and crackles like electricity, the tunnel almost floods and Harry Lime (or some lunatic with a gun imitating him) seems to reappear. What is so great here, apart from the authentic location, is the expertise of our guides. At about 3 pm brown sludge comes floating towards us. 'Do you know what this is?' our underground guide asks us. 'Around this time of the day the vats at the chocolate factory in the 3rd district are cleaned out.' No actor could deliver this kind of *authentic theming* in such a compelling fashion.

Core attraction

During the entire guided tour we are, of course, waiting to hear that famous zither melody. Finally the time has come. All of a sudden, after a speedy chase along a dark narrow passageway, we reach a huge underground tunnel through which Vienna's river flows. We see a shadow, hear a shot ringing out, then the melody can be heard from the depths of the canal system, floating over the visitors' heads to fade away in the tunnel where the Vienna river takes a bend.

The core attraction here is the ingredient that turns this trail into a trail of suspense. During our underground tour allusions designed to trigger anticipation are repeated over and over again.

Some hiking trails have professionalized the enhancement of the core attraction to such an extent that they can scarcely be distinguished from theme park rides.

On the Hawaiian island of Kauai the fern grotto, operated by the same family for 100 years, is among the most popular destinations. First you board a boat to go down river. Then you go ashore again, and follow a surprisingly tarmacked path through the jungle, passing by orchids and other tropical flora, until you finally end up in the queue waiting by the grotto. Here the group in front of us is still 'boarding' but this waiting in line merely adds to our suspense, which is made more entertaining by exotic birds flying past.

Then, suddenly, the tour continues. Within sight of the grotto people gather in front of a guide who tells them interesting facts in a kind of pre-show before the attraction proper. Finally, you wander up into the grotto. Here you look back in rows of three through the very long, very green and very wet ferns to the venue of the *pre-show*, where singers and dancers have now taken their positions to perform a Hawaiian wedding song. After 10 minutes this *main show* is over. You wander back to the boat along a different path – aha, a *loop*, I say to myself – and are swept back by boat to the starting point of the trip, while little girls dance to Hawaiian tunes – *relieving the suspense* of the show. All of this is very commercial and thoroughly organized, but works astonishingly well and is great fun.

Many hiking paths targeting children employ an old trick in order to enhance the core attraction and increase that sense of anticipation. Collecting something, stamping or scratching cards is the motto as you rush from experience point to experience point in pursuit of the next trophy. In Austria, long before new hiking was invented, badges for hats were popular collector's items, and these could be purchased at the different outing destinations.

This is why the attractions that are linked to a pronounced massage of the soul – like hiking is as such – are particularly popular.

Hiking means regaining your balance, thereby pursuing a fundamental need of all living organisms. People long for light during prolonged periods of darkness, and enjoy the first rays of sunshine when it is cold. The air and the sky, green vegetation around us, the regular rhythm of hiking that influences the alpha waves in our brains – all of this is mood management induced by hiking, fulfilling its actual purpose in this way.

Attractions try to imitate this massage of the soul in an urban environment. This is why sensual attractions are so popular. Grand feelings, like memorials, that make you feel yourself by means of emotional distress, or attractions linked to gastronomic delights, have become attractive destinations for many people.

The origin of the attractions in hiking is best demonstrated in a wine experience world opened at the Southern Austrian wine-growing town of Langenlois in 2003. Developed by scenographer Otto Steiner, the Loisium starts at a hyper-modern building, guides you through a vineyard and then takes you down to the underground cellars where you actually do something like subterranean hiking. Following a luminous strip recessed in the floor you march underground for one kilometre, touching the humid walls made of the loess in which the grapevines are planted. You are encouraged to leave your mark in the soft loess with your fingernails. You listen to the bang of a heavy sphere as it falls and rolls endlessly along a gully, thereby symbolizing the path of the moon and the time wine needs to ripen.

Towers rise to the sky, underground cathedrals are awe-inspiring, wine casks are theatrically lit, the cold air and musty smell clash with the exquisite lighting design. At the end you are lured into a ballroom with chandeliers multiplied a thousand times in the reflection of mirrors opposite. 'Glass harps' add to the glory of the subterranean ballroom. Finally, you return to the surface where that now longed-for wine tasting plus a designer store for wine shopping await you. Loisium – this is mood management using the cold, the sense of touch and smell, the delicate sounds of a glass harp and the shock of the impact of the sphere, using height and depth, glory and awe all in one grandiose attraction. (See colour plate section.)

Mood management – basically this could be the title of the entire book. Because all Third Places are essentially about doing people good, bringing them back into balance. This is the central added value to be derived from today's marketing.

In the past, if you yourself could not smile they said you shouldn't even try selling anything. Today, if you can't make your customers smile you don't stand a chance in the age of the Third Place.

SUMMARY

▌ *New hiking professionalizes the phenomenon of hiking as such.*

▌ *Hiking formerly meant: a suspense trail leading to a suspense-releasing destination.*

▌ *In-between there were nice, coincidental experiences or there was a lot of 'idle walking'.*

▌ *New hiking condenses the path by introducing purpose-made experience stops.*

▌ *It was in this way that themed hiking paths emerged to save summer tourism.*

▌ *It was also in this way that new attractions emerged revolving around history, culinary delights and culture.*

▌ *Common to both is the 'massage of the soul' as you absent-mindedly proceed along.*

▌ **Themed hiking trails.** The entry to the trail is clearly marked – by a themed gate, for instance. The different sections of the trail and its climax are named and announced in an entrance map. The final destination is linked to a reward to relieve suspense, such as authentic merchandising. In between, sensual explanatory stations are used to make historic details come to life or natural experiences accessible by means of hands-on activities.

▌ **Experience attractions.** These are 'hiking trails' within an experience-oriented museum, and they follow the dramatist's principle of the 'stations of the cross'. A typical feature here is the enhancement of the core attraction throughout the complete course of the trail. Grand feelings, like those evoked by memorials, and epicurean delights found in the attractions themed around wine, chocolate and music become a recurring principle here.

Glossary

Aha effect: disclosure revealing a concealed image core.

AIME: amount of invested mental elaboration. If the AIME value is high we feel vivacious.

All-in long shot: 'visual waste heaps' that promote flitting eye movements, weakening the aesthetic impression of a place.

Antagonistic transmission of stimuli: transmission of visual impressions via nerve channels. Each nerve channel can transmit a specific colour – as well as its contrasting colour depending on the excitation – in a plus or minus direction: red–green, blue–yellow or black–white. All other colours, colour saturation and brightness levels result from the combination of these excitation patterns.

Anticipation: this is used to whet people's appetite, thereby arousing curiosity and building suspense.

Arousal: physiological activation level of the human body.

Brain script: stereotyped patterns of activity one uses to figure out a story.

Brand land: an experience centre built around a brand.

Bricks and clicks: the fusion of virtual and real rooms: virtual ranges – clicked on the computer – are given real-life counterparts – the bricks, that is, the bricks of a real building.

Browsing: checking out every possibility at a given place.

Business entertainment: also called experience economy – experiences designed as strategic advertising, PR and sales promotion tools.

Cognitive map: the image of a place we have in our heads; we get our bearings via axes, hubs, districts and mnemonic points which all make us feel at home.

Community feeling: our feel for the very specific lifestyle in a city or region, termed 'generalized background of awareness' by psychologists.

Concept line: the recurring theme of a place serving as its all-encompassing emotional idea.

Concept store: a small store, often part of a chain, whose ranges or merchandise displays are conceived as a smart game.

Consumer benefit: product benefit, a term used in advertising.

Convenience entertainment: measures undertaken to make everyday activities more convenient so they are perceived as an experience.

Core attraction: the central attraction of a place.

Cue: a signal or piece of information that is legible purely on an emotional basis without any deeper thought process being involved.

Déjà vu: seen before.

Entrance map: a map given to visitors in the entrance area of an attraction, which makes the cognitive map visible at a glance.

Event acts: events involving actors and amateur dramatics troupes.

Event, dramatist's: makes situations that are separate from the consumer in both location and time present and tangible.

Eye-catcher: striking visual element that attracts attention and catches your eye.

Flagship store: the principal store of a retail chain.

Golden touch: an especially careful touch that upgrades a product.

Hands-on: an interactive installation is hands-on.

Header: a built 'headline' on a shopfront or the like, much like a medieval guild symbol – for example a pretzel for a baker's shop.

Image contrast: the aesthetics of old and new or of futuristic and traditional clash in such a way that image and atmosphere are created in the process.

Inferential beliefs: by figuring something out you give rise to an image and atmosphere.

Label effect: unique characteristics like the styling typical of a sales area, for example, that call up the entirety of messages or emotions by means of the 'contact effect phenomenon'.

Landmark: mnemonic point, site.

Larger than life: the Hollywood slogan ran: 'Make it big, make it right, make it class.'

Lounging: a high quality, private atmosphere in combination with extremely relaxing add-on extras.

Malling: promenading, going for a stroll.

Media literacy: being smart with the media, consumerism and modern life.

Merchandising shop: store where you buy items so as to take some of the image home and relieve any 'residual suspense'.

Mood management: massage of the soul.

Orientation reflex: anthropological survival mechanism allowing us to react to fast movements – flashing, flickering and the like – by way of our reflexes. This brings about the aesthetics of the 'visual thrill'.

Placement: the art of packaging and of image transfer. The packaging reflects on the image of the items packed (and vice versa).

PoS: point of sale, the place at which a sale is made.

Reason why: sales-promoting claim, technical term from the advertising world.

Replica: raises the question 'genuine or fake'? Toys with our perception.

Seeing is believing: the persuasive powers of appearance, seeing something with your own eyes. The art of demonstrations that create credibility.

Shop-o-tainment: shopping and entertainment merge in one place.

Slice-of-life brain scripts (SOL): cognitive scripts for everyday situations.

Suspense axis: deep perspective that pulls someone's eyes into the distance.

Teasers: lure you in, make you curious and are anticipation strategies.

Theming: walk-in stories, dream worlds.

Third Places: semi-public places used as private habitats.

Time line: someone's own time, subjective perception of time.

Urban entertainment centre: staged centres for new forms of going out featuring one core attraction (cinema, casino) and suspense-relieving add-on attractions (shops, food facilities) in the same place.

USP: Unique Selling Proposition.

Visitor centre: the centre for visitors to a particular site.

'Wow' effect: makes you marvel at something.

References

Field, Syd (1979,1982) *Screenplay: The foundation of screenwriting*, Dell, New York

Hosch, Alexander (2002) Was nun, Herr Libeskind?, *Architectural Digest*, 1

Kreft, Wilhelm (2002) *Ladenplanung. Merchandising–Architektur: Strategien für Verkaufsräume: Gestaltungs-Grundlagen, Erlebnis-Inszenierungen, Kundenleitweg-Planungen*, Verlagsanstalt Alexander Koch, Leinfelden-Echterdingen

Mikunda, Christian (2002a) *Kino spüren: Strategien der emotionalen Filmgestaltung*, WUV Universitätsverlag, Vienna

Mikunda, Christian (2002b) *Der verbotene Ort oder die inszenierte Verführung: Unwiderstehliches Marketing durch strategische Dramaturgie*, Wirtschaftsverlag Carl Ueberreuter, Frankfurt

Muschamp, Herbert (2001) Postcards from the old world gone global, *New York Times*, 12 Aug

Oldenburg, Ray (1999) *The Great Good Place: Café, coffee shops, bookstores, bars, hair salons and other hangouts at the heart of a community*, Marlowe, New York

Schulz, Denise (2000) *Das Lokal als Bühne: Die Dramaturgie des Genusses,* Metropolitan-Verlag, Düsseldorf and Berlin

Underhill, Paco (1999) *Why do we Buy? The science of shopping*, Simon & Schuster, New York

Addresses and Web sites

Adagio: Stella Musical Theater, Marlene-Dietrich-Platz 1, D-10785 Berlin, Germany; www.adagio-nightlife.de

Aladdin Hotel: 3663 Las Vegas Boulevard, Las Vegas, NV 89109, USA; www.aladdinhotelscasinoslasvegas.com

Alligator: Rotenturmstrasse 19, 1010 Vienna, Austria

Amadeus: 362 Mariahilferstrasse, A-1060 Vienna, Austria

AMLUX Toyota: 3–5 Higashi-Ikebukuro, 3chome, Toshima-ku, J-Tokyo 170, Japan; www.toyota. co.jp/Amlux

Animal Kingdom: Walt Disney World, Orlando, Florida, USA; disneyworld.disney.go.com/waltdisneyworld

Anthropology: 375 West Broadway, New York City, USA

Armani Store: Bellagio Hotel, 3600 S Las Vegas Boulevard, Las Vegas, NV 89109, USA; www.bellagio.com

Art World: Bluewater, Kent DA9 9SN, UK; www.bluewater.co.uk

Atelier Renault: 53 Avenue des Champs Elysées, F-75008 Paris, France; www.atelier-renault.com

Au Printemps: 64 Boulevard Haussmann, F-75009 Paris, France; www.printemps.com

Auréole: Mandalay Bay Resort, 3950 Las Vegas Boulevard South, Las Vegas, NV 89109, USA; www.aureolelv com

Autostadt: Berliner Strasse D-38440 Wolfsburg, Germany; www.autostadt.de

Aux Gazelles: Rahlgasse 5, A-1060 Vienna, Austria; www.auxgazelles.at

Bar 89: 89 Mercer Street, New York City, USA

Barbara Bui: 23, rue Etienne Marcel, F-75002 Paris, France; 43, rue des Francs-Bourgeois, F-75004 Paris, France; www.barbarabui.com

Barbara Bui: Galéries Lafayette, 40, Boulevard Haussmann, F-75009 Paris, France

BED: 929 Washington Avenue, Miami Beach, USA; www.bedmiami.com

Bellagio Hotel: 3600 S Las Vegas Boulevard, Las Vegas, NV 89109, USA; www.bellagio.com

Bercy Village: cour St Emilion, F-75012 Paris, France; www.bercyvillage.com

Bignet: Theobaldgasse/Mariahilferstrasse 27, A-1060 Vienna, Austria; Karntner osras 61, A-1010 Vienna, Austria; www.bignet.at

Billa, Purkersdorf: Kaiser Josef Strasse 4, A-3002 Purkersdorf, Austria; www.billa.at

Billa: 6 Singerstrasse, A-1010 Vienna, Austria

Blaha biz: Kleinengersdorferstrasse 100, A-2100 Korneuburg, Austria; www.blaha.co.at

Bluewater: Bluewater, Kent DA9 9SN, UK; www.bluewater.co.uk

British Airways: Lounge in the Sky, www.british-airways.com

Buddha Bar: 8 rue Boissy D'Anglais, F-75008 Paris, France

Buecherbogen am Savignyplatz: Stadtbahnbogen 593, D-10623 Berlin, Germany; www.buecherbogen.com

Build a Bear: Desert Passage, Aladdin Hotel, 3663 Las Vegas Boulevard, Las Vegas, NV 89109, USA; www-buildabear.com

Caesars Palace Hotel: 3570 Las Vegas Boulevard, Las Vegas, NV 89109, USA; www.caesars.com/palace

CafeCentral: Autostadt, D-38440 Wolfsburg, Germany; www.autostadt.de

Camper: Wooster Street, New York City, USA; www.camper.es

Casa la Femme: 150 Wooster Street, New York City, USA

CEBIT: Hanover, Germany

Centro: Oberhausen, Germany; www.centro.de

Chardonnay: Autostadt, D-38440 Wolfsburg, Germany; www.autostadt.de

Chiat/Day: publicity agency, New York City, USA; www.chiatday.com

China Grill: Mandalay Bay Resort, 3950 Las Vegas Boulevard South, Las Vegas, NV 89109, USA; www.mandalaybay.com

Christkindlmarkt: Rathausplatz, A-1010 Vienna, Austria, during Advent; www.christkindlmarkt.at

Church Street Station: Orlando, Florida, USA; www.churchstreetstation.com

Cinema under the Stars (Kino unter Sternen): Augarten, A-1020 Vienna, Austria, summer only

Citadium Sport: rue Caumartin, F-75008 Paris, France

Club MedWorld: in Bercy Village, 39 cour Saint Emilion, F-75012 Paris, France

Colette: 213 Rue St Honoré, F-75001 Paris, France; www.colette.fr

Colourscape: www.colourscape.org.uk

Commes des Garçons: 520 West 22nd Street, New York City, USA

Commes des Garçons: 54 rue du Faubourg St Honoré, F-75008 Paris, France

Covent Garden Market Place: Covent Garden, London, UK; www.coventgardenmarket.co.uk

Cow Culture (Kuh-Kultur): Zurich, Switzerland

Danai Beach Resort: Nikiti, Sithonia Halkidiki, 63088 Greece; www.ellada.net/danai

Das Hotel: Sempacherstrasse 14, CH-6002 Lucerne, Switzerland; www.the-hotel.ch

DB Lounge: www.bahn.de

Decoprojekt: Euroshop 2002, www.decoprojekt.de

Delano: 1685 Collins Avenue, Miami Beach, FL 33139, USA;
www.ian-schragerhotels.com/hotel delano

Desert Passage: Aladdin Hotel, 3663 Las Vegas Boulevard, Las Vegas,
NV 89109, USA; www.desertpassage.com

Diesel: Bluewater, Kent DA9 9SN, UK; www.bluewater.co.uk

Disney Store: Forum Shops at Caesars Palace Hotel, 3570 Las Vegas
Boulevard, Las Vegas, NV 89109, USA; www.forum-shops.com

Disney Village Marketplace: Walt Disney World, Orlando, Florida,
USA; www.disneyworld.disney.go.com/waltdisneyworld

DKNY: 655 Madison Avenue, New York, USA; www.dkny.com

Dussmann: Friedrichstrasse 90, D-10117 Berlin, Germany;
www.kulturkaufhaus.de

Ellis Island: Ellis Island Immigration Museum, New York, NY 10004,
USA; www.ellisisland.com

EuropaCenter: Budapester Strasse, Berlin, Germany;
www.europacenterberlin.com

Euro-Shop: Düsseldorf, Germany; www.euroshop.de

Expo 02: 15 May–20 October 2002, Drei-Seen-Land, Switzerland;
www.expo.02.ch

Expo 1998: Lisbon, Portugal

Expo 2000: 1 June–31 October 2000, Hanover, Germany

FAO Schwarz: Forum Shops at Caesars Palace Hotel, 3570 Las Vegas
Boulevard, Las Vegas, NV 89109, USA; www.forum-shops.com

FBI Tour: 9th and E streets, N W Edgar Hoover Building, Washington,
DC, USA; www.fbi.gov

Festival des Eises: start January to mid-April, Harbin, China

Finanzkaufhaus Düsseldorf: Berliner Allee 33.D-40212 Düsseldorf,
Germany; www.finanzkaufhaus-dusseldorf.de

First Austrian Nature and Environment Learning Trail for Children
(Österreichischer Natur- und Umwelterlebnispfad für Kinder):
Tourismusverband, A-8972 Ramsau am Dachstein, Austria;
www.ramsau.com

Fisherman's Wharf: Jefferson Street/Pier 39, San Francisco, USA; www.fishermanswharf.org

Forum Shops: Caesars Palace Hotel, 3570 Las Vegas Boulevard, Las Vegas, NV 89109, USA; www.forum-shops.com

French Open (tennis): Roland Garros, F-Paris, France; www.frenchopen.org

Frick Collection: 1 East 70th Street (Madison/Fifth Avenue), New York City, USA; www.frick.org

Fujita Vente: 4–6-15 Sendagaya, Shibuya-ku, Tokyo, Japan

Galéries Lafayette: 40, Boulevard Haussmann, F-75009 Paris, France; www.galerieslafayette.com

Georges: Centre Georges Pompidou, F-75004 Paris, France

Ghirardelli: 900 North Point/Larkin Street, San Francisco, USA; www.GhirardelliSq.com

Gläserne Manufaktur: Lennéstrasse, Dresden, Germany; www.glaeserne-manufaktur.de

Glacier Garden (Gletschergarten): Denkmalstrasse 4, CH-6006 Lucerne, Switzerland; www.gletschergarten.ch

Grand Optical: 138 Avenue des Champs Elysées, F-75008 Paris, France; www.grandoptical.com

G-Town, Gasometer: Guglgasse, A-1110 Vienna, Austria; www.g-town.at

Guggenheim Foundation: Venetian Hotel, 3355 Las Vegas Boulevard South, Las Vegas, NV 89109, USA; www.venetian.com

Guinness Storehouse: St James Gate, Dublin 8, Ireland; www.guinness.com

Haager Theatersommer: Höllriglstrasse 2, A-3350 Haag, Austria; www.theater-sommer.at

Hackeschen Höfe: Rosenthaler Strasse 40–41, D-10178 Berlin, Germany; www.hackesche-hoefe.com

Handwerkerhof (Craftspeople's court) Nuremberg: at the Königstor, Nuremberg, Germany, from 20 March–23 December

Hansen restaurant: Börse, Schottenring 16, 1010 Vienna, Austria; www.hansen.co.at

Haus der Musik: Seilerstätte 30, A-1010 Vienna, Austria; www.haus-der-musik-wien.at

Helmut Lang Parfum: Greene Street, New York City, USA

Hiltl vegetarian restaurant: Sihlstrasse 28, 8001 Zurich, Switzerland; www.hiltl.ch

Hollywood & Highland: 6800 Hollywood Boulevard, Hollywood, CA, USA; www.hollywoodandhighland.com

Holocaust Museum: 100 Raoul Wallenberg Place, SW, Washington, DC, USA; www.ushmm.org

Hospizalm: Arlberg Hospiz Hotel, A-6580 St Christoph, Tirol, Austria; www.hospiz.com

Hudson Hotel: 356 West 58th street, New York, USA; www-ianschrager-hotels.com/hotel hudson

Hugendubel: Steinweg 12, D-60313 Frankfurt/Main, Germany; www.hugendubel.de

Hugo Boss: Fifth Avenue/56th Street, New York, USA

IAA: Hanover, Germany

IBM Atrium: Madison Avenue between 56th and 57th Streets, New York, NY 10022, USA

Ice Dream (Eistraum): Rathausplatz, A-1010 Vienna, Austria, from January to March; www.wienereistraum.com

Ice Ring: Rockefeller Center, New York, USA, Winter only

IFA: Berlin, Germany

Interlübke 'eo': www.interluebke.com

Jäggi: Spitalgasse 47/51, Ch-3001 Berne, Switzerland; www.jaeggi.ch

Jean Claude Jitrois: 38 rue Faubourg St Honoré, F-75008 Paris, France

Just Leather: Bluewater, Kent DA9 9SN, UK; www.bluewater.co.uk

Kaufhaus Strolz: Lech am Arlberg, Austria; www.strolz.at

Kultur- und Kongresszentrum Luzern: Europaplatz 1, CH-6005 Lucerne, Switzerland; www.kkl-luzern.ch

Lederleitner: Börse, Schottenring 16, 1010 Vienna, Austria; www.lederleitner.at

Le Meridien Hotel: Opernring 13, 1010 Vienna, Austria; www.lemeridien.com

Life Ball: Rathaus, A-1010 Vienna, Austria, once a year

Loisium: Loisiumallee 1, A-3550 Langenlois, Austria; www.loisium.at

Lomography Shop: Museumsquartier, Museumsplatz, 1070 Vienna, Austria; www.lomography.com

London Eye: Westminster Road, London, UK; www.british-airways.com/londoneye

Long Night of the Museums (Die Lange Nacht der Museen): Berlin, Germany; www.lange-nacht-der-museen.de

L'oxymoron: Hackesche Höfe, Rosenthaler Strasse 40–41, D-10178 Berlin, Germany

LunAquaMarin: Paracelsus-Bad, Roedernallee 200/204, D-13407 Berlin, Germany

Lush: chain of shops including at Bluewater, Kent DA9 9SN,UK; www.lush.co.uk

Mandalay Bay Resort: 3950 Las Vegas Boulevard South, Las Vegas, NV 89109, USA; www.mandalaybay.com

Mango: Kämtner Strasse, A-1010 Vienna, Austria

Meinl am Graben: Graben 19, 1010 Vienna, Austria; www.meinlamgraben.at

Mercedes Kundencenter Rastatt: Gottlieb Daimler Strasse, D-76432 Rastatt, Germany

Meteorit: RWE Park, Essen Germany; www.meteorit.de

Millennium Dome: Greenwich, London, UK

Mirage Hotel: 3400 Las Vegas Boulevard, Las Vegas, NV 89109, USA; www.mirage.com

Moss: 146 Greene Street, New York City, USA

Muji: shops worldwide; www.muji.co.jp

Museumsquartier: Museumsplatz, A-1070 Vienna, Austria, www.mqw.at

Music Film Festival (Musikfilmfestival): Rathausplatz, A-1010 Vicnna, Austria, in Summer; www.wien-event.at

Nasdaq MarketSide Experience: 4 Times Square at Broadway and 43rd Street, New York, USA; www.nasdaq.com/reference/marketsite_about.stm

Nevada: Bluewater, Kent DA9 9SN, UK

New State Gallery (Neue Staatsgalerie): Konrad-Adenauer-Strasse 30–32, D-70173 Stuttgart, Germany; www.staatsgalerie.de

New Technology Center: Hochjoch, Montafon, A-6780 Schruns, Austria; www.snowell.com/ntc.schruns

New York New York Hotel: 3790 Las Vegas Boulevard, Las Vegas, NV 89109; www.nynyhotelcasino.com

Night of the Thick Books (Die Nacht der dicken Bücher): E Riemann'sche Hofbuchhandlung, Inh. Irmgard Clausen, Markt 9, D-96450 Coburg, Germany; http://www.riemann.de

Nike Town: 6 E 57th Street, New York City, USA; www.niketown.com

Nike Town Los Angeles: 9560 Wilshire Boulevard, Beverly Hills, CA, USA; www.niketown.com

Noodles: Bellagio Hotel, 3600 S Las Vegas Boulevard, Las Vegas, NV 89109, USA; www.bellagio.com

Nordstrom: San Francisco Shopping Centre, Market/5th Street, San Francisco, CA, USA

Oberlech tunnel system: Oberlecher Wege und Garagengesellschaft, Oberlech 266, A-6764 Lech am Arlberg, Austria

Ocean Dome: Hamayama, Yamazaki-cho Miyazaki City, 880–8945 Japan; www.seagaia.co.jp

Olympics 2002: Salt Lake City, Utah, USA

Opel Live: Friedrich-Lutzmann-Ring 2, D-65423 Rüsselsheim, Germany; www.opel-live.de

Opus One, Napa Valley: 7900 St Helena Highway Oakville, CA 94562, USA; www.opusonewinery.com

Orsay: Kärntner Strasse, A-1010 Vienna, Austria

Österreichs Wanderdörfer: Unterwollaniger Strasse 53, A-9500 Villach, Austria; www.wanderdoerfer.at

Peggy Guggenheim Museum: Palazzo Venier die Leoni, 701 Dorsoduro, 1–30123 Venice, Italy; www.guggenheim-venice.it

Pershing Hall Hotel: 49 rue Pierre Charron, F-75008 Paris, France; www.pershing-hall.com

Peugeot: 136 Avenue des Champs Elysées, F-75008 Paris, France; www.peugeot.com

Pizza Mania: Legoland, D-Giinzburg, Germany; www.legoland.de

Pleasure Island: Walt Disney World, Orlando, Florida; www.disneyworld.disney.go.com/waltdisneyworld

Pleats Please: Prince/Wooster Street, New York City, USA

Polo Ralph Lauren: 867 Madison Avenue/E 72nd Street, New York, USA

Prada: 724 Fifth Avenue, between 56th and 57th Streets, New York, USA

Quick Side Park Winter City, Dubai

Red Square: Mandalay Bay Resort, 3950 Las Vegas Boulevard South, Las Vegas, NV 89109, USA; www.mandalaybay.com

Regenwaldhaus: Herrenhäuserstrasse 4a, D-30419 Hanover, Germany; www.regenwaldhaus.de

REI: 222 Yale Avenue North, Seattle, USA; www.rei.com

Reiss: various branches including at Bluewater, Kent, UK; Trafford Centre, Manchester M17 8AA, UK; www.traffordcentre.co.uk

Résonances: Bercy Village, 9 Cour Saint-Emilion, F-75012 Paris, France

Résonances: Place de la Madeleine, 3 Boulevard Malherbes, F-75008 Paris, France

Return of the Third Man (Die Rückkehr des Dritten Mannes); Friedrichstrasse/Esperantopark, A-1010 Vienna, Austria; info.wien.at/d/event/tipps/dritter.html

Riedel Sinnfonie: Riedel Glass, A-6330 Kufstein, Austria; www.riedelcrystal.co.at

Ritz Carlton: Autostadt, D-38440 Wolfsburg, Germany; www.autostadt.de

Ritz Carlton Hotels: www.ritzcarlton.com

Royal Hotel: 5–3-68, Nakanoshima, Kita-ku, Osaka 530, Japan; www.rihga.com/osaka

Rumjungle: Mandalay Bay Resort, 3950 Las Vegas Boulevard South, Las Vegas, NV 89109, USA; www.mandalaybay.com

SSAWS Skidome: Tokyo, Japan

Santa Monica Boulevard: Los Angeles, CA, USA

Schönbrunn Castle (Schloss Schönbrunn): A-1140 Vienna, Austria: www.schoenbrunn.at

Secession: Friedrichstrasse 12, 1010 Vienna, Austria; www.secession.at

Selfridges: Bullring, Birmingham B5 4BU, UK; www.bullring.co.uk

Selfridges: 400 Oxford Street , London W1A 1AB, UK; www.selfridges.co.uk

Sephora: 70 avenue des Champs Elysées, F-75008 Paris, France; www.sephora.com

Sephora blanc: Bercy Village, Cour Saint-Emilion, F-75012 Paris, France; www.sephora.com

Sevens: Königsallee 56, D-40212 Dusseldorf, Germany; www.sevens.de

Shakespeare Globe Centre: 21 New Globe Walk, Bankside, London SE1 9DT, UK; www.shakespeares-globe.org

The Sharper Image: US shopping chain, www.sharperimage.com

Shintaro: Bellagio Hotel, 3600 S Las Vegas Boulevard, Las Vegas, NV 89109, USA; www.bellagio.com

Shopping Bahnhof: Hauptbahnhof, Willy Brandt-Platz, Leipzig, Germany

SI-Centrum: Plieninger Strasse 100, D-70561 Stuttgart, Germany; www.erlebnis-center.de

Silvester 2000: Paris, Sydney

Silvesterpfad: A-1010 Vienna, Austria, yearly on 31 December

Sketch: 9 Conduit Street, London W1, UK; www.sketch.uk.com

S Oliver: Karlsruhe, Germany

Sony: 5–3-1 Ginza, Chuo-ku, Tokyo 104, Japan

Sony Center: Potsdamer Platz, Berlin, Germany; www.sonycenter.de

Sony Metreon: 101 Fourth Street, San Francisco, CA 94103, USA; www.metreon.com

Sony Style: 550 Madison Avenue at 56th Street, New York, NY 10022, USA

Sony Wonder: 550 Madison Avenue at 56th Street, New York, NY 10022, USA; www.wondertechlab.sony.com

Sound Cloud Linz (Klangwolke): Linz, Austria, yearly; www.aec.at/festival

South Street Seaport: New York City, USA

St Jakobs Stadion: St Jakobs-Strasse 395, CH-4052 Basle, Switzerland; www.st-jakob-park.com

St Martins Lane Hotel: 45 St Martins Lane, WC2N 4HX London, UK; www.ianschragerhotels.com/hotel sml

Starbucks: corner of Karntner Strasse and Walnschgasse, A-1010 Vienna, Austria

Starthaus der Streif: A-6370 Kitzbühel, Austria; www.hahnenkamm.com

The Stinking Rose: 325 Columbus Avenue, San Francisco, CA 94133, USA; www.thestinkingrose.com

Strohzeit: Kellerberggasse, A-1230 Vienna, and Breitenleer Strasse, A-1220 Vienna, Austria; www.strohzeit.at

Swarovski Crystal World (Kristallwelten): Kristallweltenstrasse l, A-6112 Wattens, Austria; www.swarovski-kristallwelt.com

Takashimaya: Fifth Avenue/54th Street, New York, USA

Tardini: Wooster Street, New York City, USA

Tate Modern: Bankside, London SE1 9TG, UK; www.tate.org.uk

Teatriz: Calle Hermosilla 15, Madrid, Spain

Ted Baker: Bluewater, Kent DA9 9SN, UK; www.bluewater.co.uk

Temple Bar District: Dublin, Ireland

Thermenbad Vals: CH-7132 Vals/GR, Switzerland; www.therme-vals.ch

Thierry Mugler: 10 rue Boissy d'Anglais, F-75008 Paris, France

3950: Mandalay Bay Resort, 3950 Las Vegas Boulevard South, Las Vegas, NV 89109, USA; www.mandalaybay.com

Thomas Kincade: Bluewater, Kent DA9 9SN, UK; www.bluewater.co.uk

Times Square: New York, USA

Toyota E-com ride: Tokyo, Japan; www.megaweb.gr.jp

Trafford Centre: Manchester M17 8AA, UK; www.traffordcentre.co.uk

Universal City Walk: Los Angeles; www.citywalkhollywood.com; Universal Orlando; www.citywalkorlando.com

Venetian Hotel: 3355 Las Vegas Boulevard South, Las Vegas, NV 89109, USA; www.venetian.com

Versace: Fifth Avenue, New York, USA

Village Cinemas: Landstrasse Hauptstrasse, A-1030 Vienna, Austria

Waterstones: Bluewater, Kent DA9 9SN, UK; www.bluewater.co.uk

Westside: Berne Brünnen, Switzerland, opening approximately 2006

Widder Hotel: Rennweg 7, CH-8001 Zurich, Switzerland; www.widderhotel.ch

Wiener Festwochen Eroffnung: Rathausplatz, A-1010 Vienna, Austria, once a year www.festwochen.or.at

World Financial Center: Battery Park City, Lower Manhattan, New York City, USA; www.worldfinancialcenter.com

Yo! Sushi: chain of restaurants, www.yosushi.co.uk

Index

Page references in *italics* indicate illustrations

Also published by Kogan Page

Beyond Branding
How the new values of transparency and integrity are changing the world of brands, Nicholas Ind

Brand Driven
The route to integrated branding through great leadership, F Joseph LePla, Susan Davis and Lynn M Parker

Brand Failures
The truth about the 100 biggest branding mistakes fo all time, Matt Haig

Brand Management Checklist
Proven tools and techniques for creating winning brands, Brad van Auken

Brand New Brand Thinking
Brought to life by 11 experts who do, Edited by Merry Basking and Mark Earls

BRANDchild
Remarkable insights into the minds of today's global kids and their relationships with brands, Martin Lindstrom

The Essential Brand Book
Over 100 techniques to increase brand value, 2nd edition, Iain Ellwood

Global Brand Strategy
Unlocking brand potential across countries, cultures and markets, Sicco van Gelder

If You're So Brilliant…How Come Your Brand isn't Working Hard Enough?
The Essential Guide to Brand Management, Peter Cheverton

Integrated Branding
Becoming brand-driven through company-wide action, F Joseph LePla and Lynn M Parker

Living the Brand
How to transform every member of your organization into a brand champion, 2nd edition, Nicholas Ind

Media Monoliths
How great brands thrive and survive, Mark Tungate

The New Strategic Brand Management
Creating and Sustaining Brand Equity Long Term, 3rd edition, Jean-Noël Kapferer

The Philosophy of Branding
Great philosophers think, Thom Braun

Reinventing the Brand
Can top brands survive the new market realities?, Jean-Noël Kapferer

The above titles are available from all good bookshops. To obtain further information, please contact the publisher at the address below:

Kogan Page Limited
120 Pentonville Road
London N1 9JN
United Kingdom
Tel: +44 (0) 20 7278 0433
Fax: +44 (0) 20 7837 6348
www.kogan-page.co.uk